Hiking

Arizona

Help Us Keep This Guide Up to Date

Every effort has been made by the authors and editors to make this guide as accurate and useful as possible. However, many things can change after a guide is published—trails are rerouted, regulations change, techniques evolve, facilities come under new management, and so on.

We would love to hear from you concerning your experiences with this guide and how you feel it could be improved and kept up to date. While we may not be able to respond to all comments and suggestions, we'll take them to heart and we'll also make certain to share them with the authors. Please send your comments and suggestions to the following address:

The Globe Pequot Press
Reader Response/Editorial Department
P.O. Box 480
Guilford, CT 06437

Or you may e-mail us at:

editorial@globe-pequot.com

Thanks for your input, and happy travels!

Hiking

Arizona

Bruce Grubbs and Stewart Aitchison

Second Edition

FALCON®

GUILFORD, CONNECTICUT

An imprint of The Globe Pequot Press

Cover photo: Cheyenne Rouse
Interior photos: © Bruce Grubbs except pp. 4, 5, 7, 14, 24, 27, 42, 46, 47, 50, 53, 55,
57, 63, 82, 108, 135, 149, 238, 254, 265, 285, and 301 © Stewart Aitchison.
Maps: Bruce Grubbs

Library of Congress Cataloging-in-Publication Data is available.
ISBN 0-7627-1207-4

Manufactured in the United States of America
Second Edition/Second Printing

Contents

Acknowledgments

We would like to thank the many government employees who gave unselfishly of their time and expert knowledge of the natural areas of Arizona. A few are Joyce H. Wright, Business Manager, Arizona Strip Interpretive Association; Rick Best, Chief Interpreter, Navajo National Monument; Joseph Spehar, Apache-Sitgreaves National Forests; Bob Dyson, Public Affairs Officer, Apache-Sitgreaves National Forest; Conny J. Frisch, Forest Supervisor, Kaibab National Forest; John Eavis, Kaibab National Forest; Charlotte Minor, Kaibab National Forest; John Neeling, Wilderness Ranger, Kaibab National Forest; John Nelson, Recreation Officer, Coconino National Forest; Peter Pilles, Archaeologist, Coconino National Forest; Skip Larson, Coconino National Forest; Patricia Callaghan, Recreation and Lands Staff Officer, Coconino National Forest; James R. Novy, Fisheries Program Manager, Arizona Game and Fish Department; Devin J. Wanner, Public Affairs Specialist, Prescott National Forest; Dan Merritt, Receptionist, Tonto National Forest; Larry Widner, District Ranger, Globe Ranger District, Tonto National Forest; Tom Bonomo, District Ranger, Verde Ranger District, Prescott National Forest; Frank Holmes, Permit Sales Clerk, San Carlos Apache Tribe; Beverly Blair, Globe Ranger District, Tonto NF; David Weir, Information Receptionist, Coronado National Forest; Ron Morfin, Yuma Field Office, BLM; Bruce Asbjorn, Outdoor Recreation Planner, Kingman Field Office, BLM; Michael Ferguson, Deputy State Director, Resources Division, BLM; Ken Mahoney, Arizona BLM Wilderness Program Coordinator; Jackie Price, Park Ranger, Cibola National Wildlife Refuge; Charles Wahler, Editor, Grand Canyon National Park; and Chip Littlefield, Park Ranger, Saguaro National Park.

Bruce would also like to thank all his hiking friends who put up with his photography and trail mapping on hikes and backpack trips. Special thanks to Duart Martin for her unflagging support of this project, especially during the final stages of editing and map preparation.

Map Legend

Interstate		Campground	
US Highway		Cabins/Buildings	
State or Other Principal Road		Peak	9,782 ft.
National Park Route		Point	X 9,782 ft.
Interstate Highway		Hill	
Paved Road		Elevation	9,782 ft. X
Gravel Road		Gate	
Unimproved Road		Mine Site	
Trailhead		Overlook/Point of Interest	
Main Trail(s)/Route(s)			
Alternate/Secondary Trail(s)/Route(s)		National Forest/ Park/Wilderness Boundary	
Parking Area			
River/Creek		Map Orientation	N
Spring		Scale	0 0.5 1 Miles
One-Way Road	One Way		
		Meadow	
		Cliff	

Hike Locator Map

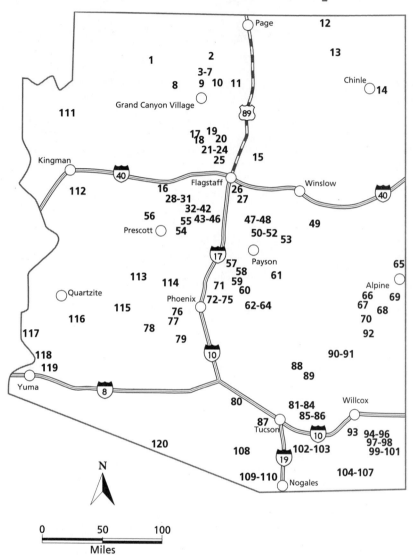

Page

12

13

1

2

3-7

9 10 11

8

Chinle

14

Grand Canyon Village

111

17 19

18 20

21-24

25

15

Kingman

112

16 Flagstaff 26

28-31 27

32-42

56 55 43-46

Prescott 54

47-48

50-52 53

49

Winslow

57

58 Payson

59 61

60

65

113

114

71

Alpine

66 69

67 68

70

92

115

Phoenix 72-75 62-64

76

77

116

78

79

117

90-91

118

119

Yuma

80

88

89

81-84

85-86

Willcox

93 94-96

97-98

99-101

120

108

87

Tucson

102-103

109-110 Nogales

104-107

N

0   50   100

Miles

Introduction

We wrote the first *Hiking Arizona* (originally titled *The Hiker's Guide to Arizona*) in 1986. Although updated a number of times since, we felt a complete revision was due, especially now as we enter a new millennium. Arizona is one of the fastest-growing states in the Union, and the number of outdoor enthusiasts has also exploded. Yet there is still no better way to explore the great state of Arizona than on foot.

In this guidebook is just a sampling of the wide variety of hikes available. Some are very popular and may require obtaining permits in advance. We included a few of these trails because they exhibit some of the very best of what Arizona has to offer in scenery, wildlife, and adventure. Other trails described are still relatively unknown and can be wonderful wilderness experiences.

All of the national parks, some of the national monuments, and many of the state, county, and city parks offer a multitude of hiking trails. The national forest and Bureau of Land Management lands, which cover much of Arizona, have designated wilderness areas and nonwilderness portions that also contain many hiking trails. Use this guidebook as a starting point to discover your own favorite areas. One lifetime is not enough to exhaust all of the possibilities.

GEOLOGY

In terms of geology, Arizona is one of the most diverse states. It can be divided into three physiographic (i.e. similar in geologic history) areas: the Colorado Plateau, the Central Highlands, and the Basin and Range Country.

The Colorado Plateau, which covers much of Utah, western Colorado, and northwestern New Mexico. takes in most of northern Arizona. The plateau is on average a mile above sea level, composed primarily of thick, colorful, horizontal beds of sandstone, limestone, and shale, and drained by the Colorado River and its myriad tributaries. This is a land of buttes, mesas, and canyons culminating in the erosional tour de force called the Grand Canyon.

The Mogollon Rim, a 1,000-foot or higher escarpment separating the plateau from the Central Highlands, demarcates the plateau's southern edge. Near this edge there is often dramatic evidence of geologically recent volcanic activity. The San Francisco Peaks and their neighboring 600 volcanoes make up one of the largest volcanic fields in the United States. In eastern Arizona, the White Mountains form another volcanic wonderland.

Stretching in a broad band across the middle of Arizona are the Central Highlands. The highlands are a transition zone between the relatively flat-lying sedimentary rocks of the Colorado Plateau and the tortured and convoluted metamorphic and igneous rocks of the Basin and Range Country. Hikers in the highlands find themselves in deep canyons or struggling up rugged mountains.

The third major physiographic province, the Basin and Range Country, covers southern and western Arizona and extends into western Utah, Nevada, eastern California, and northwestern Mexico. Broad desert valleys separate the numerous mountain ranges. To the west and southwest within Arizona, the small, corrugated ranges are typically dry desert all the way to their summit ridges. In southeastern Arizona, the mountains are higher, reaching 9,000 to 10,000 feet and harbor chaparral, woodlands, and coniferous forests.

NATURAL HISTORY

Arizona is blessed with a remarkably rich and diverse collection of habitats—everything from searing desert to alpine tundra. Each of these habitats contains special plant and animal communities.

One major factor in producing this variety of habitats is the relationship between elevation and temperature. For every 1,000 feet gained, there is a corresponding drop of about three to five degrees Fahrenheit. Additionally, getting higher usually means greater precipitation. Astoundingly, elevations in Arizona range from about 75 feet above sea level, where the Colorado River flows into Mexico, to more than 12,630 feet at the top of the San Francisco Peaks.

The sun shines 85 to 90 percent of the daytime in the lower desert regions and only slightly less in the high country. Annual temperature extremes have spanned more than 160 degrees, from a low of -37 at Maverick, in the White Mountains, to a high of 127 at Parker, along the Colorado River. Daily fluctuations commonly exceed 40 degrees, which is typical of arid climes. The low humidity allows daytime heat to dissipate quickly at night.

The annual precipitation can vary from nothing in some of the southwestern desert areas to more than 50 inches on the higher mountains. Generally, the moisture comes during one of two rainy seasons—either in the winter or in late summer. At higher elevations (those above 5,000 feet), the winter precipitation falls as snow. Flagstaff, at 7,000 feet, averages about 90 inches of snow per season. This may sound like a lot of moisture, but the 90 inches melts down to about 9 inches of water.

Summer rains usually come as afternoon thundershowers, which, although generally brief, may result in heavy runoff and flash floods because of the rocky, impenetrable nature of the ground.

All of these major environmental factors, along with minor others, set the stage for the striking array of life in the state. Arizona contains six major biotic communities; alpine tundra (12,633–11,000 feet), coniferous forest, including aspen groves (11,000–6,000 feet), woodlands (7,000–4,000 feet), chaparral (6,000–4,000 feet), grasslands (7,000–4,000 feet), and desert (6,000–75 feet). The only major North American biotic community not represented in the state is tropical. Hiking from the summit of the San Francisco Peaks to the bottom of the Grand Canyon, a horizontal distance of less than 80 miles, is biologically similar to traveling from northern Canada to northern Mexico.

Within these six communities are found more than 3,400 species of flowering plants, ferns, and fern allies, 64 species of fish, 22 species of amphibians, 97 species of reptiles, 435 species of birds, and 140 species of mammals. Arizona has 60 percent of all types of wildlife species found in North America, and this does not include the multitude of insects, arachnids, mosses, lichens, and other organisms that constitute the rest of the ecosystem. Arizona—considered by many to be a vast, lifeless desert—has a startling abundance of living, breathing, reproducing plants and creatures.

One special habitat that can be found within any of the major communities is the riparian or streamside habitat. In terms of wildlife, this is the most important habitat in the American Southwest. The vast majority of vertebrate animals utilize the riparian habitat at some point during their life cycle—to feed, to nest, to drink, or to follow the watercourse during migration. Some biologists estimate that 80 to 90 percent of Arizona's precious riparian ecosystems has been destroyed or altered in some way.

HUMAN HISTORY

Arizona's first human inhabitants were Paleo-hunters, who arrived at least 11,000 years ago, in the waning years of the last Ice Age. Arizona's weather was considerably cooler and wetter than today, and small glaciers graced the summits of the San Francisco Peaks and the White Mountains.

Using a spear-throwing device called an *atlatl,* these hunters stalked mammoths, ground sloths, giant bison, Harrington's mountain goat, tapirs (piglike mammals), cameloids, and other relics of the Pleistocene. Over several thousands of years of gradual warming and drying and, perhaps, further decimated by overhunting, the great Ice Age mammals disappeared. The hunters turned their attention to other game like deer, elk, bighorn sheep, pronghorn antelope, rabbits, squirrels and other rodents, and birds. A greater emphasis was also placed on the gathering of wild plant foods. These people had to be opportunists to survive in this unforgiving environment.

Although maize and squash were introduced into Arizona from Mexico perhaps as many as 4,000 years ago, not until about 2,000 years later did the hunter-gatherers become serious farmers. As agriculturalists, they tended to remain in one area to work and guard their small farming plots. Permanent homes were constructed. These were usually pit houses, structures that were partially subterranean with vertical poles running around the perimeter of the hole to support a roof. Later, aboveground stone and mud houses replaced the pit houses, sometimes with attached rooms and several stories high. A few dwellings were located in south-facing caves or on hilltops.

Around A.D. 600, Arizona's native people acquired several other new items from people to the south in Mexico. Beans—pinto, lima, and tepary—were introduced, as well as the technique of pottery making and the bow and arrow. These new foods, different ways of preparing them, and more efficient hunting implements apparently allowed the population to increase dramatically.

Teddy bear cholla is just one of many fascinating plants to be found in the Sonoran Desert.

Three major and distinct Indian cultures developed along with a number of smaller groups. People in the southern part of the state, whom the archaeologists call the Hohokam, engineered complex irrigation canals to carry river water onto the hot desert plains. The Anasazi (sometimes called the Ancestral Puebloans) lived on the Colorado Plateau and relied on rainstorms to water their crops. The Mogollon people lived along the Central Highlands and practiced both irrigation and dry farming.

After six or seven centuries of prosperity, the Anasazi began to abandon their area. What caused their departure is not fully understood but probably was a combination of drought, overuse of natural resources, overpopulation, and perhaps disease and warfare. By the mid-1400s, the Mogollon and Hohokam people had also left their villages.

Where did everybody go? Some probably moved out of the Arizona region entirely, while others resumed a hunting and gathering lifestyle. A few, such as the Hopi (who are likely direct descendants of the Anasazi), found different locations favorable to their dry-farming methods and continued their agricultural tradition. About this same time, new people from the north, including the Navajo and Apache, entered the American Southwest.

Arizona's historic period begins in 1539 with Estévan, a black Moor who was exploring north toward the American Southwest with the Spaniard Fray Marcos de Niza. Estévan had gone ahead of the padre and sent back word of "seven very great cities." Unfortunately, Zuni Indians killed Estévan. Hearing this news, Niza retreated back to Mexico. Niza's report of a collection of cities of unbelievable riches led Francisco Vásquez de Coronado to mount an expedition the next year to find the Seven Cities of Cíbola. The

Prehistoric petroglyphs often occur along natural routes through Arizona's canyons and mountains.

Spaniards were disappointed to discover that legendary Cíbola was in reality the stone and mud pueblos of Zuni. However, a small detachment of Coronado's men, led by García López de Cárdenas, is credited with being the first group of Europeans to see the Grand Canyon. Not long after this foray came Spanish padres seeking Indian souls instead of gold. Some Native Americans fared better than others during the Spanish invasion.

By the 1820s, fur trappers such as James Ohio Pattie, Jedediah Smith, Bill Williams, Pauline Weaver, and Kit Carson were traipsing along Arizona's streams and rivers even though the land was under Spanish and then Mexican rule. After the Mexican War of 1847–48, the Arizona territory became the property of the United States. Within a few years, prospectors, ranchers, and settlers followed, displacing the original residents, the Native Americans.

Conflict erupted as these different groups fought over Arizona's limited natural resources. However, by the end of the nineteenth century, the Old West was quickly becoming a memory. On Valentine's Day, 1912, Arizona became the nation's forty-eighth state.

PRESERVING ARIZONA'S ARCHAEOLOGICAL AND HISTORIC HERITAGE

Arizona is fortunate to have some of the best-preserved prehistoric structures and artifacts in the world. Unfortunately, many of these sites have been vandalized to some degree. Disturbing archaeological sites or collecting artifacts not only lessens their scientific value but also deeply upsets Native Americans whose ancestors left these things behind.

Two federal laws, the Antiquities Act and the Archaeological Resources Protection Act, forbid removal or destruction of archaeological and historical resources on federal land. The Arizona State Antiquities Act provides similar protection on state lands. Failure to comply with these laws can result in stiff fines and imprisonment (not to mention many years of bad luck and terrible nightmares inflicted by ancient spirits). Any vandalism should be reported immediately to the nearest federal or state resource office or law enforcement agency.

WHY HIKE?

Walking in the wilderness is not just a matter of "picking 'em up and putting `em down"! Most novice hikers try to go too fast, and then find themselves out of breath and stopping frequently. The group should move at a speed that allows easy (not breathless!) conversation among all members. Long hikes, especially uphill sections, should be paced so that rest breaks are needed only about once an hour. That's not to say that you shouldn't stop at scenic viewpoints or when you find something else that is interesting. But if you find yourself taking a great many breaks, you're probably going too fast. Keep rest stops short so that you don't become chilled. It's harder to get going after a long break.

As you walk, always pay attention to the stretch of ground immediately in front of you. Hazards such as spiny plants, overhanging sharp branches,

6

and sunbathing rattlesnakes are easy to miss if you only have eyes for the scenery on the horizon. On the other hand, daydreaming is an important part of hiking. There are always sections of trail that aren't very interesting. The experienced hiker can let his mind wander far away but still pay attention to the trail underfoot and the route ahead, or he can focus on aspects of the environment such as birdsong or identifying trees from a distance by their general shape. Either technique lets the miles pass almost unnoticed.

Hikes taken with young children should have extremely modest goals. A day hike of a few hundred yards may be far enough. Children find all sorts of interesting things in a small area, things that their parents might never notice. Seeing the natural world anew through a child's eyes is a wonderful and enlightening experience.

EQUIPMENT

A modest amount of good equipment, along with the skill and technique for using it, makes hiking safer and more enjoyable. Day hiking is very popular because it can be enjoyed without specialized equipment. On the other hand, overnight or longer backpack trips require a good pack, tent or other shelter, sleeping bag, and boots.

Essentials

On all hikes that are more than a casual stroll, you should carry certain essentials: water, food, rain/wind gear, sunglasses, sunscreen, knife, lighter or other reliable fire starter, map, compass, and flashlight. These items can easily be carried in a small fanny pack, and may save your life if you are delayed or the weather suddenly changes.

Even children can enjoy hiking in the Grand Canyon, especially if parents plan trips with short mileage days.

7

Learning to use maps is not only fun but essential when exploring much of Arizona's backcountry. Trails are often faint and hard to follow, easy to confuse with livestock and game trails. Some of the state's best wild places can only be reached by cross-country travel with map and compass. Practice map reading by obtaining a U.S. Geological Survey topographic map of an area you are already familiar with, such as your hometown.

Footwear

For short, easy hikes on good trails, nearly any comfortable footwear such as tennis shoes or running shoes will work. For difficult hiking with heavy loads, some hikers prefer all-leather boots. Many of us still prefer lightweight hiking boots even for very difficult cross-country hiking, trading durability for weight.

Good quality, well-fitting socks are critical to hiking comfort. A good combination is a light inner sock of cotton, wool, or polypropylene, with an outer medium- or heavyweight sock of wool with nylon reinforcing. The outer sock will tend to slide on the inner sock, rather than directly on your skin, reducing the chance of blisters. Incipient blisters should be treated *before* they happen! A hot spot can be protected with a piece of felt moleskin. Often a change of socks will help as well.

Clothing

Nearly any durable clothing will do for hiking in good, stable weather. On hot, sunny days, keep your skin covered and use a good sunscreen. Long pants will protect your skin from scratches when hiking a brushy trail.

Use the layer system while backpacking. In cold wet weather, the four-layer system works well: the inner layer is lightweight, synthetic, wicking long underwear; the next layer consists of sturdy pants and a sturdy shirt, which will hold up to brush and rocks; the third layer consists of an insulating jacket or parka, and the fourth layer is your rain gear.

Don't put up with being overheated or chilled while hiking. Stop to add or subtract layers as necessary to stay comfortable.

Food

You should bring some food on all but the shortest hikes. High-calorie food keeps your energy level high. Make sandwiches or bring fruit, cheese, crackers, nuts, and drink mixes.

Some suggestions for a backpacker's breakfast include low-bulk cold cereals with powdered milk, hot cereals, dried fruit, breakfast bars, hot chocolate, tea, and coffee bags. For lunch, bring munchies such as nuts, cheese, crackers, dried fruit, candy bars, athletic energy bars, dried soup, hard candy, beef or turkey jerky, sardines, and fruit-flavored drink mixes. For dinner, try dried noodle or rice-based dishes supplemented with margarine and a small can of tuna, turkey, or chicken.

Water

On day hikes, bring water from home. Water is the most important item in your pack—be sure you have enough. Each hiker may drink a gallon or more during a long, difficult hike.

On backpack trips, you will have to use water from wilderness springs, streams, or lakes; always purify it with a proven water purification system.

Pack

A well-fitting, well-made daypack goes a long way toward making your hike a pleasant experience. Packs for backpacking fall into two categories, internal frame and external frame. A good backpack of either type carefully distributes the load between your shoulders, back, and hips, with most of the weight on your hips. Correct fit is critical.

Walking sticks are helpful, especially at stream crossings or other places where the footing is uncertain.

Sleeping Bag

Your sleeping bag is one of the most important items in your pack. With a good one, you'll most likely have a comfortable sleep; a poor bag will guarantee a miserable experience. The occasional user may be happy with a backpacker-style mummy bag insulated with one of the current synthetic fills. People who backpack often tend to prefer down bags because of their lighter weight and easier packing. Sleeping bags are rated by temperature and sometimes by recommended seasons.

Sleeping Pad

Lightweight sleeping bags don't provide much insulation or padding underneath; you'll need a sleeping pad. Closed-cell foam pads are cheap and durable, but not very comfortable. Self-inflating foam pads are comfortable, but check carefully for cactus spines before you put one down.

Shelter

Most hikers depend on a tent for shelter. Sound construction and high quality are important. A three-season, two-person dome or freestanding tent is the most versatile. Some hikers avoid the weight and expense of a tent by carrying a tarp with a separate groundsheet.

Getting it all together. A typical assortment of gear for an Arizona backpack trip.

First-aid Kit

A small first-aid kit will do for day hikes, but you'll definitely need a more complete kit for backpacking. Make sure that you get one intended specifically for wilderness sports. And take a first-aid class. Knowledge is your best defense.

Equipment Sources

Local outdoor shops staffed by people who use the gear and are willing to share their knowledge with you are a valuable resource and are worth supporting. If you can't find a good local shop, mail order is a good alternative. Check the ads in outdoor magazines for addresses and phone numbers.

Making It a Safe Trip

Wilderness can be a safe place, if you are willing to respect your limitations. You'll gain confidence and self-reliance safely if you start out with easy hikes and progress to more difficult adventures.

TRIP PLANNING

Individuals or parties pushing too hard often suffer wilderness accidents. Always set reasonable goals, allowing for delays caused by weather, deteriorated trails, unexpectedly rough country, and dry springs. Remember that the group moves at the speed of the slowest member. Be flexible enough to eliminate part of a hike if your original plans appear too ambitious. Do not fall into the trap of considering a trip plan cast in stone; rather, take pride in your adaptability. Plan your trip carefully using maps, guidebooks, and information from reliable sources such as experienced hikers and backcountry rangers.

When backpacking, consider alternatives to traditional campsites. Dry camping—that is, away from water sources—virtually eliminates the possibility of contaminating wilderness streams and lakes. It also allows you to avoid heavily used campsites and their camp-robbing animal attendants such as skunks, mice, rock squirrels, jays, and insects, and enjoy beautiful, uncrowded campsites. The technique is simple: Use a collapsible water container to pick up water at the last reliable source of the day, and then use minimum water for camp chores. With practice it will become second nature.

WATER ESSENTIALS

Backcountry water sources are not safe to drink. Infections from contaminated water are uncomfortable and can be disabling. Giardiasis, for example, is a severe gastrointestinal infection caused by small cysts that can result in an emergency evacuation of the infected hiker. Purify all backcountry water sources. Iodine tablets are effective and lightweight. Water filters are popular, but not all of them kill viruses. The term "water purifier" usually means a filter with an active iodine element that kills viruses. You can also purify water by bringing it to a rolling boil. This produces safe water at any altitude. After boiling, pour the water back and forth between containers to cool it and improve its taste.

BACKCOUNTRY NAVIGATION

Maps are essential for finding your way in the backcountry. Don't depend on trail signs, which are often missing.

Topographic maps are the most useful for backcountry navigation because they show the elevation and shape of the land. All of Arizona is covered by a 7.5-minute quadrangle series published by the U.S. Geological Survey. Each hike description in this book lists the USGS topographic maps that cover the hike. Keep in mind that USGS maps are not updated very often, so man-made details such as trails and roads may be inaccurate.

The U.S. Forest Service and several private companies publish recreational and wilderness area topographic maps with more up-to-date trail information. The U.S. Forest Service and the Bureau of Land Management publish a series of road maps that cover national forests and other public lands. These maps are useful for navigating roads and finding trailheads.

Before entering the backcountry, study the maps to become familiar with the general lay of the land. This is a good time to establish a baseline, a long, unmistakable landmark such as a road or highway that borders the area. In the rare event that you become totally disoriented, you can always use your compass to follow a general course toward your baseline. Although hiking to your baseline will probably take you out of your way, it's comforting to know you can find a route back to known country.

While hiking, refer to the map often and locate yourself in reference to visible landmarks. Use trail signs to confirm your location. If you do this consistently, you will never become lost.

The satellite-based Global Positioning System is very useful in areas where landmarks are few, such as pinyon-juniper flats or dense forest, and when bad weather hides landmarks. Although GPS makes it possible to find your location nearly anywhere, a GPS receiver is no substitute for a good map and a reliable compass. With GPS alone, you will know your coordinates to a few feet, but still may not know where you are, let alone where you need to go. You'll need map and compass to plot your location and determine the route you need to travel. Also, as with any mechanical or electronic device, it can fail. Bring spare batteries.

TRAIL COURTESY

Don't cut switchbacks. It takes more effort and increases erosion. Give pack animals the right-of-way by stepping off the trail on the downhill side, avoiding sudden movements or loud noises and following any instructions given by the wrangler. You will encounter mountain bikes outside designated wilderness areas. Because they're less maneuverable than you, it's polite to step aside so the riders can pass without having to veer off the trail.

Smokers should stop at a bare spot or rock ledge, then make certain that all smoking materials are out before continuing. Due to fire hazard, it may be illegal to smoke while traveling in a national forest. Never smoke or light any kind of fire on windy days or when the fire danger is high, because wildfires can start easily and spread explosively.

Although dogs are allowed in national forests and designated wilderness areas, it is your responsibility to keep them from bothering wildlife or other hikers. In national parks and monuments, dogs are generally not allowed on trails. In national forests, dogs must be kept under control, and on a leash when required.

Don't cut live trees or plants of any kind, carve on trees or rocks, pick wildflowers, or build structures such as rock campfire rings.

Motorized vehicles and bicycles, including mountain bikes, are prohibited in all designated wilderness areas. State parks and other areas may also have restrictions.

CAMPING

Choose campsites on durable, naturally drained surfaces, such as forest duff, sand, gravel, or rock. In forest, look above you for dead branches that could break off. Avoid fragile meadows and sites next to springs and creeks. Never dig drainage ditches or make other "improvements." Rangers sometimes close specific areas to camping or entry to allow it to recover from heavy use.

CAMPFIRES

Don't build campfires except in an emergency. There are far too many fire scars in Arizona's backcountry. If you have good equipment, you'll be warmer without a fire.

Campfires are prohibited in certain areas, and during periods of high fire danger. Check with the land management agency listed with each hike for current regulations.

TRASH

If you carried it in, you can also carry it out. Do not bury food or trash; animals will dig it up. Feeding wild creatures makes them dependent on human food, which can lead to unpleasant encounters and cause the animals to starve during the off-season.

SANITATION

A short walk in any popular recreation area will show you that few people seem to know how to answer the call of nature away from facilities. Diseases such as giardiasis are spread by poor human sanitation. If facilities are available, use them. In the backcountry, select a site at least 100 yards from streams, lakes, springs, and dry washes. Avoid barren, sandy soil, if possible. Next, dig a small "cat hole" about 6 inches down into the organic layer of the soil. (Some people carry a small plastic trowel for this purpose.) When finished, refill the hole, covering any toilet paper. In some areas, regulations require that you carry out used toilet paper.

WEATHER

During the summer, heat is a hazard at lower elevations. In hot weather, each hiker will need a gallon of water or more every day. To avoid dehydration, drink more water than required merely to quench your thirst. Sport drinks, which replace electrolytes, are very useful. Eating a small amount of salty food, such as nuts, is helpful in replacing salts lost through heavy exercise.

Protection from both the heat and the sun is important; a lightweight sun hat is essential. During hot weather, hike in the mountains at higher elevations or hike early in the day to avoid the afternoon heat. Thunderstorms, which bring high wind, heavy rain and hail, and lightning, are common from July through September, and may occur any time of year. When

The desert mountain ranges of southwestern Arizona are best hiked in the cooler months of winter.

thunderstorms form, stay off exposed ridges and mountaintops and away from lone trees.

Hypothermia is a life-threatening condition caused by continuous exposure to chilling weather. Rainy, windy weather causes an insidious heat loss and is especially dangerous. Snowfall and blizzard conditions can occur at any time of year in the higher mountains. Hypothermia may be prevented by adjusting your clothing layers to avoid chilling or overheating, and by eating and drinking regularly so that your body continues to produce heat.

INSECTS AND THEIR KIN

A few mosquitoes appear after wet spring weather, but generally aren't a problem. Although most scorpions can inflict a painful sting, only the small, straw-colored scorpion found in the lower desert is dangerous. Black widow and brown recluse spiders can also be a hazard, especially to young children and adults who are allergic. Susceptible individuals should carry insect sting kits prescribed by their doctors. Kissing bugs and other obnoxious insects are dormant during cool weather but are active in warm weather. Use a net tent to keep nighttime prowlers away when camping in warm weather in the desert. You can avoid most scorpion and spider encounters by not placing your hands or bare feet where you can't see. Kick over rocks and logs before picking them up.

Aggressive Africanized bees are found throughout the state and are indistinguishable from domesticated honeybees. The best way to avoid being stung is to give all bees a wide berth. If attacked, drop your pack, protect your eyes, and head for brush or a nearby building or vehicle.

SNAKES

Arizona boasts eleven species of rattlesnakes—more than any other state—and several varieties. Rattlesnakes are most common at lower elevations but may be encountered anywhere. Rattlesnakes can strike no further than approximately half their body length, so avoid placing your hands and feet in areas that you cannot see, and walk several feet away from rock overhangs and shady ledges. Because bites often occur on feet, ankle-high hiking boots and loose fitting long pants will help. Snakes, which are cold-blooded, prefer surfaces at about 80° F, so watch for snakes in shady places during hotter weather. In cool weather be alert for sunning snakes.

OTHER WILDLIFE

Wild animals normally leave you alone unless molested or provoked. Black bears, mountain lions, and coyotes are shy and usually not a problem. Do not feed any wild animals, as they rapidly get accustomed to handouts and then will vigorously defend their new food source. Around camp, problems with rodents can be avoided by hanging your food from rocks or trees.

PLANTS

Poison ivy grows along streams and dry washes at intermediate elevations. The leaves, stems, and berries of poison ivy are poisonous to the touch. It is easily recognized by its leaves, which grow in groups of three. Contact causes a rash that later starts to blister. Unless large areas of skin are involved or the reaction is severe, no specific treatment is required. Calamine lotion will relieve the itching.

Cactus and other spiny plants occur at all but the highest elevations. Some cacti, especially cholla, have tiny barbs on their spines, which cause the burrs to cling ferociously. Use a pair of sticks to quickly pluck the burr or joint from your skin or clothing. A pair of tweezers is essential for removing spines.

Never eat any wild plant unless you know its identity. Many common plants, especially mushrooms, are deadly.

RESCUE

Anyone entering remote country should be self-sufficient and prepared to take care of emergencies such as equipment failure and minor medical problems. Very rarely, circumstances may create a life-threatening situation that requires a search effort or an emergency evacuation. Always leave word of your hiking plans with a reliable individual. For backpack trips, you should provide a written itinerary and a map. In your instructions, allow extra time for routine delays, and always make contact as soon as you are out. The responsible person should be advised to contact the appropriate authority if you are overdue. County sheriffs are responsible for search and rescue; you can also contact forest or park rangers.

Don't count on a cellular phone for communications in the backcountry. The cellular phone system is designed for use along highways and in cities, not the backcountry.

Authors' Recommendations

Easy Day Hikes	2 Dog Lake
	14 White House Ruin Trail
	19 Walker Lake
	27 Mormon Lake
	35 Bear Sign Canyon
	37 West Fork Trail
	41 Huckaby Trail
	47 Kinder Crossing Trail
	52 Horton Creek Trail
	55 Woodchute Trail
	72 Go John Trail
	74 Cholla Trail
	81 Wilderness of Rocks
	90 Ash Creek Falls
	91 Webb Peak
	93 Cochise Stronghold East
	101 Rucker Canyon
	105 Ramsey Canyon
	107 San Pedro River Trail
	111 Cherum Peak Trail
	114 Vulture Peak
Very Easy Day Hikes for Parents with Small Children	15 Wupatki Ruin
	19 Walker Lake
	51 Tunnel Trail
	73 Lookout Mountain
	76 Mayors Loop Trail
	94 Sugarloaf Mountain
	95 Echo Canyon
	97 Buena Vista Peak
	107 San Pedro River Trail
	116 Palm Canyon
	117 Squaw Lake Nature Trail
	118 Betty's Kitchen Interpretive Trail
First Night in the Wilderness	31 Parsons Trail
	32 Secret Mountain Trail
	43 Bell Trail
	46 Fossil Springs Trail
	47 Kinder Crossing Trail
	49 Chevelon Canyon
	52 Horton Creek Trail
	57 Pine Mountain
	63 Dutchmans Loop
	70 Bear Wallow Trail
	78 Margies Cove Trail
	82 Butterfly Trail
	88 Aravaipa Canyon
	109 Sycamore Creek

Authors' Recommendations

Authors' Recommendations

Authors' Recommendations

Hikes with Lots of Side Trips and Exploring (continued)	50 Highline National Recreation Trail
	58 Y Bar Basin–Barnhardt Canyon Loop
	63 Dutchmans Loop
	64 Fireline Loop
	68 KP Creek
	69 Bear Mountain
	71 Cave Creek Trail
	81 Wilderness of Rocks
	85 Mica Mountain
	86 Tanque Verde Ridge
	88 Aravaipa Canyon
	89 Powers Garden
	92 Safford–Morenci Trail
	103 Santa Rita Crest Trail
Hikes for Peak Baggers	16 Bill Williams Mountain Trail
	17 Bull Basin–Pumpkin Trails
	18 Kendrick Peak Trail
	21 Humphreys Peak Trail
	60 Browns Peak
	65 Escudilla Mountain
	67 Mount Baldy
	77 Quartz Peak Trail
	91 Webb Peak
	98 Chiricahua Peak
	99 Silver Peak
	100 Monte Vista Peak
	102 Mount Wrightson
	103 Santa Rita Crest Trail
	104 Carr Peak
	106 Miller Peak
	108 Summit Trail
	111 Cherum Peak Trail
	112 Wabayuma Peak
	113 Harquahala Mountain Trail
	114 Vulture Peak
Hikes for Backpackers	1 Ranger Trail
	6 North Kaibab Trail
	7 Clear Creek Trail
	8 Boucher–Hermit Trails
	9 South Kaibab–Bright Angel Trails
	11 Tanner–Grandview Trails
	12 Rainbow Bridge Trail
	13 Keet Seel Trail
	30 Taylor Cabin Loop
	31 Parsons Trail
	32 Secret Mountain Trail

Authors' Recommendations

Using This Guide

The hikes are presented in an easy-to-read format with at-a-glance information at the start. Each hike description contains the following information:

Hike number and name. The hike number is also shown on the overview map, to help you visualize the general location of the hike. We have used the official, or at least the commonly accepted, name for a trail or hike wherever possible. Hikes that use several trails are usually named for the main trail.

Description. This is a general description of the hike, including special attractions, and the name of the designated wilderness or other specially protected area, if any.

Location. This is the distance in miles, and direction from the nearest large town.

Type of hike. Out-and-back hikes are two-way hikes; you'll return by backtracking the trail. Loop hikes start and end at the same trailhead, but avoid retracing the trail. There may be some repeated sections in order to connect a loop hike. Shuttle hikes are one-way hikes starting and ending at different trailheads. You will have to leave a vehicle at both trailheads, or arrange for reliable pickup at the exit trailhead. Some day hikes can be expanded into easy backpack trips, and ambitious hikers may cover a backpack trip in one day.

Difficulty. All the hikes are rated as easy, moderate, or difficult. This is a subjective rating, but in general, easy hikes can be done by nearly anyone and take a few hours at most. Moderate hikes take all or most of a day and require moderate physical abilities. Difficult hikes are long, with significant elevation change, requiring a full day or several days to accomplish, and may involve cross-country hiking and route finding. Only experienced hikers in good physical condition should attempt these hikes.

Total distance. For out-and-back hikes, this distance in miles includes the return. For loops and shuttle hikes, this is the one-way distance.

Elevation change. The total altitude change in feet, not including ups and downs along the way, is given for each hike.

Water. Known and usually reliable sources are listed. Don't ever depend on a single water source, no matter how reliable it's been in the past. Remember that all backcountry water should be purified.

Best Months. This is the recommended time of year to do the hike. The season may be longer or shorter in some years. "Year-round" hikes may be hot in summer; you may want to hike early in the morning.

Maps. The appropriate USGS 7.5-minute topographic quadrangles are always listed, and other maps if useful.

Permit. Camping and other restrictions are also noted here.

For more information. The name of the land management unit having jurisdiction over the hike. For the address and phone number, refer to the Appendix.

Finding the trailhead. Driving directions are given from the nearest large town for all of the hikes. Distances are in miles.

Key points. This is a listing of trail junctions and important landmarks along the hike. You should be able to follow the route by reference to this section. Distances are given from the start of the hike in miles. All but a few level hikes have a corresponding elevation profile, to provide a picture of the climbs and descents of the hike.

The hike. In this narrative, we describe the hike in detail, along with interesting natural and human history. The description uses references to landmarks rather than distances wherever possible, because distances are listed under key points.

Grand Canyon

Nearly 300 miles long and averaging 10 miles wide, the Grand Canyon is truly the master canyon of the Colorado Plateau. A lifetime can easily be spent exploring its depths. As you descend through the layered geology of the canyon, you'll also be traveling southward in climate. On the South Rim, mixed ponderosa pine and pinyon-juniper forest identify the transition life zone. Midway in your descent, you'll be passing through the upper Sonoran life zone, identifiable by its pygmy forest of junipers. Near the river, you'll be hiking in the lower Sonoran life zone, characterized by low desert shrubs and grasses. The North Rim of the canyon is formed by the south edge of the Kaibab Plateau, a scenic alpine plateau that is 8,000 to 9,000 feet in elevation. The plateau receives more rain and snow than the South Rim and so is covered with a forest of ponderosa pine, Douglas fir, and quaking aspen.

Spanish conquistadors under the command of Coronado, who was riding north from Mexico City in 1540, were the first Europeans to visit the Grand Canyon. They probably reached the South Rim somewhere between the present Tanner and Grandview trailheads. A number of days were spent trying to find a way to the Colorado River, without success. Undoubtedly their native guide knew of several routes but chose to keep the information to himself. More than 200 years would pass before Europeans would see the canyon again. During the 1840s, mountain men roamed the Southwest in search of beaver, but apparently none of these intrepid explorers got below the rims of the canyon. Major John Wesley Powell carried out the first scientific exploration of the great canyon on two Colorado River float trips between 1869 and 1871. His group, conducting one of several government-sponsored surveys of the West, also extensively explored the region surrounding the canyon. Major Powell popularized the name Grand Canyon and many of its features. After Powell's explorations, miners and prospectors began to establish trails into the canyon. Most of them eventually found that guiding tourists was more profitable than mining.

Several hikes on the Kaibab Plateau are featured in this section. These are great hikes for summer or early fall, as the plateau is high enough to be pleasantly cool even during the hottest summer days. In addition, several of the best hikes into the canyon are featured. These routes are historic trails that have been abandoned and receive only minimum maintenance. It is strongly suggested that hikers carry the topographic maps on these hikes, as sections of trail may not be obvious. The hikes listed are within the Grand Canyon National Park, and overnight camping requires a permit that can be obtained from the backcountry office on the South Rim. Hike reservations can be made in person at the backcountry office, or in advance by mail. For information contact the National Park Service at the address listed in Appendix A. Campfires are not allowed in the park's backcountry, so plan to cook on a backpacking stove.

These hikers enjoy another wonderful sunset at the Grand Canyon.

1 Ranger Trail

Description:	An overnight backpack trip into the Kanab Creek Wilderness.
Location:	About 30 miles south of Fredonia.
Type of hike:	Out-and-back backpack.
Difficulty:	Moderate.
Total distance:	About 9.6 miles.
Elevation change:	1,400 feet.
Water:	Upper Jumpup and Lower Jumpup Springs.
Best months:	March–May, September–November.
Maps:	Jumpup Point USGS; North Kaibab National Forest.
Permit:	None for wilderness area; permit required if you continue south into Grand Canyon National Park.
For more information:	Kaibab National Forest, North Kaibab Ranger District.

Finding the trailhead: From Fredonia, drive south on Forest Road 422 (Ryan Road) about 23.3 miles then turn right (west) onto Forest Road 423. Follow it for 3.3 miles to Forest Road 235. Continue on Forest Road 235 about 7 miles until it becomes Forest Road 423 again. Drive another 8 miles to the end of the road at Jumpup Cabin and the Ranger Trailhead. A high-clearance vehicle is recommended, and the dirt forest service roads may be impassable when wet.

Key points:
- 0.0   Trailhead.
- 0.4   Upper Jumpup Spring.
- 4.2   Junction of Ranger Trail. with Sowats Point Trail.
- 4.8   Lower Jumpup Spring.

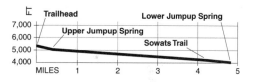

The hike: The Ranger Trail is only one of a number of routes into the magnificent Kanab Creek Wilderness. The trail begins at an old cabin and quickly drops into Jumpup Canyon. After a few switchbacks through the cross-bedded Coconino sandstone, the trail reaches the canyon bottom where a side canyon joins from the east. Upper Jumpup Spring emerges here and is piped into a concrete trough. This is a lovely spot with large box elders and fragrant big sage. There are stands of wolfberry, which often indicates that Native Americans frequented the location. They liked to eat the juicy, tart berries and probably encouraged their growth.

The trail continues down the main canyon bottom, in places climbing up on the right or left bank or bench. But if you don't notice it leaving the dry streambed, don't worry. Simply continue along the bottom.

Scan the cliff faces, especially under overhangs, and you might discover some intriguing prehistoric rock art. There are pictographs (paintings) dating as far back as several thousand years, as well as historic Southern Paiute drawings. Please do not touch them. Oils from your fingers can degrade the image.

Ranger Trail

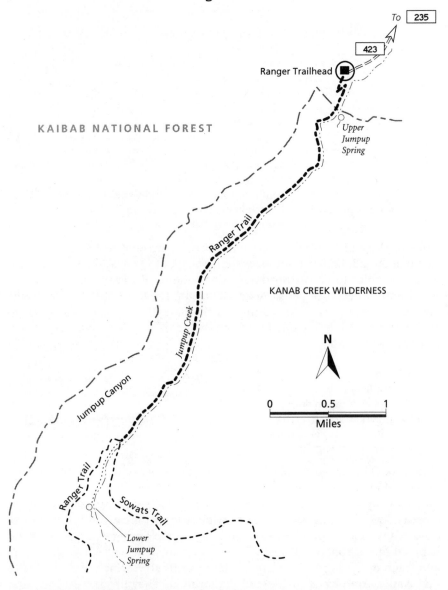

To 235

423

Ranger Trailhead

Upper Jumpup Spring

KAIBAB NATIONAL FOREST

Ranger Trail

KANAB CREEK WILDERNESS

Jumpup Creek

N

Jumpup Canyon

0   0.5   1

Miles

Ranger Trail

Sowats Trail

Lower Jumpup Spring

Continuing down canyon, the walls rise higher and higher. Beneath the buff Coconino sandstone, the dark red Hermit shale appears and begins to form a slope down to the canyon bottom. After about 4 miles, the canyon walls fold back, revealing the grand expanse called the Esplanade. This relatively flat bench covers hundreds of square miles in western Grand Canyon. The resistant upper member of the Supai Group, a collection of sandstones, shale, and limestone, has created this remarkable feature.

Backpackers of all ages enjoy the Ranger Trail in the Kanab Creek Wilderness.

Keep a sharp lookout for a sign and/or rock cairns that signal the Ranger Trail's exit from the canyon floor to go southwest along the Esplanade. To the southeast, the Sowats Trail follows the Esplanade. For now though, continue downstream to the stand of Fremont cottonwoods ahead. This is Lower Jumpup Spring. The exact point of emergence for this spring varies from year to year. Sometimes water is seeping out just below the first trees. Other years, you may have to walk another 0.5 mile to find water. The best camping is around the area where you first encounter the cottonwoods.

The Ranger Trail across the Esplanade and the Sowats Trail both make great day hikes or longer. But remember to carry plenty of water. Many of the springs shown on the topo maps are unreliable. Get the latest information from the North Kaibab Ranger District Office.

—Stewart Aitchison

2 Dog Lake

Description:	A scenic walk on a section of the Arizona Trail through alpine meadows on the Kaibab Plateau.
Location:	30 miles south of Jacob Lake.
Type of hike:	Out-and-back day hike.
Difficulty:	Easy.
Total distance:	3.8 miles.
Elevation change:	100 feet.
Water:	None.
Best months:	June–October.
Maps:	Dog Point USGS, Kaibab National Forest (North Kaibab Ranger District).
Permit:	None.
For more information:	Kaibab National Forest, North Kaibab Ranger District.

Finding the trailhead: From Jacob Lake, go south approximately 26 miles on Arizona 67, then turn left (east) on Forest Road 611. (This signed turnoff is 0.9 mile south of Kaibab Lodge.) Follow Forest Road 611, a maintained dirt road, 1.4 miles then turn right (east) to remain on Forest Road 611. After a few yards turn left to remain on Forest Road 611. This road is signed for East Rim View. Continue 2.5 miles to the signed trailhead, which is about 0.25 mile past the East Rim Viewpoint.

Key points:

- 0.0   Trailhead.
- 0.2   Dog Lake.
- 0.5   Dog Canyon.
- 1.3   East rim of Upper Tater Canyon.
- 1.9   Upper Tater Canyon

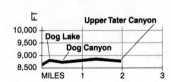

Along the Arizona Trail near Dog Lake.

Dog Lake

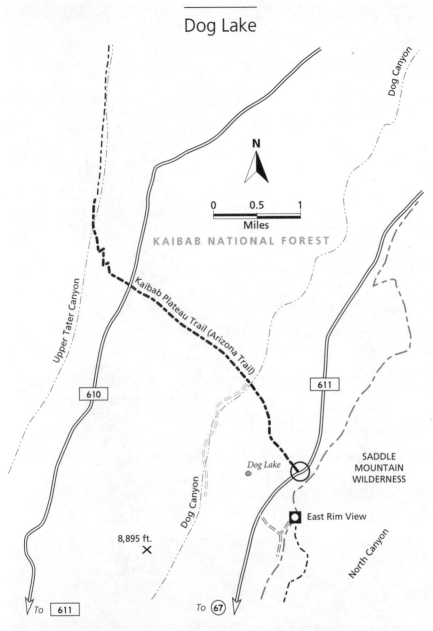

The hike: Before starting the hike, walk to the rim of North Canyon for the great view from the east side of the Kaibab Plateau. This hike follows a portion of the Arizona Trail, which when completed will traverse Arizona from Utah to Mexico. The northernmost section has been completed across the Kaibab Plateau from the Utah border to the Grand Canyon National Park boundary. This section of the trail is especially scenic, traversing two of the alpine meadows that grace the high plateau.

The Arizona Trail crosses the state from Utah to Mexico.

The trail crosses Forest Road 611 here, and is signed KAIBAB PLATEAU TRAIL and marked with small Arizona Trail signs. Follow the trail across the road to the northwest. After about 0.2 mile through the fir forest, the trail (an old road) passes Dog Lake, a small shallow pond ringed by aspen. Although the Kaibab Plateau lies at 8,000 to 9,000 feet above sea level and receives much more precipitation than the surrounding desert, the limestone bedrock is porous and soaks up all the moisture. There are no running streams on the plateau; the only water sources are a few springs and small ponds.

Just after the pond, the trail enters a meadow and then crosses a road that comes down Dog Canyon. The trail, still marked by Arizona Trail posts, continues northwest and enters the forest again after more than a mile of meadow. It crosses the east ridge of Upper Tater Canyon and Forest Road 610, then descends into Upper Tater Canyon via a series of switchbacks and enters another fine meadow. This expansive alpine setting makes a good turnaround point for an easy day hike.

—Bruce Grubbs

3 Widforss Trail

Description: A hike along the North Rim of the Grand Canyon with good views. This is a good walk if you have limited time but still wish to escape the crowds.
Location: 40 miles south of Jacob Lake.
Type of hike: Out-and-back day hike.
Difficulty: Moderate.
Total distance: 8.8 miles.
Elevation change: 300 feet.
Water: None.
Best months: June–October.
Maps: Bright Angel Point USGS; Kaibab National Forest, North Kaibab Ranger District.
Permit: Required for overnight hikes.
For more information: Grand Canyon National Park.

Finding the trailhead: From Jacob Lake, drive south approximately 40 miles on Arizona 67, then turn right on the signed road for the Widforss Trail. (If you miss this turnoff, turn around at the better-marked Kaibab Trailhead about 0.5 mile farther.) Continue 0.5 mile to the signed trailhead for the Widforss Trail, with parking on the left.

Key points:
0.0 Trailhead.
0.4 First view of the Transept.
1.8 Cross a drainage at the head of the Transept.
2.4 Trail leaves the rim.
4.4 Widforss Point.

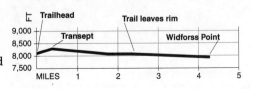

Widforss Trail

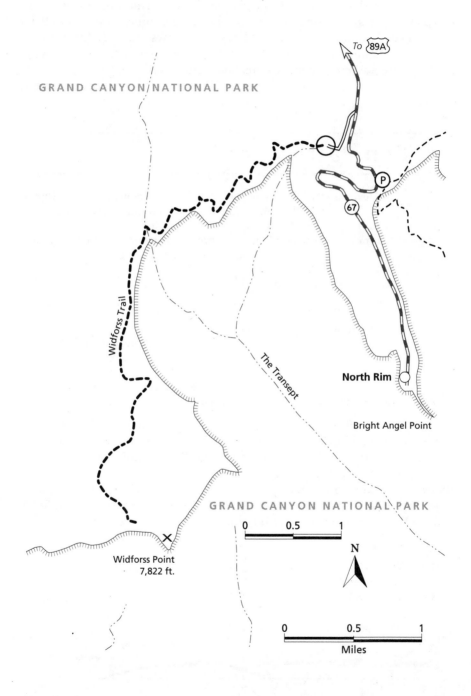

To 89A

GRAND CANYON NATIONAL PARK

P

67

Widforss Trail

The Transept

North Rim

Bright Angel Point

GRAND CANYON NATIONAL PARK

Widforss Point
7,822 ft.

0   0.5   1

N

0   0.5   1
Miles

The hike: The well-maintained trail climbs along a slope, then skirts a drainage that soon opens out into the Transept, a side canyon. The trail continues along the rim with occasional views through the dense forest, and then crosses a shallow drainage at the head of the Transept. Shortly after this point, the trail veers away from the rim and continues to Widforss Point at the head of Haunted Canyon. Although the views are more limited than some of the famous viewpoints, the opportunity to enjoy the canyon without the noise and crowds makes this hike very rewarding.

—Bruce Grubbs

4 Ken Patrick Trail

Description:	This is a cool and scenic hike along the North Rim of the Grand Canyon, in Grand Canyon National Park.
Location:	40 miles south of Jacob Lake.
Type of hike:	Shuttle if the entire trail is hiked. The first 2.7 miles make a great out-and-back day hike.
Difficulty:	Moderate.
Total distance:	7.4 miles one-way.
Elevation change:	780 feet.
Water:	None.
Best months:	June–October.
Maps:	Bright Angel Point, Wahalla Plateau, Point Imperial USGS; Grand Canyon National Park Trails Illustrated.
Permit:	Required for overnight hikes.
For more information:	Grand Canyon National Park.

Finding the trailhead: If you do the entire hike, you'll need to shuttle a vehicle to the end of the hike. From Jacob Lake, drive south approximately 40 miles on Arizona 67, then turn left to the Kaibab Trailhead, just before entering the North Rim village. To reach the start of the hike from the Kaibab Trailhead, go north on Arizona 67 about 1 mile, then turn right on Cape Royal Road. Drive about 5 miles, then turn left on Point Imperial Road, and continue 2.5 miles to Point Imperial.

Key points:
- 0.0 Trailhead at Point Imperial.
- 2.7 Trail leaves the rim.
- 3.2 Cape Royal Road.

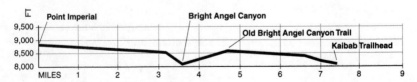

Ken Patrick Trail

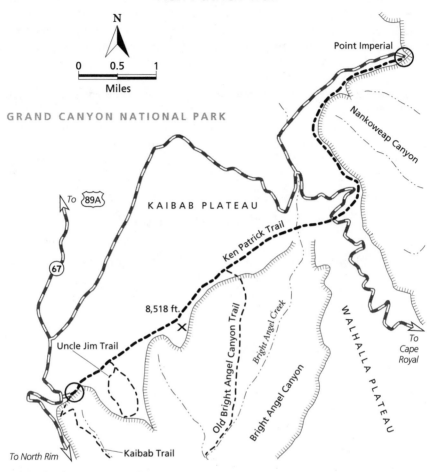

N

0   0.5   1

Miles

GRAND CANYON NATIONAL PARK

To 89A

KAIBAB PLATEAU

Point Imperial

Nankoweap Canyon

Ken Patrick Trail

67

8,518 ft.

X

Old Bright Angel Canyon Trail

Bright Angel Creek

To
Cape
Royal

Uncle Jim Trail

WALHALLA PLATEAU

Bright Angel Canyon

To North Rim

Kaibab Trail

3.6   Bright Angel Canyon.
4.7   Junction with Old Bright Angel Canyon Trail.
6.6   Junction with Uncle Jim Trail.
7.0   Roaring Springs Canyon.
7.4   Kaibab Trailhead.

The hike: The trail, named for a park ranger killed in the line of duty, follows the rim west from Point Imperial. There are occasional views, but the thick alpine forest grows right to the edge most of the way. Nevertheless, you'll see tooth-shaped Mount Hayden and the sharp spire of Sullivan Peak. This section of the trail skirts the many heads of Nankoweap Canyon, a major side canyon. The trail follows the rim around the head of the arm west of Sullivan Peak and heads southeasterly. After passing a point where the Cape Royal Road nearly touches the rim, the trail veers west, away from the rim, and crosses the road. This would be a good goal for an easy day hike.

After crossing the road, the trail gets less use and can be hard to follow though the fir and spruce forest. It drops down to cross the head of Bright Angel Creek, and then loosely follows the rim of Bright Angel Canyon southeast. Most of the time, the trail stays on the top of the broad ridge back from the rim. You'll pass the junction with the Old Bright Angel Canyon Trail, which goes left and descends into the canyon. After a couple more miles, the Uncle Jim Trail joins from the left, and the trail becomes more distinct. It dips into the head of Roaring Springs Canyon, and then ends at the North Kaibab Trailhead.

—Bruce Grubbs

5 Nankoweap– Saddle Mountain Trail

Description:	This is a great day hike to a seldom visited overlook of the Grand Canyon.
Location:	About 40 miles southwest of Lees Ferry.
Type of hike:	Out-and-back day hike.
Difficulty:	Moderate.
Total distance:	6.0 miles.
Elevation change:	1,145 feet.
Water:	None.
Best months:	March–May, September–November.
Maps:	Point Imperial USGS; Kaibab National Forest, North Kaibab Ranger District.
Permit:	None.
For more information:	Kaibab National Forest, North Kaibab Ranger District.

Finding the trailhead: Turn off U.S. 89A about 20 miles east of Jacob Lake. Head south 27 miles on the House Rock Valley/Buffalo Ranch Road (Forest Road 8910) to the wilderness boundary and signed trailhead.

Key points:
0.0   Trailhead.
0.75 Traverses hill.
1.25 Bottom of Saddle Canyon and junction with Saddle Mountain Trail going east.
3.0   Rim.

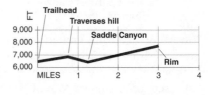

The hike: At the end of Forest Road 8910, a sign marks the beginning of the Nankoweap/Saddle Mountain Trail. The trail starts off as an old road heading uphill. Pinyon pines and junipers grow along the rocky slope. Eventually the trail turns left and traverses the slope before dropping into the upper reaches of Saddle Canyon. Already the scenery is taking on a grand scale.

Nankoweap–Saddle Mountain Trail

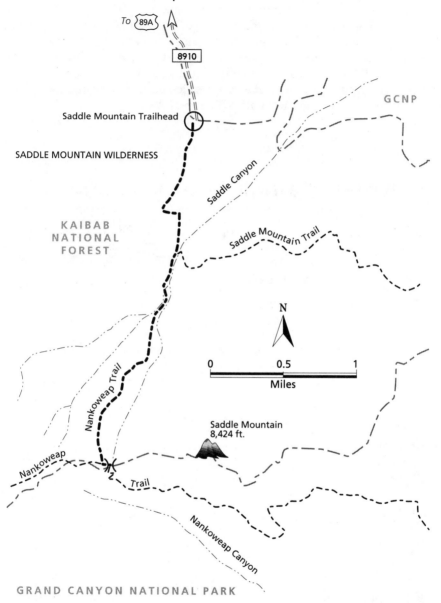

To 89A

8910

Saddle Mountain Trailhead

SADDLE MOUNTAIN WILDERNESS

GCNP

Saddle Canyon

KAIBAB
NATIONAL
FOREST

Saddle Mountain Trail

N

0   0.5   1
Miles

Saddle Mountain
8,424 ft.

Nankoweap Trail

Nankoweap

Trail

Nankoweap Canyon

GRAND CANYON NATIONAL PARK

Off to the north are the Vermilion Cliffs. To the east are the Echo Cliffs. Between the two sets of cliffs and slicing into the Marble Platform is Marble Canyon, the beginning of the Grand Canyon.

Closer at hand, mule deer tracks are common on the trail. Also, be alert for mountain lion tracks and scat. These magnificent predators are rarely seen. From the canyon bottom, the Saddle Mountain Trail ascends to the east (and is a delightful 5-mile walk one-way to Marble Canyon), but the

Nankoweap Trail begins to work its way upstream. Rock cairns and blazes on tree trunks mark the route.

After another 2 miles and climbing a thousand vertical feet, the trail tops out in the saddle of Saddle Mountain overlooking Nankoweap Canyon, a major drainage into the Grand Canyon. You have also entered Grand Canyon National Park and reached the trailhead for the park's Nankoweap Trail, an extremely difficult route into Nankoweap. Remember that there is no camping allowed within the park without a Park Service permit. No camping permit is required in the Saddle Mountain Wilderness Area.

—Stewart Aitchison

6 North Kaibab Trail

Description:	This is a strenuous but rewarding backpack to the very bottom of the Grand Canyon.
Location:	About 2 miles north of Grand Canyon Lodge on the North Rim.
Type of hike:	Out-and-back backpack.
Difficulty:	Difficult.
Total distance:	28.4 miles.
Elevation change:	5,850 feet.
Water:	Roaring Springs, Cottonwood Camp, Phantom Ranch, and Bright Angel Campground.
Best months:	Mid-May–October; summers are hot.
Maps:	Bright Angel Point, Phantom Ranch USGS.
Permit:	Backcountry permit required.
For more information:	Grand Canyon National Park.

Finding the trailhead: From the Grand Canyon Lodge on the North Rim, drive about 2 miles north on the main entrance road (Arizona 67) to the trailhead parking area on the right.

Key points:
- 0.0 Trailhead.
- 4.7 Roaring Springs.
- 6.8 Cottonwood Campground.
- 8.3 Side trip to Ribbon Falls.
- 11.0 The Box.
- 13.8 Phantom Ranch.
- 14.4 Bright Angel Campground.
- 14.6 Colorado River.

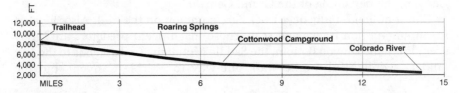

North Kaibab Trail • Clear Creek Trail

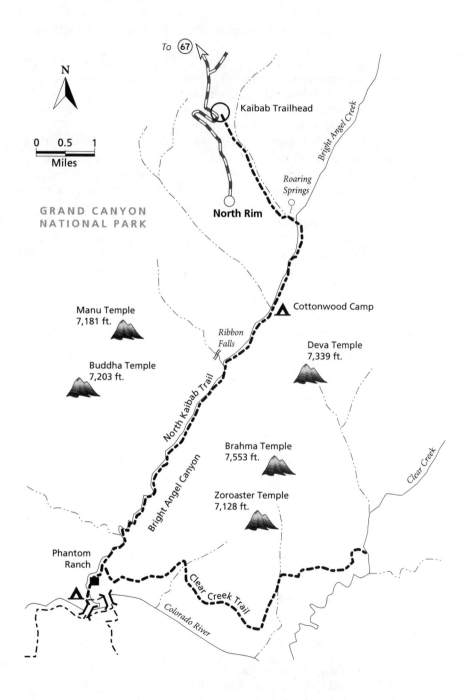

To (67)

N

0   0.5   1
Miles

Kaibab Trailhead

Bright Angel Creek

Roaring Springs

North Rim

GRAND CANYON
NATIONAL PARK

Manu Temple
7,181 ft.

Cottonwood Camp

Ribbon
Falls

Deva Temple
7,339 ft.

Buddha Temple
7,203 ft.

North Kaibab Trail

Brahma Temple
7,553 ft.

Clear Creek

Bright Angel Canyon

Zoroaster Temple
7,128 ft.

Phantom
Ranch

Clear Creek Trail

Colorado River

The hike: For the first 4.7 miles, the North Kaibab Trail quickly descends into Roaring Springs Canyon to meet Bright Angel Creek. Roaring Springs, as the name suggests, can be heard long before it is seen. Water gushes out of a cave in the Redwall limestone and cascades down to Bright Angel Creek. Water from the springs is pumped to both the North and South Rims to serve tourists and residents.

About 2.1 miles down the creek is Cottonwood Campground, which is good destination for first-time canyon hikers. Fremont cottonwood, box elder, pale hoptree, Knowlton hop hornbeam, and coyote willow line the creek banks. American dippers may be seen doing their kneebends on boulders in the stream or "flying" underwater in search of aquatic invertebrates to eat.

About 1.5 miles downstream from the campground is a short side trip to Ribbon Falls. The waters of Ribbon Creek are highly mineralized with calcium carbonate derived from the limestone formations above. As the mineral slowly precipitates from the creek water, an apron of calcium carbonate or travertine is formed behind the falls. Moss, maidenhair ferns, yellow columbine, and scarlet monkeyflowers thrive in the spray from the falls.

Back on the main trail, travel another 3 miles to reach the entrance of The Box, where vertical walls of black Precambrian schist tower 1,000 feet above the creek. After 2.8 miles more, you reach Phantom Ranch. Built in 1922, it's the only lodge within the Grand Canyon. Mail can be sent out from the ranch, and it will be postmarked "Mailed from the bottom of the Canyon." The delightful booklet *Recollections of Phantom Ranch,* written by Elizabeth Simpson, delves into the fascinating history of this isolated guest ranch.

The Bright Angel Campground is 0.6 miles beyond Phantom Ranch. The Colorado River is another 0.2 mile past the campground.

Strong hikers could do this as a two-day backpack, but breaking it up into three or four days would give you more time to enjoy this remarkable place.
—Stewart Aitchison

7 Clear Creek Trail

Description:	A rugged hike that requires going to the bottom of the Grand Canyon just to reach the trailhead.
Location:	About 0.5 mile north of Phantom Ranch.
Type of hike:	Out-and-back backpack.
Difficulty:	Difficult.
Total distance:	17.4 miles.
Elevation change:	1,000 feet.
Water:	Only at Bright Angel and Clear Creeks; purify before drinking.
Best months:	September–May.
Maps:	Phantom Ranch USGS.
Permit:	Required.
For more information:	Grand Canyon National Park.

See Map on Page 39

Finding the trailhead: This trail is reached via the North Kaibab Trail (see Hike 6). About 0.5 mile north of Phantom Ranch, the signed Clear Creek Trail begins its ascent through the somber Precambrian schist.

Key points:
   0.0   Trailhead.
   1.6   Reach top of Tonto Platform.
   8.0   Begin descent into Clear Creek.
   8.7   Clear Creek.

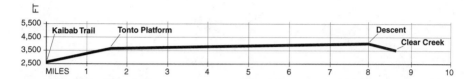

The hike: The hike starts off with several switchbacks, after which you begin to have great views up and down Bright Angel Canyon and beyond. The Civilian Conservation Corps built this well-constructed trail in 1933. At one switchback corner, there is a stone bench, a good place to take off the pack and enjoy the scenery.

The trail eventually rounds a bend, and the Colorado River, entrenched in the Inner Gorge, is directly below you. Across the way you can see the South Kaibab Trail making its steep descent into the gorge. Notice the near canyon wall. Here is the contact between the very ancient foliated and shiny (due to mica) Precambrian schist and the coarse, dark brown Cambrian Tapeats sandstone. The contact represents a gap in geologic time of about one billion years, known to geologists as the Great Unconformity.

Once gaining the Tonto Platform, which is essentially the top of the Tapeats sandstone formation, the Clear Creek Trail meanders eastward around Sumner Butte and Bradley and Demaray Points. On a hot day with a heavy backpack, the trail can become tedious, but remember that you are slowly climbing almost all the way to Clear Creek, so the return trip is slightly downhill and therefore faster.

The trail must travel north into Clear Creek Canyon quite a way before making its final descent to the creek. Along the stream are a number of campsites among the Fremont cottonwood trees. There is also a pit toilet located between the camp area and where the trail meets the canyon bottom.

From the camp area, there are several options for day hikes. Going downstream, the Colorado River is about 4 miles distant. Most springtime hikers decide to walk upstream about 4 miles in hopes of getting a glimpse of Cheyava Falls, one of the tallest in the Grand Canyon but intermittent. Its flow depends on the amount of rain and snow the North Rim receives.

Going upstream can be problematic, however. In some years, the stream flow is so high and vegetation so thick that upstream progress may be impossible or at least very dangerous. Other years, flash floods may have scoured out the vegetation and the stream may be nearly nonexistent. Walking along the creek at these times is no problem, but the falls may be no

The Clear Creek Trail within Grand Canyon National Park crosses the Tonto Platform north of the Colorado River and gives hikers awesome panoramas on the inner gorge.

more than a damp stain on the canyon wall. When you pick up your hiking permit, ask the ranger for the latest information.

—Stewart Aitchison

8 Boucher-Hermit Trails

Description:	A three- to five-day hike on historic trails in Grand Canyon National Park.
Location:	8 miles west of Grand Canyon Village.
Type of hike:	Loop backpack.
Difficulty:	Difficult.
Total distance:	19.7 miles.
Elevation change:	3,680 feet.
Water:	Boucher Creek, Hermit Creek.
Best months:	October–April.
Maps:	Grand Canyon USGS; Grand Canyon National Park Trails Illustrated.
Permit:	Required for overnight hikes.
For more information:	Grand Canyon National Park.

Finding the trailhead: From Grand Canyon Village, drive west 4.5 miles to the end of Hermit Road. The signed trailhead for the Hermit Trail is west of the main parking area. During the summer the road is closed to private vehicles, and access is via the free Hermit Road Shuttle. Check with the Park Service when you get your hiking permit for the shuttle schedule and current vehicle restriction. Usually there is a hiker's special, which runs early in the morning.

Key points:

0.0	Trailhead at Hermits Rest.
1.2	Junction with Waldron Trail.
1.5	Turn left on Dripping Spring Trail.
2.4	Turn right on Boucher Trail.
5.2	Start the Supai descent.
6.0	Cross Travertine Canyon.
6.7	Start the Redwall descent.
7.6	Turn right on the Tonto Trail.
10.3	Cross Travertine Canyon.
12.2	Hermit Creek.
13.1	Turn right on Hermit Trail.
14.3	Top of the Redwall.
16.9	Santa Maria Spring.
17.3	Junction with Dripping Spring Trail.
18.5	Junction with Waldron Trail.
19.7	Trailhead at Hermits Rest.

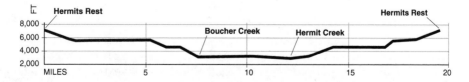

Boucher–Hermit Trails

The hike: In hot weather, carry plenty of water, as it is a long hike to the first water at Boucher Creek. Keep in mind that the temperature rises as you descend. One gallon per person is not excessive. In cool weather two quarts per person is sufficient.

Descend into the canyon on the Hermit Trail. The trail is named for Louis Boucher, a solitary prospector who developed a small mine at nearby Boucher Creek. After a few switchbacks through the cliff-forming Kaibab limestone and the sloping Toroweap formation, the trail turns west and descends into Hermit Basin. Impressive trail construction was done in the Coconino sandstone; the trail was paved with slabs of rock set on edge. Cross-bedded layers of rock and sandblasting of the individual grains of sand prove that the Coconino sandstone had its origin in a Sahara-like sand dune desert. Watch for fossil reptile tracks along this section of the trail as well.

In Hermit Basin, the trail passes the junction with Waldron Trail and then meets Dripping Spring Trail. Turn left (west) and follow the Dripping Spring Trail as it contours around the head of Hermit Canyon. There are impressive views down this narrow gorge. After contouring around several side canyons, you'll meet the Boucher Trail, where you'll turn right. (Dripping Spring is about 0.4 mile west of the junction). Louis Boucher constructed this trail to reach his mines at Boucher Creek. The Boucher Trail stays on the same level past Yuma Point, giving a view of the Hermit Trail and Hermit Canyon to the east. The soft red Hermit shale forms this terrace, which the trail remains on until it takes advantage of a break in the cliffs below to descend. About 0.6 mile west of Yuma Point, the trail finds the break and descends abruptly through the layered red Esplanade and Supai sandstones as it drops into the head of Travertine Canyon. After passing through the saddle south of Whites Butte, it descends the massive Redwall limestone cliff through a fault to the north. The Redwall limestone is actually a translucent gray rock composed entirely of the shells of millions of microscopic animals. These tiny ocean creatures died and fell to the deep sea floor as a constant rain. The Redwall gets its name from the red stain that seeps down from the overlying red formations and coats the surface of the cliff.

As the slope moderates, the Boucher Trail descends through the greenish Muav limestone and ends at the junction with the Tonto Trail. Turn left (west) to descend about 0.2 mile to Boucher Creek, where you'll find water and campsites. If time allows, it is easy to walk cross-country about 2 miles to the Colorado River by descending Boucher Creek into the Granite Gorge. As you near the river, you'll be greeted by the roar of Boucher Rapid. It's a small one on the Grand Canyon scale, but impressive nevertheless.

The loop continues on the Tonto Trail to the north and east. From the rim the Tonto Trail looks flat, but it is constantly climbing and descending to avoid small drainages. It zigs into side canyons and zags back out again. The trail is much longer than the horizontal distance would suggest. Allow plenty of time when hiking this section, especially since you'll be distracted by the occasional spectacular views of the Granite Gorge and the Colorado River. The Tonto Plateau, which the trail follows, is formed by the greenish-purple Bright Angel shale, which is soft and erodes into slopes. In contrast, the underlying Japeats sandstone is resistant and forms cliffs. The trail crosses Travertine Canyon, where huge deposits of travertine rock indicate the former presence of a large natural spring, now dry. After Travertine it swings into Hermit Canyon and drops into Hermit Creek.

Where the Hermit Trail passes through the Coconino Sandstone, the original builders carefully placed sandstone slabs on edge to create a beautiful and durable trail.

There is always water in Hermit Creek, and there's designated camping at the Park Service campsite. The trail down Hermit Canyon is about 1.5 miles, and descends through ancient rock formations to the Colorado River. The Tapeats sandstone, a rock that was derived from beach sand, forms the rim of lower Hermit Creek. The somber dark gray rocks of the gorge are Vishnu schist, among the oldest rocks on earth. The hard, twisted schist is the result of extreme pressures deep in the earth, probably caused by movement of the continental plates. The side canyon ends at Hermit Rapid, one of the largest in the Grand Canyon. For modern river craft, Hermit Rapid is fun but not difficult, because the water is deep and free of rocks. At high water the waves reach heights of 20 feet or more.

During the walk along Hermit Creek, you'll see sections of trail construction from the tourist resort days. Up until about 1930, Hermit Camp on the Tonto Trail at Hermit Creek was the primary tourist resort in the Grand Canyon. A long aerial tram from Pima Point was used to ferry supplies to the camp. A Model T Ford was even sent down and used on a short network of roads. When the transcanyon Kaibab Trail was completed, the tourism focus quickly switched to the Bright Angel Creek area, the present site of Phantom Ranch resort.

From Hermit Camp, start the ascent out of the canyon by hiking northeast on the Tonto Trail. The Hermit Trail is clearly visible ahead, climbing the slopes above the Tonto Plateau. When you reach the junction, turn right (east). At first the climb is gentle, but the grade rapidly becomes steeper as the trail picks its way up the shale slopes. At the foot of the Redwall limestone, the trail begins a series of short switchbacks known as the Cathedral Stairs. At the top

Weather within the Grand Canyon can vary dramatically. On this early spring day on the Clear Creek Trail, the morning started with snow flurries but the day ended with the hot sun bearing down.

of the Redwall, the trail then swings southwest around Breezy Point, and passes a section where the original horse trail was destroyed by a landslide.

The trail climbs slowly until south of Breezy Point, where it takes advantage of a weakness in the Supai sandstone cliffs and abruptly climbs to the base of the Esplanade sandstone. (Breezy Point is an easy, short side hike with great views of Hermit Camp.) An old rest house marks Santa Maria Spring, which usually has water. Shortly after the spring, the Hermit Trail climbs through the Esplanade sandstone and passes the Dripping Spring Trail junction. Turn left (east) and continue on the Hermit Trail to the rim and the trailhead.

—Bruce Grubbs

9 South Kaibab– Bright Angel Trails

Description:	This is one of the easier backpacks in the Grand Canyon but still not to be taken lightly.
Location:	Near the Grand Canyon Village on the South Rim.
Type of hike:	Shuttle backpack.
Difficulty:	Difficult.
Total distance:	16.6 miles.
Elevation change:	4,780 feet.
Water:	Treated water is available at Bright Angel Campground, Indian Gardens, and—in summer only—Three-Mile and One-and-a-half-Mile Rest Houses.
Best months:	September–May.
Maps:	Phantom Ranch USGS.
Permit:	Required.
For more information:	Grand Canyon National Park.

Finding the trailhead: The South Kaibab Trail begins near Yaki Point, 3 miles east of the Grand Canyon Village. Access is limited to park shuttle vans; check at the Backcountry Information Center for the schedule. You'll end the trip at Bright Angel Trailhead at the west end of Grand Canyon Village; park in the designated trailhead parking and ride the park shuttle to the Kaibab Trailhead.

Key points:
- 0.0   South Kaibab Trailhead.
- 1.3   Cedar Ridge.
- 6.3   Colorado River.
- 7.3   Bright Angel Campground.

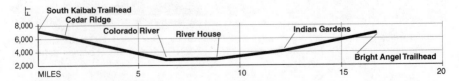

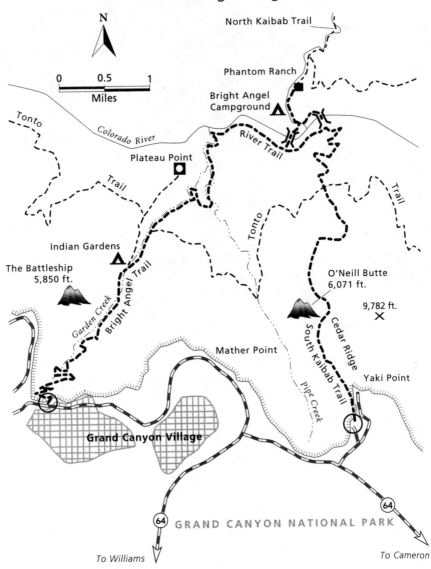

South Kaibab–Bright Angel Trails

North Kaibab Trail

Phantom Ranch

Bright Angel Campground

N

0   0.5   1
Miles

Tonto

Colorado River

River Trail

Plateau Point

Tonto

Trail

Trail

Indian Gardens

The Battleship
5,850 ft.

O'Neill Butte
6,071 ft.

9,782 ft.
✕

Garden Creek

Bright Angel Trail

South Kaibab Trail

Cedar Ridge

Mather Point

Yaki Point

Pipe Creek

Grand Canyon Village

64   GRAND CANYON NATIONAL PARK

64

To Williams

To Cameron

8.8   River House.
12.1 Indian Gardens.
16.6 Bright Angel Trailhead.

The hike: This is the backpack trip that many first-timers to the Grand Canyon give a try. Most go down the South Kaibab because it is steeper than the Bright Angel. This hike can be done as an overnight, but you will have more time to look around (and rest those sore muscles) if you make it a three-day trip.

The South Kaibab Trail begins near Yaki Point, several miles east of the Grand Canyon Village. Like most Grand Canyon trails, this one starts by steeply

Families enjoy the Bright Angel Trail. Camping part way down at Indian Gardens helps break up a trip to the bottom.

switchbacking through the upper cliffs of the Kaibab, Toroweap, and Coconino formations. At about 1.3 miles you reach Cedar Ridge, where there is a toilet. The ridge makes a good turnaround spot for day hikers.

The South Kaibab Trail leaves Cedar Ridge, circles under O'Neill Butte, and then plunges through the Redwall, Muav, and Bright Angel layers before leveling off on the Tonto Platform. But relief is short-lived because the trail suddenly begins another set of steep switchbacks leading down to the Colorado River. The Kaibab Suspension Bridge (a.k.a. Black Bridge), built in 1928, takes you across the river, and another 0.5 mile brings you to the Bright Angel Campground, which has designated sites, drinking water, and a rest room with running water. Phantom Ranch, where mule riders stay, is located just north of the campground. There is also the Hiker's Dorm for those hikers who have made reservations and don't want to camp out. Hot and cold drinks are available at Phantom Ranch.

To get out of this big hole in the ground, hike from the campground area toward the river. Instead of returning to the Black Bridge, cross the wooden Bright Angel Creek Bridge and follow the trail to the Silver Bridge, built in the late 1960s to support the pipeline carrying water from Roaring Springs to the South Rim. On the far side of this bridge, turn right and follow the River Trail for 1.5 miles to its junction with the Bright Angel. From here it's only 7.8 miles and 4,400 vertical feet to the South Rim.

At Indian Gardens, 4.5 miles from the South Rim, are toilets, drinking water, a picnic area, ranger station, and campground. During the warmer months, there is drinking water available at 3 miles and 1.5 miles from the rim.

The trail passes through a short tunnel just below the rim. Before entering the tunnel, look up to your right. There under an overhang are some red pictographs presumably painted by ancient Indians. Once you reach the South Rim, you will find yourself near the historic Kolb Studio at the west end of Grand Canyon Village.

—Stewart Aitchison

10 Horseshoe Mesa

Description:	A hike to a historic mining district in Grand Canyon National Park.
Location:	14 miles east of Tusayan.
Type of hike:	Out-and-back day hike.
Difficulty:	Difficult.
Total distance:	4.0 miles.
Elevation change:	2,400 feet.
Water:	None.
Best months:	March–May, October–November.
Maps:	Grandview Point, Cape Royal USGS; Grand Canyon National Park Trails Illustrated.
Permit:	Required for overnight hikes.
For more information:	Grand Canyon National Park.

Horseshoe Mesa • Tanner-Grandview Trails

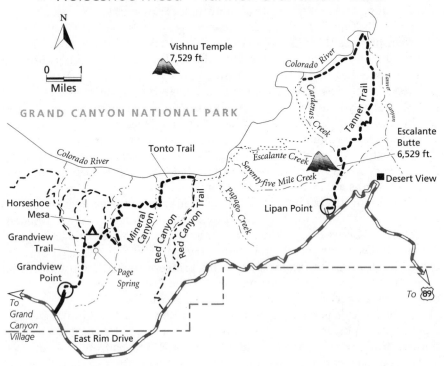

Finding the trailhead: From Tusayan, drive 8.2 miles north on Arizona 64, then turn east on Desert View Drive. 8.6 miles from the turnoff, turn left (north) on the signed Grandview Point road, and park in the signed trailhead parking area.

Key points:
- 0.0 Trailhead at Grandview Point.
- 2.0 Last Chance Mine on Horseshoe Mesa.

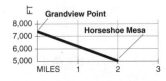

The hike: This a strenuous hike and the short distance is deceiving; the trail descends 2,400 feet. You will have to climb this distance on the way out. The Grandview Trail is well named, as it features an expansive view right from its start at the east side of the stone wall at the viewpoint. A series of switchbacks leads through the cliffs of the Kaibab limestone and out onto the steep slopes of the Toroweap formation. Clever trail construction is used in sections through the Coconino sandstone. Parts of the trail are paved with blocks of sandstone fitted on edge, and in other places the trail is built up with log cribbing. These places can become interesting when a winter storm leaves 2 feet of snow on the trail. After reaching the red slopes of the Hermit shale, the trail descends east, then north around the head of Cottonwood Creek and finally comes out onto Horseshoe Mesa.

The Inner Gorge of the Grand Canyon is only accessible to hikers and river runners.

When you reach the top of the Redwall limestone, it appears that you should be on the same level as Horseshoe Mesa, which is formed on the upper surface of the Redwall, but you'll still descend another 200 feet onto the mesa. This difference is caused by the displacement along the Grandview Fault, which you cross as you descend onto Horseshoe Mesa. The Park Service campground is near the abandoned Last Chance Mine, which is interesting to explore. (Do not enter the old mine shafts, which are very dangerous.) Pete Berry established the old copper mine before 1900, and the Grandview Trail was constructed to service the mine. The stone cookhouse still stands several hundred yards west of the campground. A vertical shaft on the mesa provided air to one of the mines, but the main access was via a horizontal shaft just below the rim to the southeast. Another shaft is located near the base of the Redwall limestone farther to the east. Water was obtained either from Page Spring or from a spring in Cottonwood Creek.

—Bruce Grubbs

11 Tanner-Grandview Trails

See Map on Page 52

Description: A hike featuring interesting geology on two of the most scenic trails in Grand Canyon National Park.

Location: 16 miles east of Grand Canyon Village.

Type of hike: Shuttle backpack.

Difficulty: Difficult.

Total distance: 24.8 miles one-way.

Elevation change: 4,800 feet.

Water: Colorado River, Hance Creek, Page Spring (shown as Miners Spring on the USGS map).

Best months: March–May, October–November.

Maps: Desert View, Cape Royal, Grandview Point USGS; Grand Canyon National Park Trails Illustrated.

Permit: Required for overnight hikes.

For more information: Grand Canyon National Park.

Finding the trailhead: See map for Hike 10. This one-way hike requires a car shuttle. To reach the end of the hike from Tusayan, drive 5.2 miles north on Arizona 64, and then turn east on Desert View Drive. 8.6 miles from the turnoff, turn left (north) on the signed Grandview Point road, and park in the signed trailhead parking area. To reach the start of the hike from Grandview Point, turn left (east) on the Desert View Drive, and go about 11 miles to Lipan Point. Turn left into the parking area.

Key points:

0.0	Trailhead at Lipan Point.
1.2	Head of Seventyfive Mile Creek.
3.4	Start of the Redwall descent.
4.3	Start down the ridge above Tanner Canyon.
6.5	Colorado River at Tanner Canyon.
8.9	Cardenas Creek.
10.7	Start of traverse into Escalante Creek.
12.8	Escalante Creek.
14.6	Nevills Rapids.
15.3	Papago Creek.
16.1	Red Canyon.
18.3	Cross Mineral Canyon.
21.5	Cross Hance Creek.
22.8	Horseshoe Mesa.
24.8	Trailhead at Grandview Point.

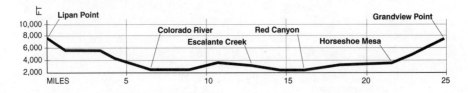

The hike: The Tanner Trailhead is signed and starts on the east side of the parking lot to the south of the viewpoint. A steep series of switchbacks descends rapidly through the rim formations to the saddle at the head of Seventyfive Mile Creek. After the confinement of the upper section of the trail, the sudden view to the west is startling. The trail now contours around Escalante and Cardenas Buttes on the gentle slopes of the red Supai sandstone. At the north end of Cardenas Butte, the trail descends abruptly through the Redwall limestone in a series of switchbacks, then works its way through the greenish Muav limestone and greenish-purple Bright Angel shale slopes. Massive fallen blocks of Tapeats sandstone mark the level of the rim of the Granite George in the central Grand Canyon, but here the gorge is replaced by rolling hills.

As the Tanner Trail descends the long ridge west of Tanner Canyon, the reason for the change in the canyon's topography is apparent. In the central canyon, the hard Vishnu schist is found at this level, and the resistant rock forms cliffs. Here, the Vishnu schist is replaced by the softer shales of the Grand Canyon supergroup, which erode into relatively gentle slopes and valleys.

There are a few small campsites scattered around the mouth of Tanner Canyon at the Colorado River. The sand dune at the mouth of Tanner Canyon is closed to camping to protect its micro-environment. Tanner Canyon is normally dry, but water can be obtained from the river. The route now turns south, and follows the bench just above the river. Although there has never been a formal trail between Tanner Canyon and Red Canyon, enough hikers have traveled the route in recent years to create a trail most of the way. Tanner Rapid, visible below, is shallow and rocky and creates more of a problem for riverboats than some of the larger rapids do. After skirting a narrow

The Tanner Trail often follows ridge lines which allows hikers to have great views, but no shade.

section where the river presses against its left bank, the trail moves inland and follows the foot of the shale slopes to the mouth of Cardenas Creek. Campsites are more plentiful here than back at the mouth of Tanner Canyon.

The actual trail crosses Cardenas Creek and continues down river, but dead-ends with a view of Unkar Rapid, which makes it a worthwhile side trip of about a mile round-trip. Our route goes up the dry bed of Cardenas Creek about 0.2 miles, and then leaves the bed to climb onto the ridge above the river. Walk to the west edge for a spectacular view of Unkar Creek Rapid, 200 feet straight down.

Turn south and climb the gentle red shale ridge directly toward Escalante Butte. Stay on the crest of the ridge to pick up the trail again as the ridge narrows. The trail turns west and heads along the nameless canyon west of Cardenas Creek at about the 3,800-foot level.

After rounding the west end of the point, the trail turns back to the east to descend into Escalante Creek. Cross the bed of Escalante Creek, and climb through a low saddle to the south. Descend into the unnamed south fork of Escalante Creek and follow it to the Colorado River (a barrier fall has an obvious bypass on the left). As the river enters the Granite Gorge ahead, it crashes though some of the hardest rapids in the canyon.

Turn left along the river's left bank. Notice how a rising ramp of hard rock forms a cliff right into the river and forces our route to climb. The bench is Shinumo quartzite, a resistant layer of rock near the bottom of the Grand Canyon series. As the river rolls downstream through this section, the rocks at river level become harder and the gorge becomes steeper-walled and deeper. The contrast between this section and the river valley at the foot of the Tanner Trail is already impressive, but the narrowest section is still downstream. After about 0.5 mile, the route reaches the rim of Seventyfive Mile Canyon and turns east along the edge of the narrow, impassable gorge. About 0.4 mile up this side canyon, the route drops into the bed and follows it back to the river, passing almost directly underneath the trail 200 feet above. At the river, turn left (downstream) again and walk about 0.6 mile along the easy beach to the mouth of Papago Creek. There are several good campsites here for small groups.

Just downstream of Papago Creek, a cliff falls directly into the river and appears to block the route. Go up Papago Creek a few yards and climb up a steep gully, which will require some scrambling. Work your way up easier ledges to a point about 300 feet above the river, and then traverse east. If you are on the correct level, you will be able to reach the head of a steep, loose gully that can be used to descend back to river level. The usual error is to traverse too low. If this happens, retrace your steps until you can climb to a higher level. Once the river is reached, a good trail follows the bank to the mouth of Red Canyon.

There is limited, sandy camping at Red Canyon. The Red Canyon Trail goes up the bed here and could be used for an early exit if necessary, but is steeper and harder to follow than the Grandview Trail. At this point, start on the Tonto Trail, which climbs the slopes to the west. The view of mile-long Hance Rapid is great. Hance is one of the hardest Grand Canyon rapids

The rock layers in the Grand Canyon span 1.82 billion years of the earth's history.

due to the numerous rocks. As you continue to climb above the river on the Tonto Trail, note the trail climbing the slope on the opposite side of the river. This trail goes to Asbestos Canyon and was used to reach the asbestos mines on the north side of the river.

About a mile from Red Canyon, the Tonto Trail turns south. After crossing dry Mineral Canyon, the trail turns west again and climbs a bit more to reach the greenish-gray shale slopes below Ayer Point. This terrace is called the Tonto Plateau, and forms a prominent shelf about 1,200 feet above the Colorado River. The rim of the Tonto Plateau is formed from the hard Tapeats sandstone, and overlooks the dark, narrow Granite Gorge, already impressive in this area. The Tonto Trail follows the Tonto Plateau for about 60 miles. After Ayer Point, the Tonto Trail turns south into Hance Canyon along the Tapeats sandstone rim. Hance Creek may be dry where the trail crosses, but there is always water a short distance downstream. There is also camping downstream, below the impressive Tapeats narrows.

After crossing Hance Creek, the Tonto Trail continues northwest about a half mile to a side canyon coming from the east side of Horseshoe Mesa. Turn west here, onto the East Grandview Trail. Page Spring, shown as Miners Spring on the USGS map, is reliable. It is reached from a spur trail about a mile from the Tonto Trail junction. The final section of the trail climbs the high Redwall limestone cliff at the canyon head to reach Horseshoe Mesa and the junction with the main Grandview Trail. There is a Park Service campground on Horseshoe Mesa, but water will have to be carried from Hance Creek or Page Spring.

Turn left onto the Grandview Trail, and climb 2.0 miles to the rim at Grandview Point. For more information on this section, see Hike 10, Horseshoe Mesa.

—Bruce Grubbs

Northeast Plateaus

This part of the Colorado Plateau is Navajo and Hopi country. Hiking for non-Indians is limited and requires a permit, and sometimes a local guide, but the scenery is spectacular and the cultural experience unrivaled.

12 Rainbow Bridge Trail

Description:	A challenging backpack into some spectacular canyon country.
Location:	About 35 miles east of Page.
Type of hike:	Out-and-back backpack.
Difficulty:	Moderate.
Total distance:	23 miles.
Elevation change:	2,800 feet.
Water:	Cliff Canyon, Bridge Canyon; purify before using.
Best months:	March–May, September–November.
Maps:	Chaiyahi Flat, Rainbow Bridge USGS.
Permit:	Required from Navajo Nation.
For more information:	Navajo Nation Parks and Recreation Department.

Finding the trailhead: Getting to the trailhead can be an adventure in itself. From Page, take Arizona 98 about 56 miles southwest to Indian Route 16 (the Inscription House/Navajo Mountain Road). Turn left (north) and drive about 32 miles to a major fork. The right takes you to the old Navajo Mountain Trading Post and Rainbow City, a government housing area. Take the left fork. In about 4 miles you will see a large dome of naked sandstone, Haystack Rock, looming ahead. Take the road to the right of it. Pass a Navajo home, and shortly you will see a well. Park here unless you have a four-wheel-drive vehicle; the last mile of the road is badly washed out, It's difficult to imagine that ordinary cars used to make it easily to the trailhead at the ruins of the old Rainbow Lodge, once owned by the late Senator Barry Goldwater.

Key points:
- 0.0 Trailhead.
- 0.6 First Canyon.
- 2.0 Horse Canyon.
- 4.6 Cliff Canyon rim.
- 6.3 Cliff Canyon.
- 7.6 Redbud Canyon.
- 9.6 Bridge Canyon.
- 11.8 Rainbow Bridge.

The hike: Rock cairns mark the trailhead on the west side of the parking area. At first the trail is an old road, but it quickly becomes a narrow path.

Rainbow Bridge Trail

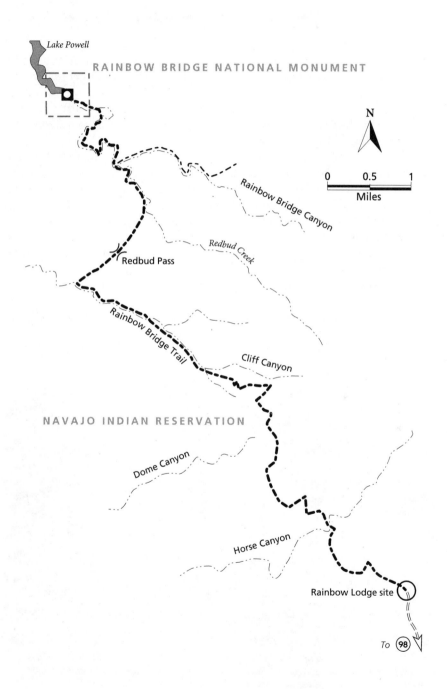

Lake Powell

RAINBOW BRIDGE NATIONAL MONUMENT

N

0   0.5   1
Miles

Rainbow Bridge Canyon

Redbud Creek

Redbud Pass

Rainbow Bridge Trail

Cliff Canyon

NAVAJO INDIAN RESERVATION

Dome Canyon

Horse Canyon

Rainbow Lodge site

To (98)

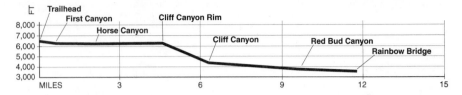

In about 0.5 mile the trail descends and crosses First Canyon. A mile and a half farther, it crosses Horse Canyon. At both crossings you may notice several paths. They all eventually rejoin the main trail. The trail continues to skirt the rugged slopes around the base of Navajo Mountain until it reaches a pass near the head of Cliff Canyon. The trail rapidly descends a steep talus slope to the floor of the canyon.

A mile or so farther down canyon, a seasonal spring may be found. A sign usually marks where to turn right into Redbud Pass, a narrow, spectacular crack in the Navajo Sandstone walls, but it won't hurt to refer to your map often. In the last few years Redbud Pass has suffered from landslides. You probably will have to take off your pack and lower it in one place and then scramble down.

Once over the pass, the trail meets Redbud Creek, which may be dry, then joins the permanent Bridge Creek. Along Bridge Creek are some excellent campsites. From here down to Rainbow Bridge, the canyon walls grow higher and higher and the scenery more and more amazing. About 0.5 mile before the bridge, the trail passes a huge cave called Echo Camp, where horse pack trips would camp in the days before Lake Powell was created.

Although Rainbow Bridge is one of the largest natural bridges in the world—290 feet high and 275 feet wide—in some ways, reaching the bridge

Although Rainbow Bridge is located in Utah, the described hike begins in Arizona and traverses some of the most fantastic sandstone canyon country anywhere. In the background is snow-covered Navajo Mountain, a volcanic laccolith reaching over 10,000 feet above sea level.

60

is anticlimactic. The surrounding cliffs dwarf the bridge, and there may be a lot of tourists who arrived by boat. Yet the hike in is worth every step.

As shown on the topo, another longer trail skirts the north slopes of Navajo Mountain. This is the route used by the 1909 Rainbow Bridge Discovery Expedition. It is not used as much as the Rainbow Bridge Trail, but does offer access to the labyrinth of canyons flanking the mountain.

—Stewart Aitchison

13 Keet Seel Trail

Description:	This is a backpack to one of the largest and best-preserved cliff houses in Arizona.
Location:	28 miles west of Kayenta.
Type of hike:	Out-and-back backpack.
Difficulty:	Moderate.
Total distance:	14 miles.
Elevation change:	680 feet.
Water:	Seasonal creek water; best to bring your own.
Best months:	Usually only open between Memorial Day and Labor Day.
Maps:	Betatakin Ruin, Keet Seel Ruin, Marsh Pass USGS.
Permit:	Required; reservations can be made up to 60 days in advance.
For more information:	Navajo National Monument.

Finding the trailhead: From Kayenta, drive about 20 miles southwest of U.S. 160. Turn right (north) onto Arizona 564 and drive another 10 miles to Navajo National Monument. When you pick up your hiking permit at the Visitor Center, the Park Service will give you directions to the trailhead. Before receiving your permit, you must attend a trail orientation meeting either at 4:00 p.m. the day before your hike or at 8:15 a.m. the day of your hike. You must be on the trail no later than 9:15 a.m.

Key points:

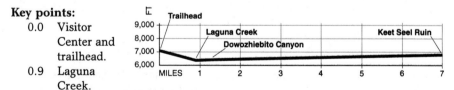

- 0.0 Visitor Center and trailhead.
- 0.9 Laguna Creek.
- 1.3 Dowozhiebito Canyon.
- 7.0 Keet Seel Ruin and campground.

The hike: This trail takes you to one of the largest and most spectacular prehistoric cliff houses in Arizona, the 160-room Keet Seel, tucked under a huge overhang in a remote canyon. People of the Anasazi culture lived for more than a thousand years in the Four Corners region, the area where Utah, Colorado, New Mexico, and Arizona join at a common point.

Keet Seel Trail

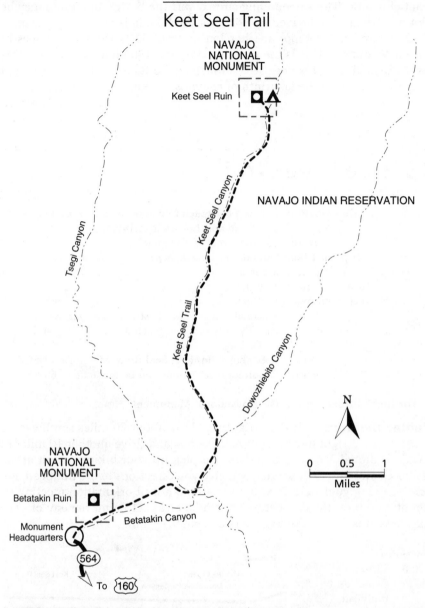

NAVAJO NATIONAL MONUMENT

Keet Seel Ruin

NAVAJO INDIAN RESERVATION

Tsegi Canyon

Keet Seel Canyon

Keet Seel Trail

Dowozhiebito Canyon

N

0   0.5   1
Miles

NAVAJO NATIONAL MONUMENT

Betatakin Ruin

Monument Headquarters

Betatakin Canyon

564

To 160

The trail begins with a short but steep and sandy descent to Laguna Creek in Tsegi Canyon. Then the trail crosses the creek and heads up Keet Seel Canyon. Most of the route traverses reservation land, and it's not uncommon to encounter Navajos on horseback or on foot tending flocks of sheep or goats. Remember that the park service permit does not give you permission to deviate from the trail onto other Navajo land.

The route up Keet Seel Canyon is between towering walls of Navajo sandstone stained with long dark stripes of desert varnish. The ledge-forming Kayenta formation underlies the Navajo. Rainwater easily soaks into the porous sandstone and is pulled downward by gravity. When this groundwater encounters the shales and clay beds in the Kayenta, its downward journey is interrupted. The water then begins to migrate horizontally and if it comes to a cliff face, emerges as a seep or spring. Look for these seeps at the contact between the Navajo and Kayenta. Remember, too, to treat all water before drinking.

Along the trail grow high desert plants typical of the Colorado Plateau country: four-wing saltbush, big sage, virgin's bower, Mormon tea, rabbitbrush, snakeweed, skunkbush, juniper, and pinyon. You may be lucky and spot a rock squirrel or chipmunklike antelope squirrel, although most of the canyon country's mammals tend to be nocturnal. Common raven, turkey vulture, scrub jay, canyon wren, rock wren, red-tailed hawk, and other birds may be seen or heard.

Keet Seel is a Navajo phrase meaning "broken pottery," and you may see pottery shards and other artifacts eroding out of the sand along the trail. Admire and photograph them, but please return them to exactly where you found them. Visitors sometimes pile artifacts on a rock for a picture and then leave them there. These "museum rocks" do not reveal as much information to archaeologists as leaving artifacts where they are discovered. Of course, all prehistoric artifacts are protected by federal, state, and tribal laws and should not be collected. Besides, the canyon spirits will haunt you.

From the mid–tenth century to the late thirteenth, several hundred Anasazi people occupied Tsegi Canyon and its tributary Keet Seel. Here they

The prehistoric Anasazi Indians lived in northern Arizona from about the time of Christ until the fourteenth century. During this 1,300-year span only the last century saw extensive use of cliff houses such as this one, known today as Keet Seel. Earlier Anasazi lived in pit houses, which were partially subterranean huts, or in mud-and-stone pueblos.

grew corn and several kinds of beans and squash, tended turkeys, and created exquisite pottery painted with geometric and animal designs. Then in the late 1200s, the people began to abandon the area. The exact cause is uncertain, but is likely a combination of drought, disease, warfare, overpopulation, and the attraction of a new religion emerging in New Mexico.

About 0.5 mile from Keet Seel there is a primitive campground but no purified water. You may enter the cliff house only with the ranger on duty.

—Stewart Aitchison

14 White House Ruin Trail

Description:	A pleasant, short day hike to one of the Southwest's best-preserved cliff houses.
Location:	About 6 miles east of Chinle in Canyon de Chelly National Monument.
Type of hike:	Out-and-back day hike.
Difficulty:	Easy.
Total distance:	2.5 miles.
Elevation change:	560 feet.
Water:	None.
Best months:	March–May, September–November.
Maps:	Del Muerto USGS.
Permit:	None.
For more information:	Canyon de Chelly National Monument.

Finding the trailhead: From the Canyon de Chelly National Monument Visitor Center, drive east 6.4 miles on the South Rim Drive. Turn left onto the White House Ruin Overlook road. Park in the lot, and walk down the paved path toward the White House Overlook. About 50 yards from the parking lot, there is a sign marking the trail on your right.

Key points:
  0.0 Trailhead.
  1.25 White House Ruin.

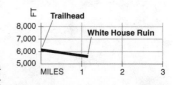

The hike: This is the only trail that visitors can use in Canyon de Chelly National Monument without a local guide. The monument is unique in that most of the land is still Navajo Reservation with locals still living in the canyon. Guides are necessary in most parts of the canyon to protect the privacy of the residents.

The trail at first crosses slickrock, paralleling the rim for 100 yards or so before turning sharply to drop off the rim. Rock cairns and painted symbols on the sandstone mark the trail.

Off the rim, the trail descends nearly 600 vertical feet in a series of sweeping, not too steep switchbacks. Wonderful close-up views of the distinctly cross-bedded de Chelly sandstone are possible. Try to imagine this

White House Ruin in Canyon de Chelly is a well-preserved Anasazi site. Above the ruin are long, black streaks of desert varnish staining the sandstone cliff. Desert varnish, or patina, is a surface deposit of manganese or iron oxide. It usually forms where water periodically washes down the cliff, but the exact processes involved are still poorly understood.

White House Ruin Trail

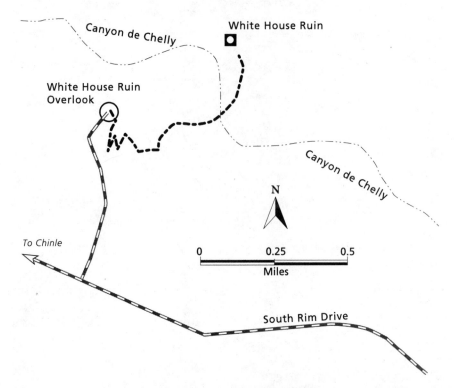

rock as golden sand dunes piled up by strong desert winds some 270 million years ago. Later, over an almost unimaginable amount of time, these dunes were buried under other sediments and the sand grains became cemented into sandstone. More time passed, the region was uplifted, and erosion eventually exposed this layer. Relatively recently, Chinle Creek and its tributaries sliced down through this layer to create the intricate Canyon de Chelly complex.

At the canyon bottom, the trail passes a Navajo camp (the term for a traditional home site) and crosses Chinle Creek, delivering you at the base of a tremendous overhanging cliff. Partway up this face, White House Ruin, named for its white plastered walls, is tucked into a cave. Below White House, at the base of the cliff, is another masonry pueblo. Ladders allowed access to the cave from the rooftops of the lower pueblo. Perhaps fifty or more people lived in this village between A.D. 1040 and 1275. They planted corn, beans, and squash along Chinle Creek much like the Navajo people do today.

—Stewart Aitchison

15 Wupatki Ruin

Description:	A short walk around an extensive, well-preserved Sinagua Indian ruin in Wupatki National Monument.
Location:	44 miles northeast of Flagstaff.
Type of hike:	Out-and-back day hike.
Difficulty:	Easy.
Total distance:	0.5 mile.
Elevation change:	None.
Water:	Visitor Center.
Best months:	All year.
Maps:	Wupatki SE USGS.
Permit:	None.
For more information:	Wupatki National Monument.

Finding the trailhead: From Flagstaff, drive north about 30 miles on U.S. 89, then turn right (east) at the signed Wupatki National Monument turnoff. Follow this paved road east 14 miles, and park at the visitor center.

Key points:

0.0   Visitor center.
0.2   Start of loop around ruin.

The hike: The paved trail may be reached either by walking through the visitor center or by walking around the right (north) side of the building. It is worthwhile spending time in the visitor center to learn about the Sinagua

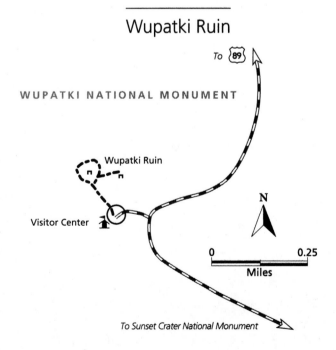

Wupatki Ruin

Present-day Wupatki National Monument—it was a thriving community 1,000 years ago.

Indians who built Wupatki and many other structures in the area. The trail first passes an overlook with a good view of the ruin and its setting, then descends slightly to the ruin itself. The trail forms a loop around the hilltop, and there is a spur trail to an amphitheater.

—Bruce Grubbs

San Francisco Peaks Area

The San Francisco Peaks are the highest mountains in Arizona. They, along with about 600 neighboring cinder cones, stratovolcanoes, and shield volcanoes, make up one of the largest volcanic fields in the United States. Much of the land is managed by the U.S. Forest Service, which maintains a complex of trails.

16 Bill Williams Mountain Trail

Description:	This trail takes you through cool alpine forest to the summit of Bill Williams Mountain. It's a fine choice for a hot summer day.
Location:	1 mile west of Williams.
Type of hike:	Out-and-back day hike.
Difficulty:	Moderate.
Total distance:	6.8 miles.
Elevation change:	2,380 feet.
Water:	None.
Best months:	May–November.
Maps:	Williams South USGS; Kaibab National Forest (Williams, Chalender, and Tusayan Ranger Districts).
Permit:	None.
For more information:	Kaibab National Forest, Williams Ranger District.

Finding the trailhead: From Williams, drive west on Bill Williams Avenue (Business I–40). Just before the I–40 interchange west of town, turn left at the turnoff for the Forest Service Ranger Station. Turn left again at the next signed turnoff for the ranger station, and then follow the signs to the Bill Williams trailhead, next to the ranger station.

Key points:
- 0.0 Bill Williams Mountain trailhead.
- 0.6 Junction with the Clover Spring Trail.
- 2.9 Turn left at Bill Williams Road.
- 3.4 Bill Williams Mountain.

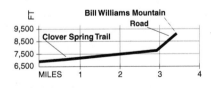

The hike: The trail is not shown on the topographic map, but it's a good trail and easy to follow. Follow the signed Bill Williams Mountain Trail as it leaves the parking area and crosses a meadow. The trail soon begins to climb moderately in a series of switchbacks. The forest is especially fine in this area, with an interesting mixture of the ever-present ponderosa pine, Gambel oak, alligator juniper, and even a few white fir.

Bill Williams Mountain Trail

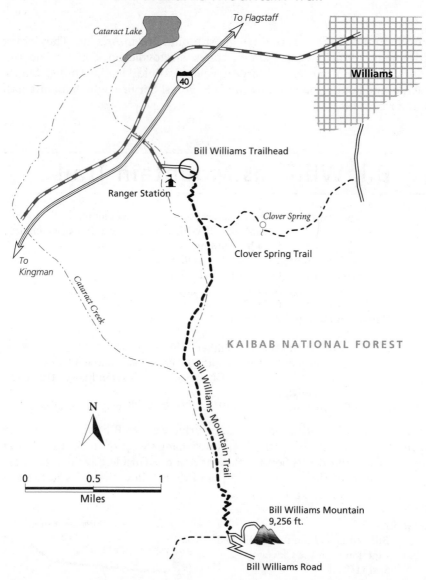

White fir is much less common than Douglas fir, and seems to favor cool drainage bottoms. Usually it can be distinguished from the Douglas fir by its blue-green color. When white fir is growing next to Douglas fir, the color difference is obvious; otherwise, you may have to look more closely. White fir cones grow upward from the branches, as do all true firs, while the Douglas fir cones hang down. Some people also confuse white fir with blue spruce, but if you attempt to roll a few needles in your fingers you'll discover that they are flat. Spruce needles are square in cross section and easily roll in your fingers.

Old-growth pondersosa pine on Bill Williams Mountain.

After the switchbacks end and the Bill Williams Mountain Trail levels out a bit, you'll pass the Clover Spring Trail junction. The Bill Williams Mountain Trail continues south, climbing gradually. As it nears the steep north slopes of the mountain, it heads into a north-facing canyon and starts to climb more steeply. The forest changes from open ponderosa pine stands to denser Douglas fir with a scattering of aspen. A series of switchbacks leads up to the trail's end at the Bill Williams Road. To reach the summit, turn left and walk 0.5 mile to the end of the road.

—Bruce Grubbs

17 Bull Basin–Pumpkin Trails

Description:	A rugged hike on less-used trails through beautiful alpine forest with excellent views of the Kendrick Peak Wilderness.
Location:	28 miles northwest of Flagstaff.
Type of hike:	Loop day hike.
Difficulty:	Difficult.
Total distance:	10.6 miles.
Elevation change:	3,160 feet.
Water:	None.
Best months:	May–November.
Maps:	Kendrick Peak, Moritz Ridge USGS; Kaibab National Forest (Williams, Chalender, and Tusayan Ranger Districts).
Permit:	None.
For more information:	Kaibab National Forest, Williams Ranger District.

Finding the trailhead: From Flagstaff, drive north 17 miles on U.S. 180, then turn left (west) on a maintained dirt road (Forest Road 193). Continue 3.2 miles, and then turn right (northwest) on another maintained dirt road (Forest Road 171). Drive 7.8 miles to the Pumpkin Trailhead, which is on the right.

Key points:
- 0.0   Pumpkin Trailhead.
- 1.6   Go left at junction with Connector Trail.
- 2.4   Turn right on Bull Basin Trail.
- 4.6   Saddle.
- 5.6   Old lookout cabin; turn right on Kendrick Peak Trail.
- 5.9   Kendrick Lookout; continue on Pumpkin Trail.
- 9.0   Turn left at Connector Trail junction.
- 10.6 Pumpkin Trailhead.

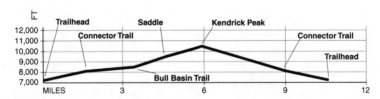

The hike: This is a strenuous hike on steep trails with no water. Hikers planning an overnight trip will have to carry water or do the hike in late spring when there are still snowdrifts near the summit. The rewards are worth the effort. The trails are not shown on the topographic maps, except for the short segment of the Kendrick Peak Trail used by this loop.

The Pumpkin Trail follows an old road east through the ponderosa pine forest. It almost immediately starts climbing toward the west ridge of Kendrick Peak. After 1.6 miles, the trail climbs into a saddle and meets the

72

Bull Basin–Pumpkin Trails • Kendrick Peak Trail

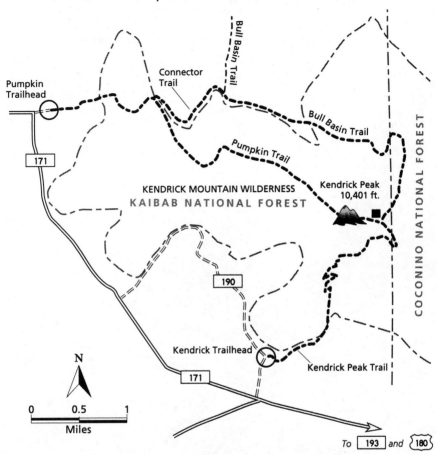

Connector Trail. Turn left (east) here and continue as the Connector Trail contours the north slopes of the mountain along the wilderness boundary. The Forest Service has logged right up to the boundary, but this section is soon left behind. After about a mile the trail passes through another saddle and crosses into Bull Basin. The Connector Trail ends at the junction with the Bull Basin Trail.

Turn right (southeast) on the Bull Basin Trail. The trail contours across the head of Bull Basin, then climbs through a beautiful forest as it heads toward the north ridge of Kendrick Peak. The dense forest gives way to a series of alpine meadows just before the trail reaches the ridge crest at a saddle. Here the trail turns south and climbs steeply to the 10,000-foot east shoulder of the mountain.

Now the trail climbs more gradually, and ends near the old lookout cabin at the junction with the Kendrick Peak Trail. There are campsites along the tree line at the north edge of the meadow. In early summer or late spring, lingering snowdrifts make it possible to camp without carrying water. The

Along the Bull Basin Trail, Kendrick Peak.

alpine meadow and splendid sunset and sunrise views south are worth the effort of carrying overnight gear up here. Campfires are not recommended. Trees grow very slowly in the Arctic environment and should not be burned. Carry a backpacking stove to melt snow and cook meals.

Turn right (west) on the Kendrick Peak Trail, and follow it as it climbs to the summit. Look on the west side of the lookout building for the beginning of the Pumpkin Trail, which begins descending immediately. The views are excellent from the upper part of the trail as it switchbacks though several meadows. As the trail enters denser forest, it tends to follow the broad west ridge of the mountain. Watch for the junction with the Connector Trail as the forest becomes nearly pure ponderosa pine once again. This closes the loop; continue on the Pumpkin Trail to the trailhead.

—Bruce Grubbs

18 Kendrick Peak Trail

See Map on Page 73

Description: This hike follows a well-graded trail to the summit of the second highest mountain in northern Arizona, in the Kendrick Mountain Wilderness.
Location: 23 miles northwest of Flagstaff.
Type of hike: Out-and-back day hike.
Difficulty: Moderate.
Total distance: 8.0 miles.
Elevation change: 2,720 feet.
Water: None.
Maps: Kendrick Peak USGS; Kaibab National Forest (Williams, Chalender, and Tusayan Ranger District).
Permit: None.
Best months: May–November.
For more information: Kaibab National Forest, Chalender Ranger District.

Finding the trailhead: From Flagstaff, drive north about 17 miles on U.S. Highway 180, then turn left (west) on a maintained dirt road (Forest Road 193). Continue 3.2 miles, then turn right (northwest) on another maintained dirt road (Forest Road 171). Drive 2.0 miles, then turn right onto Forest Road 190 and continue 0.4 mile to the signed trailhead on the right side of the road.

Key points:
0.0 Trailhead.
0.7 Join old trail.
1.5 Saddle.
3.7 Old lookout cabin and Bull Basin Trail junction.
4.0 Kendrick Lookout and Pumpkin Trail junction.

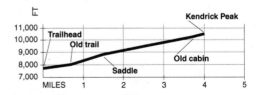

The hike: The Kendrick Peak Trail is the easiest of the three trails to the summit of Kendrick Peak. Built for maintenance of the Forest Service fire lookout, it climbs the south side of the mountain in gradual switchbacks.

A new trailhead was constructed recently, moving the beginning of the trail about 0.5 mile to the west. The trail climbs the slope to the northeast, through ponderosa pine stands, to join the original trail just above the old trailhead. This next section of trail was used as a road during a forest fire many years ago, and it is noticeably wider than the remainder of the trail. At first, the trail follows the left side of a drainage, then it begins to switchback. Notice that Douglas fir appears as the trail climbs this section.

Soon the trail reaches a saddle and becomes narrower again. The trail climbs a short distance up the ridge to the northeast, then starts to ascend the south-facing slope in a series of switchbacks. Limber pine and Arizona corkbark fir appear, as well as quaking aspen. Occasional open meadows offer extensive views of the forested Coconino Plateau to the south. Eventually, the trail makes a major switchback to the northwest, and there are glimpses of the summit and the squat lookout building. The trail enters a meadow on the east ridge of the peak, and meets the Bull Basin Trail near an old cabin.

The cabin was built in the early part of the century by the fire lookout, who then lived in the cabin and rode his horse to the summit each day to watch for fires. The lookout obtained water from a spring to the south, which is unreliable today. In the early days of the Forest Service, fire lookouts often sat on the bare mountaintop to watch for fires. Amenities like lookout buildings and towers were constructed gradually as the need for permanent fire watches developed.

Continue on the Kendrick Peak Trail about 0.3 mile to the summit. The lookout welcomes visitors unless he or she is busy; ask permission before climbing the stairs. From either the catwalk or the ground, the views are stunning. The San Francisco Peaks to the east dominate the scenery, and you can also see many of the hundreds of old volcanoes and cinder cones that dot the plateau. The beautiful pine forest stretches in all directions, scarred here and there by old forest fire burns. To the north, the cliffs of the Grand Canyon's north rim are visible 50 miles away.

—Bruce Grubbs

19 Walker Lake

Description:	A short hike to a lake in a volcanic crater near the San Francisco Peaks.
Location:	22 miles northwest of Flagstaff.
Type of hike:	Out-and-back day hike.
Difficulty:	Easy.
Total distance:	1.0 mile.
Elevation change:	140 feet.
Water:	None.
Best months:	April–November.
Maps:	White Horse Hills USGS, Coconino National Forest.
Permits:	None.
For more information:	Peaks Ranger District, Coconino National Forest.

Finding the trailhead: From Flagstaff, drive north 20 miles on U.S. 180, then turn right (east) on the north end of Hart Prairie Road (Forest Road 151). Continue on this maintained dirt road 1.5 miles, then turn left (east) on another maintained road (Forest Road 418). Drive 0.2 mile, then turn

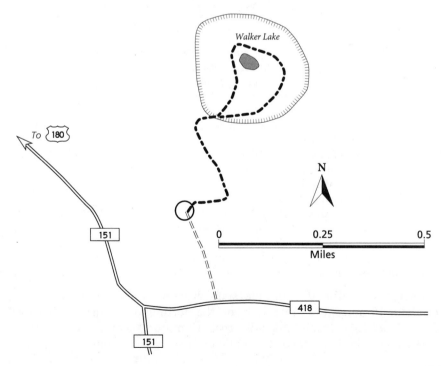

Walker Lake

8,511 ft.

COCONINO NATIONAL FOREST

left again (north) on an unmaintained road. Park at the end of the road, in another 0.2 mile.

Key points:
- 0.0   Trailhead.
- 0.3   Saddle on crater rim.
- 0.5   Walker Lake.

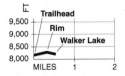

The hike: The trail follows the old road, closed now, up the southwest slope of the cinder cone. It passes through a broad saddle after 0.3 mile and drops gently into the volcanic crater. Walker Lake is fullest in late spring after a snowy winter. In late summer it is little more than a marsh. Considering how porous this volcanic area is, it's surprising that the runoff from the small watershed formed by the crater is enough to form even a small pond.

It is worthwhile to walk around the lake. A man-caused forest fire burned the now-barren north slope of the crater. The fire started near the lake, and high winds swept it up over the rim, where it traveled another 5 miles before being contained by firefighters. A larger fire in 1996 burned much of the area again. The views of Humphreys Peak, the highest of the San Francisco Peaks, are great from the northwest side of the lake, and even better if you climb up the slope through the old burn.

—Bruce Grubbs

20 Bear Jaw–Abineau Canyon Loop

Description:	This is a hike on the north side of the San Francisco Peaks, in the Kachina Peaks Wilderness. It's a cool hike on a hot summer day, and also great for aspen color during October.
Location:	23 miles north of Flagstaff.
Type of hike:	Loop day hike.
Difficulty:	Moderate.
Total distance:	7.4 miles.
Elevation change:	2,000 feet.
Water:	None.
Best months:	May–November.
Maps:	White Horse Hills, Humphreys Peak USGS; Coconino National Forest.
Permit:	Cross-country hiking is prohibited above 11,400 feet (the approximate level of timberline).
For more information:	Coconino National Forest, Peaks Ranger District.

Finding the trailhead: From Flagstaff, drive north on U.S. Highway 180 for about 18 miles, then turn right on the north end of Hart Prairie Road (Forest Road 151), a maintained dirt road. Continue 1.6 miles, then turn left on the Hostetter Tank Road (Forest Road 418), also maintained dirt. Drive

Bear Jaw–Abineau Canyon Loop

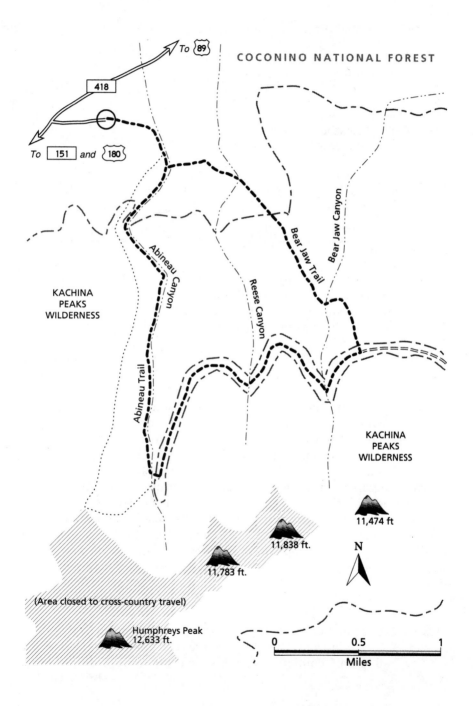

To ⑧⑨

COCONINO NATIONAL FOREST

418

To 151 and ⑱⓪

KACHINA
PEAKS
WILDERNESS

Abineau Canyon

Bear Jaw Trail

Bear Jaw Canyon

Reese Canyon

Abineau Trail

KACHINA
PEAKS
WILDERNESS

11,474 ft

11,838 ft.

N

11,783 ft.

(Area closed to cross-country travel)

Humphreys Peak
12,633 ft.

0   0.5   1
Miles

3.1 miles to the signed Abineau Trail turnoff, turn right, and go 0.3 mile to the trailhead.

Key points:
- 0.0   Abineau Trailhead.
- 0.5   Turn left at Bear Jaw Trail.
- 0.9   Cross Reese Canyon.
- 2.1   Cross Bear Jaw Canyon.
- 2.5   Turn right on Abineau Canyon Road.
- 2.8   Cross Bear Jaw Canyon.
- 3.7   Cross Reese Canyon.
- 4.7   Turn right at Abineau Trail.
- 6.9   Stay left at junction with Bear Jaw Trail.
- 7.4   Abineau Trailhead.

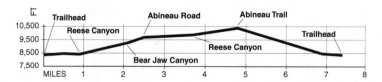

The hike: Start off on the Abineau Trail, which soon drops into Abineau Canyon. A half mile up the canyon, turn left onto the Bear Jaw Trail, which traverses east through open ponderosa pine forest to cross Reese Canyon. Now you'll start to climb as the trail ascends the north slopes of the mountain. The pure pine forest gradually gives way to a pleasing mix of pine, quaking aspen, Douglas fir, and white fir. After the trail crosses Bear Jaw Canyon, it's only a short climb to the Abineau Canyon Road, where you'll turn right.

The road, part of the Flagstaff watershed project, was built in an attempt to tap a spring in Abineau Canyon. Parts of the abandoned pipeline can still be seen in the roadbed. Although the road is in a narrow, nonwilderness corridor, it is open only to official vehicles, and rarely used. It makes a pleasant, easy hike along the north side of the mountain. Shortly, you'll cross Bear Jaw Canyon, and then the road swings around into Reese Canyon, climbing gradually. The fir-aspen forest is a riot of color during the fall, and the road is often paved with golden aspen leaves for a couple of weeks.

The view opens up as you reach the end of the road in Abineau Canyon. The lack of trees in the canyon is due to numerous snow avalanches that roar down the northeast slopes of Humphreys Peak. Some of these slides reach the bottom of the canyon with such power that they continue below the road, crossing back and forth several times before the snow finally loses its momentum. Such a large avalanche will destroy any small trees attempting to grow in its path.

Just before the end of the road, turn right on the Abineau Trail, which descends Abineau Canyon. After a little more than 2 miles, you'll pass the Bear Jaw Trail turnoff; continue on the Abineau Trail to reach the trailhead.

—Bruce Grubbs

21 Humphreys Peak Trail

Description: This popular hike takes you to the highest summit in Arizona, which is in the Kachina Peaks Wilderness. On a clear day, the views are incredible.

Location: 14 miles northwest of Flagstaff.

Type of hike: Out-and-back day hike.

Difficulty: Difficult.

Total distance: 8.8 miles.

Elevation change: 3,330 feet.

Water: None.

Best months: May–October.

Maps: Humphreys Peak USGS; Coconino National Forest.

Permit: Cross-country hiking is prohibited above 11,400 feet (the approximate level of timberline). Camping is not allowed in the Interior Valley above Lockett Meadow.

For more information: Coconino National Forest, Peaks Ranger District.

Finding the trailhead: From Flagstaff, drive 7 miles north on U.S. Highway 180, then turn right (north) on Arizona Snowbowl Road. Continue 6.5

Humphreys Peak Trail • Kachina Trail • Weatherford Trail

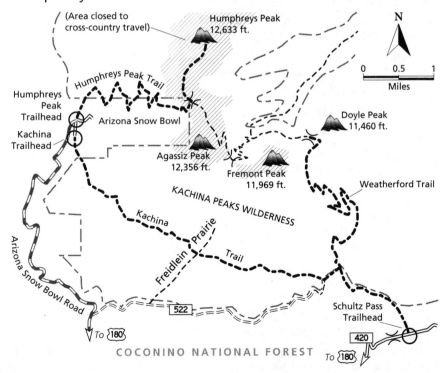

Near the top of Arizona, Humphreys Peak in the Kachina Peaks Wilderness Area—here shown on an early March hike and ski—averages more than two hundred inches of snow each winter.

miles to the ski area lodge, and turn left into the parking lot below the lodge. Park at the north end, where you will see the signed trailhead.

Key points:
0.0   Trailhead.
3.4   Agassiz Saddle.
4.4   Humphreys Peak.

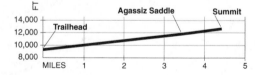

The hike: Note that cross-country hiking is prohibited by the U.S. Forest Service above 11,400 feet in the San Francisco Peaks. Above timberline, you must stay on the trail. This trail was completed in 1985 and is not shown on the topographic map.

The trail starts near the base of a chairlift in upper Hart Prairie, then crosses into the forest on the north side of the meadow. The trail ascends in a series of long but well-graded switchbacks through the dense forest. At first, the forest is a mixture of ponderosa pine, Douglas fir, and quaking aspen trees associated with the Canadian life zone. These give way to limber pine and Engelmann spruce in the higher sections of the forest. Near timberline, the forest is mostly subalpine fir, Arizona corkbark fir, and bristlecone pine, which represent the classic subalpine life zone. Near timberline, the trail crosses the west-facing ridge and climbs up to Agassiz Saddle at 11,800 feet. The few trees in this area show the effect of the harsh Arctic climate. They grow in low mats to conserve heat and protect themselves from wind. In winter, snow collects around the dense foliage, forming drifts that further protect the trees. The climate in this Arctic life zone is similar to that in the far northern regions of Canada and Alaska.

From Agassiz Saddle, the Weatherford Trail branches south along the ridge. The Humphreys Peak Trail turns north and skirts the west side of the ridge. The next mile of the trail is above timberline with no shelter and should not be attempted if thunderstorms, high wind, or snowstorms threaten. After about 0.2 mile the last struggling trees are left behind as the trail continues to climb along the ridge toward the invisible summit. You'll pass several false summits, each appearing to be the final one. There are choice views of the Interior Valley to the east along the way, a good excuse to stop to catch your breath in the thin air.

Low stone walls mark the summit. A large portion of northern Arizona is visible from this lofty perch. If the air is clear, you can see Utah's 10,300-foot Navajo Mountain to the north-northeast, and the 11,400-foot White Mountains in east central Arizona near the New Mexico border. The Mogollon Rim and some of its canyons can be seen to the south, as well as the rugged mountain ranges of central Arizona.

—Bruce Grubbs

22 Kachina Trail

See Map on Page 81

Description: This relatively new trail offers an easy hike through fine alpine forest, ending at a scenic meadow. The hike is on the southwest slopes of the San Francisco Peaks in the Kachina Peaks Wilderness.

Location: 14 miles northwest of Flagstaff.

Type of hike: Out-and-back day hike.

Difficulty: Moderate.

Total distance: 10.6 miles.

Elevation change: 800 feet.

Water: None.

Best months: May–November.

Maps: Humphreys Peak USGS; Coconino National Forest.

Permit: Cross-country hiking is prohibited above 11,400 feet (the approximate level of timberline). Camping is not allowed in the Interior Valley above Lockett Meadow.

For more information: Coconino National Forest, Peaks Ranger District.

Finding the trailhead: From Flagstaff, drive northwest on U.S. Highway 180 about 7 miles, then turn right (north) on the paved and signed Arizona Snowbowl Road. Continue 6.5 miles to the ski area lodge, and turn right into the first parking lot. Drive to the far end of the parking lot and park at the signed trailhead for the Kachina Trail.

Key points:

0.0 Kachina Trailhead.

2.7 Freidlein Prairie.

5.3 Weatherford Trail.

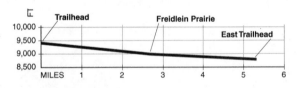

The hike: The Kachina Trail was one of several trails built during the mid-1980s as part of a new recreational trail system on the Peaks, and it is not shown on the topographic map. After a short distance on the Kachina Trail, you'll cross under a power line and enter Kachina Peaks Wilderness. The trail winds in and out of small canyons and through meadows as it traverses the southwest slopes of Mount Agassiz. The forest is an attractive mixture of quaking aspen, Douglas fir, and limber pine. In fall, the aspen leaves change to beautiful shades of yellow, orange, and red. This is a good hike to view those colors.

After about a mile you'll cross a rocky canyon; the trail beyond this point crosses a steeper, more rugged slope. After crossing several small draws, the trail traverses the deeper canyon coming down from Fremont Saddle, then enters into Freidlein Prairie, an alpine meadow on the southwest slopes of Fremont Peak. The junction with Freidlein Prairie Trail is in this meadow. The meadow is much larger than depicted on the topographic map, extending all the way down to the Freidlein Prairie Road.

Aspen glades along the Kachina Trail, on the south slopes of the San Francisco Peaks.

Now the trail descends gradually eastward across the slopes of Fremont Peak, traversing several beautiful aspen-lined meadows. Watch for elk; at times there are more elk tracks than human tracks on the trail. The trail ends at the wilderness boundary and the junction with the Weatherford Trail, which is the turnaround point for the hike.

—Bruce Grubbs

23 Weatherford Trail

See Map on Page 81

Description: An enjoyable hike on a well-graded trail that winds around Fremont and Agassiz Peaks in the Kachina Peaks Wilderness.

Location: 8 miles north of Flagstaff.

Type of hike: Out-and-back day hike.

Difficulty: Moderate.

Total distance: 14.8 miles.

Elevation change: 2,800 feet.

Water: None.

Best months: May–November.

Maps: Humphreys Peak USGS; Coconino National Forest.

Permit: Cross-country hiking is prohibited above 11,400 feet (the approximate level of timberline). Camping is not allowed in the Interior Valley above Lockett Meadow.

For more information: Coconino National Forest, Peaks Ranger District.

The Weatherford Trail above timberline in the Kachina Peaks Wilderness.

Finding the trailhead: From Flagstaff, drive northwest about 3 miles on U.S. Highway 180, then turn right (north) on the Schultz Pass road (Forest Road 420). Continue past the end of the pavement on a maintained dirt road to the signed Weatherford Trail at Schultz Pass, about 5.5 miles from U.S. 180. Park on the right (south) in the parking area next to Schultz Tank.

Key points:
- 0.0 Trailhead at Schultz Tank.
- 1.7 Kachina Trail.
- 7.4 Doyle Saddle.

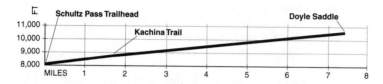

The hike: The walk begins across the road from the east end of the parking area and follows the Weatherford Trail, an old road. The trail crosses a cleared pipeline corridor and continues to climb gradually north on a ponderosa pine–covered slope. When the trail emerges into a large meadow at the foot of Fremont Peak, it starts to switchback. You'll pass the Kachina Trail turnoff after one of these switchbacks, and then the trail crosses the meadow and enters the forest. The slope steepens as the trail swings around a small meadow. A series of broad switchbacks takes you up the southeast slopes of Fremont Peak. The old road crosses several large avalanche paths, and a final switchback leads into Doyle Saddle, the goal for the hike. The view from this saddle is especially fine, overlooking the Interior Valley with its surrounding alpine peaks, and the lower Mount Elden–Dry Lake Hills complex to the south.

Option: The Weatherford Trail continues around Fremont Peak, through Fremont Saddle, around the east slopes of Agassiz Peak, and ends at the Humphreys-Agassiz Saddle. If you continue to the end, you'll add 1,000 feet of elevation and 4.2 round-trip miles to the hike.

—Bruce Grubbs

24 Inner Basin Trail

Description:	A hike through an alpine forest to a large avalanche path on the southeast face of Humphreys Peak, in the San Francisco Peaks.
Location:	22 miles northeast of Flagstaff.
Type of hike:	Loop day hike.
Difficulty:	Moderate.
Total distance:	6.7 miles.
Elevation change:	1,900 feet.
Water:	Watershed cabins (summer only).
Best months:	May–November.
Maps:	Sunset Crater West, Humphreys Peak USGS; Coconino National Forest.
Permit:	Cross-country hiking is prohibited above 11,400 feet (the approximate level of timberline). Camping is not allowed in the Interior Valley above Lockett Meadow.
For more information:	Coconino National Forest, Peaks Ranger District.

Finding the trailhead: From Flagstaff, drive north on U.S. Highway 89, the main street through town, and continue about 17 miles to Schultz Pass Road (Forest Road 520), and turn left (west). This maintained dirt road is opposite the Sunset Crater National Monument turnoff. Drive 0.4 mile, then turn right at a T intersection. Continue 0.8 mile to another T intersection, and then turn left. Abut 0.6 mile further, just before a locked gate at a cinder pit, turn right on the Locket Meadow Road. Continue 2.8 miles to Lockett Trailhead at the southwest corner of the loop road around Lockett Meadow.

Key points:
- 0.0 Lockett Trailhead.
- 1.5 Watershed cabins; continue straight on Inner Basin Trail.
- 1.6 Go right on the Flagstaff Spring road.
- 2.3 Stay right at fork.
- 3.1 Flagstaff Spring.
- 3.9 Turn right.
- 4.4 Turn left on Inner Basin Trail.
- 5.2 Watershed cabins.
- 6.7 Lockett Trailhead.

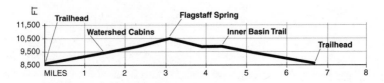

The hike: Start on Inner Basin Trail, and hike southwest up the Interior Valley to the watershed cabins. The trail, which is not shown on the topographic

Inner Basin Trail

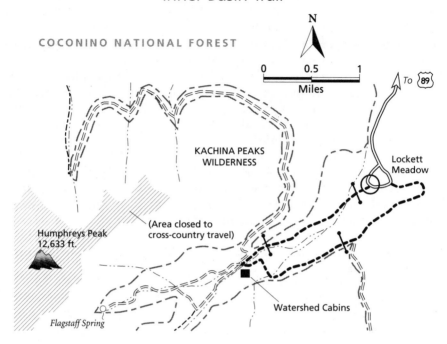

N

COCONINO NATIONAL FOREST

0   0.5   1
Miles

To {89}

KACHINA PEAKS
WILDERNESS

Lockett
Meadow

Humphreys Peak
12,633 ft.

(Area closed to
cross-country travel)

Watershed Cabins

Flagstaff Spring

map, climbs gradually southwest through fine stands of quaking aspen, ponderosa pine, and the occasional limber pine. The valley floor is broad and fairly flat, though cut by numerous small gullies. If you take the time to walk to either side of the valley, you'll notice that the bordering slopes are very steep. This is characteristic of valleys carved by glaciers. The moving ice shapes the entire valley into broad U-shape. Valleys carved entirely by water have a V-shaped cross section. Another glacial characteristic is the unsorted debris composing the valley floor. Rocks and boulders of all sizes are randomly scattered around, instead of being sorted by size as they are when carried and deposited by running water. As a glacier moves down hill, it scours rock from its bed. More rock falls from the slopes above and is carried by the glacier. When the ice melts, the sand, gravel, rocks, and boulders are dropped in an unsorted heap, called "glacial till." After 1.5 miles, the trail reaches a small group of cabins at the junction of several roads. There is untreated spring water at a tap near the largest cabin.

From the cabins, take Inner Basin Trail, the road that continues west-southwest up the Interior Valley. This road is not open to private vehicles; the city of Flagstaff uses the road only to maintain its water system, so there is very little traffic. One hundred yards beyond the cabins, the road forks. Take the right fork, which goes to Bear Paw and Flagstaff Springs. The road climbs steadily through the dense alpine forest, which sometimes opens up for glimpses of the high peaks. Along the way, you will see old signs of construction dating from the beginnings of the watershed project.

Flagstaff has outgrown its water supply many times. In the early part of the century, only a couple of decades after the city's founding, someone had an idea: tap the springs in the Interior Valley of the San Francisco Peaks. In an area with very few springs, this water was worth considerable effort to reach. A pipeline was built up Schultz Creek, west of the Dry Lake Hills, to Schultz Pass, then around the east slopes of Doyle Peak and into the Interior Valley. From the present site of the watershed cabins, branch pipelines were built to all of the springs in the valley. An attempt was even made to tap a spring in Abineau Canyon on the northeast side of Humphreys Peak.

In the 1950s, in an effort to find more water, the city drilled a number of exploratory wells in the Interior Valley. A few were successful, and diesel-powered pumps were installed. Most of the old roads dating from the exploration period are overgrown now, but the valley still lacks a wilderness feeling. Until the mid-1970s, the entire watershed was closed to all public access, including hiking and cross-country skiing. Increasing public interest in outdoor activities finally caused the Forest Service to open the area to day hiking, skiing, and snowshoeing. Locked steel covers protect the springs, so there are no water sources in the Interior Valley except for the tap at the watershed cabins.

About 0.8 mile from the watershed cabins, a road forks left. This will be the return loop, but for now continue on the main road (right), which ends below Flagstaff Spring in another 0.8 mile. The most notable feature here is the incredible swath of destruction of the 200-year-old fir and spruce. The winter of 1972–73 was an unusually snowy one, and sometime during that winter a large avalanche came down the southeast face of Humphreys Peak, destroying the trees.

An 0.5 mile optional cross-country side hike to Humphreys Cirque is worth doing. Continue up the forested slope, proceeding southwest from Flagstaff Spring, to reach the rim of the cirque at 11,200 feet. You are near timberline, and there are excellent views of the stark alpine ridges above. (The mountain is closed to cross-country hiking above 11,400 feet.) Return to Flagstaff Spring the way you came.

To continue on the main hike from Flagstaff Spring, retrace your steps east down the road 0.8 mile to the junction mentioned above, and then turn right. This road goes south 0.5 mile to the south branch of the Interior Valley, passing through some fine aspen stands before reaching a broad open meadow just west of one of the city well site with its noisy diesel pump. This meadow has the best views in the Interior Valley. From left to right the summits are Doyle Peak, Fremont Peak, Agassiz Peak, and Humphreys Peak. From this vantage point Fremont Peak is the most striking, with its pyramidal northeast face.

Turn left at the road junction in the meadow, and descend to the east-northeast, following the road back to the watershed cabins. Then return to the trailhead via the Inner Basin Trail, the way you came.

—Bruce Grubbs

90

25 Sunset-Brookbank Trails

Description:	This hike features easy access and cool alpine forest and meadows in the Dry Lake Hills.
Location:	8 miles northwest of Flagstaff.
Type of hike:	Loop day hike.
Difficulty:	Moderate.
Total distance:	5.4 miles.
Elevation change:	900 feet.
Water:	None.
Best months:	April–November.
Maps:	Humphreys Peak, Sunset Crater West USGS; Coconino National Forest.
Permit:	None.
For more information:	Coconino National Forest, Peaks Ranger District.

Finding the trailhead: From Flagstaff, drive northwest about 3 miles on U.S. Highway 180, then turn right (north) on the Schultz Pass road (Forest Road 420). Continue past the end of the pavement on the maintained dirt road to the Sunset Trailhead at Schultz Pass, 5.3 miles from the highway.

Key points:

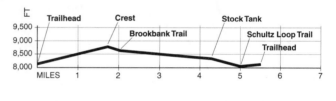

- 0.0 Sunset Trailhead.
- 0.2 Stay right at Little Elden Trail junction.
- 1.7 Cross the crest of the Dry Lake Hills.
- 2.0 Go straight ahead onto Brookbank Trail.
- 3.8 Turn right, uphill, onto an unsigned trail.
- 4.2 Join an old road below the stock tank, and turn right downhill.
- 4.9 Go right at the junction with Schultz Loop Trail.
- 5.4 Sunset Trailhead.

The hike: The trails on this hike are not shown on the topographic maps. From the trailhead, the Sunset Trail first crosses the gentle slope above Schultz Tank through beautiful ponderosa pine and aspen forest. The Little Elden Trail goes left; continue straight ahead. Now the trail enters a small drainage and turns uphill. Climbing steadily but at a moderate grade, the trail stays on the right side of the drainage for more than a mile. It then crosses a road, veers out of the drainage to the left, and enters a more open forest. The openness is due to the fact that the area was once logged. The trail reaches the crest of the Dry Lake Hills, where there are good views of the San Francisco Peaks to the north, then descends west on the south side of the ridge to meet the Brookbank Trail.

Sunset-Brookbank Trails

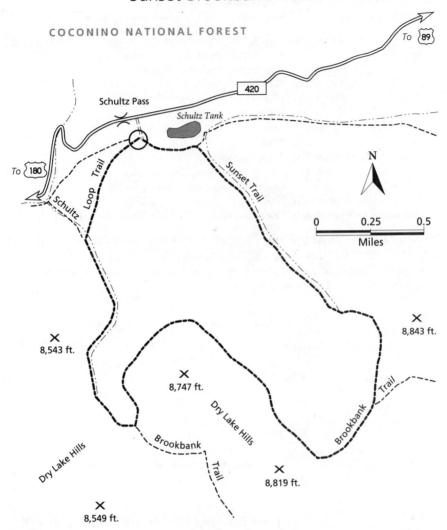

COCONINO NATIONAL FOREST

From this junction, continue straight ahead on the Brookbank Trail as it contours the slope westward. Here the forest is a pleasing mixture of ponderosa pine, Douglas fir, and aspen. Soon the trail crosses over a broad saddle and turns north. It descends though a small meadow then descends northwest via several switchbacks through dense fir forest. The trail passes through another saddle and meadow, and then contours around a hill to the north. The forest is so dense here that there are very few views.

Continuing around the hill, the trail heads south, then meets a T intersection. Turn right, uphill, on the unsigned trail. After a hundred yards, the trail levels out into a large meadow with a seasonal lake, the largest in the Dry Lake Hills. The next section of trail crosses private land. It is open to hikers at present. Please respect private property and all posted signs.

View of the San Francisco Peaks from the Brookbank Trail.

The trail turns into an old road as it crosses the meadow. Watch for a good trail branching right (north) before the road crosses the meadow. Take this trail directly toward the San Francisco Peaks, skirting a small stock tank on the east, and then join an old road just west of the stock tank. Follow the road downhill to the north. At the junction with Schultz Loop Trail, turn right and continue to Sunset Trailhead.

—Bruce Grubbs

26 Walnut Canyon Rim

Description:	This long and scenic hike follows a section of the Arizona Trail along the north rim of Walnut Canyon.
Location:	8 miles southeast of Flagstaff.
Type of hike:	Out-and-back day hike.
Difficulty:	Moderate.
Total distance:	13.6 miles.
Elevation change:	300 feet.
Water:	None.
Best months:	April–November.
Maps:	Flagstaff East USGS; Coconino National Forest.
Permit:	None.
For more information:	Coconino National Forest, Peaks Ranger District.

Finding the trailhead: From Flagstaff at the junction of Interstate 40 and U.S. 89, drive 4 miles east on I–40 to the Walnut Canyon National Monument exit. Go right (south) 2.5 miles on Walnut Canyon Road. Just before

Walnut Canyon Rim

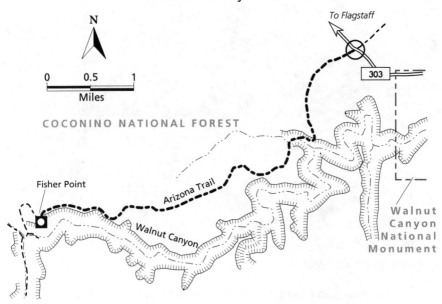

entering the monument, turn right on Old Walnut Canyon Road (Forest Road 303). Continue 1.8 miles to the Arizona Trail parking area.

Key points:
- 0.0   Trailhead.
- 1.9   Cross a side canyon.
- 2.4   First Walnut Canyon viewpoint.
- 5.5   The trail reaches the Walnut Canyon rim again.
- 6.8   Fisher Point.

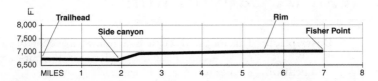

The hike: This hike follows a section of the Arizona Trail. Parts of the trail follow old roads, while other sections are new trail construction. Pay close attention to the trail markers. The trail starts off heading southwest though open ponderosa pine–Gambel oak forest, climbing gradually. It turns south, then joins an old road for a short distance.

After almost 2 miles, new trail construction takes you across a side canyon. On the far side, you'll join another old road. Watch for a spur trail on the right: it goes to a viewpoint overlooking Walnut Canyon. The trail then follows old roads for more than a mile, and wanders away from the rim. After the trail leaves the road again, it soon hits the north rim of Walnut Canyon, and follows it closely all the way to Fisher Point. This viewpoint, reached by a few yards of spur trail, overlooks the point where the canyon makes an abrupt 90-degree change in direction. It makes an ideal goal for a hike on this portion of the Arizona Trail.

—Bruce Grubbs

27 Mormon Lake

Description:	A hike along the shore of Mormon Lake, Arizona's largest natural lake. This is a great place to view wildlife.
Location:	27 miles southeast of Flagstaff.
Type of hike:	Out-and-back day hike.
Difficulty:	Easy.
Total distance:	6.4 miles.
Elevation change:	None.
Water:	Mormon Lake, but it may be muddy and difficult to reach.
Best months:	April–November.
Maps:	Mormon Lake USGS; Coconino National Forest.
Permit:	None.
For more information:	Coconino National Forest, Mormon Lake Ranger District.

Finding the trailhead: From Flagstaff, drive 27 miles southeast on Lake Mary Road (Forest Highway 3). The highway skirts the east side of Mormon Lake then descends through a cut. Watch for the turnoff to Kinnikinick Lake

Mormon Lake is Arizona's largest natural lake, and it's a great place to view wildlife.

Mormon Lake

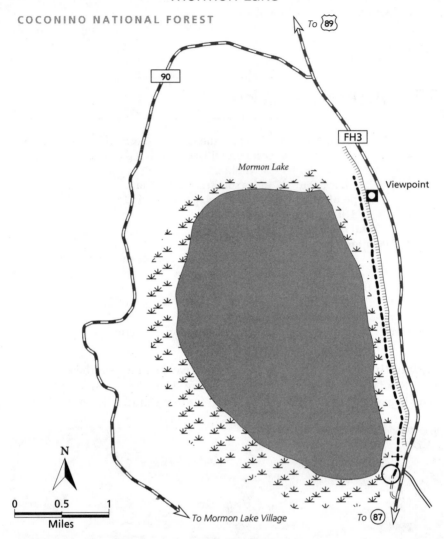

To (89)

90

FH3

Mormon Lake

Viewpoint

N

0   0.5   1
Miles

To Mormon Lake Village

To (87)

on the left, then turn right (east) onto an unmarked, unmaintained dirt road, which descends toward the lake then turns right. Go through the gate (low-clearance cars should be parked here), then drive a short distance to a fork; turn right, drive a few yards uphill to a second gate, and park. This gate is normally locked to protect the area's wildlife.

Key points:

0.0	Trailhead.
3.2	North end of old highway.

The hike: The walk follows on old road along the shore of the lake. (The topographic map shows this old road, but not the present highway, which is to the east, above the lakeside cliffs.) The old road is nearly level and is about 20 feet higher than the lake, so there is a good view. This hike is best done at sunrise or sunset, which are good times for wildlife viewing.

The road can be followed more than 3 miles along the eastern shore, to a point just past the viewpoint on the new highway. Cottonwood and aspen trees grow here in an unusual association, and there are fine views of the distant San Francisco Peaks. Most of the year, Mormon Lake is more a marsh than a lake. When full, after the spring snowmelt, it is the largest "natural" lake in Arizona.

Although there is no dam (in contrast with Upper and Lower Lake Mary), man has still influenced the lake. The area was first settled by Mormons who started dairy farming here. In the pioneer days the lake area was never more than a marsh, so the settlers ran cattle on the rich forage. Eventually, the hooves of the cattle compacted the soil and made it less porous, so that the marsh flooded and became a lake in wet years. Today, the lake and its marshes are important havens for wildlife.

—Bruce Grubbs

Mogollon Rim Country

The thousand-foot-plus escarpment known as the Mogollon Rim sweeps across central Arizona, separating the Colorado Plateau from the Central Highlands. Scores of canyons have been eroded into the Rim. Many contain permanent streams and lovely riparian habitats that are popular with fishermen and birders.

28 Sycamore Rim Trail

Description:	A long and enjoyable walk on a scenic trail along the rim of Sycamore and Big Springs Canyons. Part of the trail is within Sycamore Canyon Wilderness.
Location:	28 miles southwest of Flagstaff.
Type of hike:	Loop day hike.
Difficulty:	Moderate.
Total distance:	9.6 miles.
Elevation change:	790 feet.
Water:	None.
Best months:	April–November.
Maps:	Davenport Hill, Garland Prairie USGS; Kaibab National Forest (Williams, Chalender, and Tusayan Ranger Districts).
Permit:	None.
For more information:	Kaibab National Forest, Williams Ranger District.

Finding the trailhead: From Flagstaff, drive about 16 miles west on Interstate 40, then turn left (south) at the Parks exit onto the maintained Garland Prairie Road (Forest Road 141). Drive 12 miles, then turn left (south) on Forest Road 131, a signed, maintained road. Continue about 1.5 miles to Dow Trailhead.

From Williams, drive east on I-40 about 4 miles, then turn right (south) at the Garland Prairie Road exit (this is not the same exit for Garland Prairie mentioned above). Drive 8.5 miles on Forest Road 141 to reach Forest Road 131, then turn right (south) and continue 1.5 miles to the trailhead.

Key points:
- 0.0   Dow Trailhead.
- 0.1   Turn right on Sycamore Rim Trail.
- 1.4   Forest Road 56.
- 2.1   KA Hill.
- 4.4   Pomeroy Tanks.
- 5.2   Sycamore Falls.
- 6.6   Sycamore Vista.
- 9.6   Dow Trailhead.

Sycamore Rim Trail

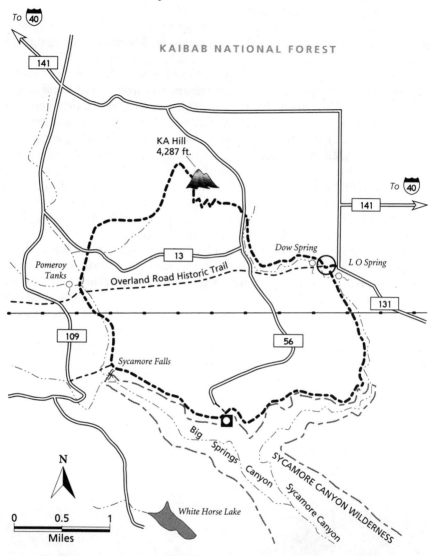

The hike: The Sycamore Rim Trail is a relatively new recreation trail and is not shown on the topographic map. Almost immediately after you leave the parking lot, you'll cross the route of the historic Overland Road. The old road was built in 1858 as part of a route across northern Arizona from east to west. Long abandoned, the route has recently been retraced by the U.S.

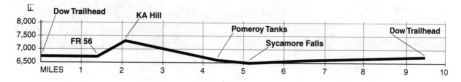

Forest Service, and marked with wood posts, brass caps, and rock cairns. From this trailhead, you could also follow the old route either east into Garland Prairie or west toward Pomeroy Tanks.

Continuing on our hike, you meet the Sycamore Rim Trail at a T intersection, where you'll turn right to start the loop. The trail follows the rim of Sycamore Canyon, which is a shallow drainage at this point. A Forest Service sign points out the location of an old lumber mill. Not much is visible now except a few rotting timbers. These temporary logging mills and camps were moved to follow the active logging. The logs were transported on temporary railroad spurs. After the transcontinental railroad reached the area in 1883, railroads were the most economical method of moving cut timber to the mills, as well as men and supplies into the forest. When logging was complete in an area (meaning that all the accessible large trees were cut), the rails would be removed and reused on another spur railroad. The roadbeds were built to the minimum standard necessary for their short-lived purpose. Today these old railroad grades can be traced for miles through the forest; some have been rebuilt into modern dirt roads.

The shallow canyon gradually broadens into a meadow, which the trail crosses to meet Forest Road 56. On the west side of the road, the trail starts to climb KA Hill in a series of switchbacks. After crossing the forested summit, the trail drops southwest down the gentle, pine-forested slopes and into a shallow drainage. It crosses a road (Forest Road 13), and then passes Pomeroy Tanks, a series of natural basins in the drainage that sometimes hold water. A spur trail goes southwest to Pomeroy Tanks Trailhead on Forest Road 109.

Now the trail follows the drainage, soon crossing back to the east side. The canyon gradually deepens, and the trail meets another spur trail. This

The Sycamore Rim Trail runs along the northern edge of the Sycamore Canyon Wilderness.

one goes to Sycamore Falls Trailhead, also on Forest Road 109. The drainage we've been following is joined by Big Spring Canyon, which soon drops over the falls. The basalt cliffs here are a popular rock climbing area.

As the canyon deepens, the trail heads southeast along its rim, climbing gradually. At Sycamore Vista, you'll have a fine view of Sycamore Canyon Wilderness to the south. Another short spur trail goes to Sycamore Vista Trailhead on Forest Road 56. At this point, the canyon is more than 500 feet deep. Now, the trail heads east across the broad point separating Big Spring Canyon from Sycamore Canyon. After it meets the rim of Sycamore Canyon, it follows the rim back to the junction near Dow Trailhead. Turn right to return to the trailhead.

—Bruce Grubbs

29 Kelsey-Dorsey Loop

Description:	A scenic, remote hike in the Sycamore Canyon Wilderness.
Location:	21 miles southwest of Flagstaff.
Type of hike:	Loop day hike.
Difficulty:	Moderate.
Total distance:	6.4 miles.
Elevation change:	1,080 feet.
Water:	Kelsey, Babes Hole, and Dorsey Springs.
Best months:	April–November.
Maps:	Sycamore Point USGS; Coconino National Forest.
Permit:	None.
or more information:	Coconino National Forest, Peaks Ranger District.

Finding the trailhead: From Flagstaff, drive west on West U.S. 66 (Business Interstate 40) about 2 miles, then turn left (south) on the Woody Mountain Road (Forest Road 231). This road starts out paved but soon becomes maintained dirt. Continue 13.7 miles, then turn right (west) at Phone Booth Tank onto a narrower, maintained dirt road (Forest Road 538). Continue on the main road 5.3 miles, and then turn right (northwest) onto an unmaintained road (Forest Road 538G), which is signed for the Kelsey Trail. Go 0.6 mile, then turn right at a junction to continue on Forest Road 538G 1.3 miles to the end of the road at the Kelsey Trailhead.

Key points:
0.0	Kelsey Trailhead.
0.4	Kelsey Spring.
1.0	Babes Hole Spring; turn left onto the Dorsey Trail.
2.5	Dorsey Spring; turn left onto the Dorsey Spring Trail.
4.0	Dorsey Trailhead.
4.6	Turn left at road junction.
5.1	Turn left on Forest Road 538G.
6.4	Kelsey Trailhead.

Kelsey-Dorsey Loop

Kelsey Spring

Kelsey Trailhead

Geronimo Spring

Dorsey Trail

Babes Hole Spring

538G

Dorsey Spring Trail

To 231

~O Dorsey Spring

Hog Hill 7,220 ft.

538

Sycamore Canyon

SYCAMORE CANYON WILDERNESS

Winter Cabin Spring

COCONINO NATIONAL FOREST

Sycamore Creek

Ott Lake

N

0   0.5   1
Miles

The hike: The Kelsey Trail drops over the upper rim of Sycamore Canyon and descends steeply for a couple of switchbacks, then reaches gentler terrain as it swings west through the pine-oak forest. In a half mile the trail reaches Kelsey Spring, where it turns sharply left (south) to cross a drainage. The trail follows this drainage to the northwest to Babes Hole Spring. Just past the spring, go left on the Dorsey Trail, up the hill, at a junction marked by a huge, ancient

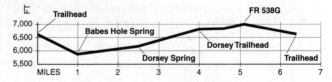

Sycamore Canyon near the foot of the Kelsey Trail.

ponderosa pine. There are good views as the trail contours along the inner rim of rugged Sycamore Canyon. At Dorsey Spring, turn left (east) onto the Dorsey Spring Trail. The trail climbs over a low ridge and drops into a drainage, which it follows nearly to the outer rim before swinging north. The trail goes through a low saddle in the forest before turning east again and climbing gradually to the Dorsey Trailhead.

Continue along the seldom traveled dirt road 0.6 mile, and then turn left (northeast) at the junction. In another 0.5 mile you will reach Forest Road 538G. Turn left (north) and walk 1.3 miles to the end of the road and your car. It is possible to do a car shuttle to avoid the hike on the road, but not really necessary as there is almost no traffic on these roads, and they form a pleasant loop hike.

—Bruce Grubbs

30 Taylor Cabin Loop

Description:	This is a fine hike through the remote red rock canyons of the Sycamore Canyon and Red Rock–Secret Mountain Wildernesses. A bonus is the return trail across the top of Casner Mountain, which gives you outstanding views of Sycamore Canyon.
Location:	19 miles west of Sedona.
Type of hike:	Loop backpack.
Difficulty:	Difficult.
Total distance:	18.8 miles.
Elevation change:	2,560 feet.
Water:	Seasonal in Sycamore Creek.
Best months:	April–May, October–November.
Maps:	Sycamore Point, Sycamore Basin, Loy Butte USGS; Coconino National Forest.
Permit:	Red Rock Pass required for parking.
For more information:	Coconino National Forest, Sedona Ranger District.

Finding the trailhead: From Sedona, drive about 8 miles south on Arizona 89A, then turn right (northwest) on Forest Road 525, a maintained dirt road. Go 2.2 miles, and then turn left (west) onto Forest Road 525C. Continue 8.8 miles to the end of the road at the Dogie Trailhead. The last mile or two frequently washes out and may be very rough, but the rest is passable to ordinary cars. The Casner Mountain Trail, which is the return trail for the loop, meets Forest Road 525C 0.8 mile east of Sycamore Pass Trailhead.

Key points:
- 0.0   Dogie Trailhead.
- 0.4   Sycamore Pass.
- 4.9   Sycamore Creek.
- 5.0   Turn right on Taylor Cabin Trail.

Taylor Cabin Loop • Parsons Trail

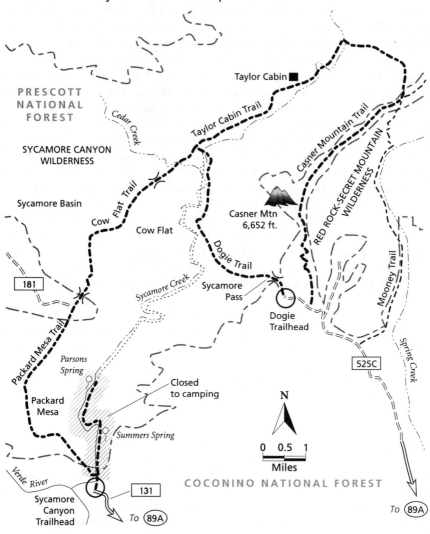

7.9   Taylor Cabin.
9.7   Trail turns right, up an unnamed side canyon.
12.0   Turn right on Casner Mountain Trail.
15.6   Casner Mountain.
18.0   Turn right on Forest Road FR 525C.
18.8   Sycamore Pass Trailhead.

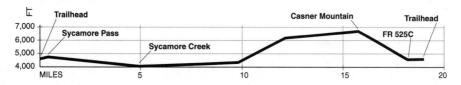

The hike: There is usually water in Sycamore Creek during the spring, but it is dry later in the year. Enough water should be carried for a dry camp if the creek is dry. On the other hand, Sycamore Creek may be flooding and be impassable during snowmelt or after a major storm. In this case you'll have to make the hike an out and back, which you can do in a day.

The start of the Dogie Trail is shown on the Loy Butte quad, but the trail is missing from the Sycamore Basin quad. You'll climb a short distance to cross Sycamore Pass, and then descend gradually to the west. The trail turns north and works its way along a sloping terrace through pinyon-juniper forest. The inner gorge of Sycamore Canyon is visible to the west, and the cliffs of Casner Mountain rise on the east. Finally, the trail descends to Sycamore Creek and crosses it to join the Cow Flat and Taylor Cabin Trails on the west bank. There are several campsites for small groups on the bluff just to the south. (In an emergency, you may be able to find water in Cedar Creek. See Hike 31, Parsons Trail, for details.)

Turn right (northeast) on the Taylor Cabin Trail, which stays on the bench to the west of Sycamore Creek. After about 2 miles, the trail descends to the creek and becomes harder to find. Watch for Taylor Cabin on the west bank; the trail passes right by this old rancher's line cabin. The trail stays on the west side of the creek after Taylor Cabin. If the trail is lost, then boulder-hop directly up the creekbed.

About 1.8 miles from Taylor Cabin, the trail turns right (east) and climbs out of Sycamore Canyon. Watch carefully for the turnoff, which is usually marked by cairns. The topographic maps are essential for finding this trail. Most of the trail follows the major drainage south of Buck Ridge, often staying right in the bed of this very pretty canyon. Near the top, the trail turns more to the south and climbs steeply through a fine stand of ponderosa pine and Douglas fir. A single switchback leads to the top of the ridge, where there are excellent views of Sycamore Canyon and the Taylor Basin. The trail reaches a pass and ends at the junction with the Casner Mountain and Mooney Trails.

Turn right (southwest) on the Casner Mountain Trail, which is an old road built during power line construction. The road is now closed to vehicles and makes a scenic finish to this loop hike. Follow the trail southwest along the narrow ridge leading to Casner Mountain. There are views of Sycamore Canyon on the west and Mooney Canyon on the east. The trail climbs onto Casner Mountain, a broad plateau capped with dark volcanic rocks. A gradual descent leads to the south edge of the plateau, where the trail descends rapidly in a series of switchbacks. Near the bottom of the descent, the trail is shown as ending on the topographic map; if you lose it, follow the power line down to Forest Road 525C. Turn right and walk 0.8 mile up the road to the Sycamore Pass Trailhead.

—Bruce Grubbs

31 Parsons Trail

See Map on Page 105

Description:	A challenging trail and cross-country hike through the remote red rock canyons of the Sycamore Canyon Wilderness.
Location:	10 miles north of Cottonwood.
Type of hike:	Loop backpack.
Difficulty:	Difficult.
Total distance:	21.4 miles.
Elevation change:	1,200 feet.
Water:	Sycamore Creek downstream from Parsons Spring; seasonal pools upstream.
Best months:	April–May, October–November.
Maps:	Clarkdale, Sycamore Basin USGS; Coconino National Forest.
Permit:	Camping is not allowed in Sycamore Canyon from Parsons Spring downstream to the Verde River.
For more information:	Coconino National Forest, Sedona Ranger District; Prescott National Forest, Chino Valley Ranger District.

Finding the trailhead: From Cottonwood, drive to the north end of town on Arizona 89A and into the town of Clarkdale, then turn right (east) on the road to Tuzigoot National Monument. After 0.2 mile, just after crossing the Verde River bridge, turn left (north) on County Road 139 (it becomes Forest Road 131), a maintained dirt road. Drive 10 miles to the end of the road at the Sycamore Canyon Trailhead.

Key points:
0.0	Sycamore Canyon Trailhead.
0.2	Sycamore Creek.
1.2	Summers Spring.
3.6	Parsons Spring.
11.2	Turn left on Sycamore Pass Trail.
11.3	Turn left on Cow Flat and Taylor Cabin Trail.
11.7	Cedar Creek.
12.7	Pass into Sycamore Basin.
15.8	Pass.
19.8	Sycamore Canyon Rim.
21.2	Sycamore Creek.
21.4	Sycamore Canyon Trailhead.

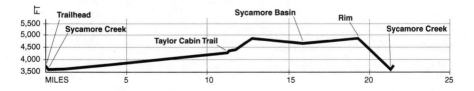

The hike: Sycamore Creek is usually dry above Parsons Spring. In the spring, seasonal pools above this point make it possible to do this loop without carrying water. During summer and fall, you'll have to pick up enough water at Parsons Spring for your camp farther up the canyon. The catch is that during early spring, Sycamore Creek may be flooding from snowmelt in the high country and this loop trip may be impossible. If the creek is running muddy at the trailhead, content yourself with a short day hike to Summers Spring or Parsons Spring. Do not attempt to cross the creek when it is flooding. In summer, this loop is recommended only for hikers experienced at dry camping in hot weather.

From the trailhead, follow the good trail 0.2 mile north into Sycamore Creek. On the left, the Packard Trail crosses the creek; this is our return trail. Please note that Sycamore Canyon is closed to camping between the trailhead and Parsons Spring, due to overuse. Continue following Sycamore Creek on the broad, easy trail along the east bank. Sycamore Creek flows all year and supports a rich variety of riparian trees, including the Arizona sycamore for which the canyon is named.

About 1.5 miles from the trailhead, the canyon swings sharply left, then right. During the winters of 1993 and 1994, massive flooding completely rearranged the creekbed. Evidence of the flooding is everywhere: saplings leaning downstream, piles of driftwood and even huge logs far above normal stream level, and collapsed stream banks.

Above Parsons Spring, the source for Sycamore Creek, the creekbed dries up. Continue up Sycamore Creek by boulder hopping along the broad dry wash. You may see seasonal pools of water in the bends of the creek. Also,

The many canyons incised into the Mogollon Rim offer outstanding opportunities for exploring and camping.

Several springs keep a year-round flow in lower Sycamore Creek.

watch for petroglyphs along the rock walls of the canyon. Although strenuous, progress up the creekbed is relatively fast because the periodic floods keep the bed clear of brush. The gorge becomes shallower after about 6 miles.

The Sycamore Pass Trail crosses Sycamore Creek 7.6 miles above Parsons Spring. Turn left (west) on the Sycamore Pass Trail, which joins the Taylor Cabin and Cow Flat Trails above the west bank. Turn left (south) on the Cow Flat Trail. There are several good campsites for small groups on the bluffs overlooking the creek to the east. There is no water except for possible seasonal pools in Sycamore Creek.

After the confines of Sycamore Creek and the rugged boulder hopping, it is a pleasure to walk the easy Cow Flat Trail southwest through the open pinyon-juniper forest. Shortly, the trail crosses Cedar Creek. (This creek is usually dry at the crossing, but water can sometimes be found upstream about a mile.) The trail climbs gradually for another mile and passes through a broad saddle to enter Sycamore Basin. The walking is very easy through this open basin, with fine views of the surrounding red rock formations. Camping is unlimited if you carry water for a dry camp.

The trail crosses Cow Flat, skirts the head of a side canyon, then climbs gradually to another pass. On the far side of the pass, the trail ends at a trailhead at the end of Forest Road 181. To continue, go south on the Packard Trail. Packard Mesa forms the west rim of lower Sycamore Canyon, and the trail generally stays near the crest as it works its way south through open pinyon pine and juniper stands. About 4 miles from Forest Road 181, the trail turns east and descends into Sycamore Canyon. It crosses the creek and meets the Parsons Trail; turn right to return to the trailhead.

—Bruce Grubbs

32 Secret Mountain Trail

Description:	This trail wanders out onto Secret Mountain, an isolated mesa in the Red Rock–Secret Mountain Wilderness. It features a historic cabin and some good views of the canyons in the wilderness area.
Location:	20 miles southwest of Flagstaff.
Type of hike:	Out-and-back day hike or backpack.
Difficulty:	Moderate.
Total distance:	9.8 miles.
Elevation change:	240 feet.
Water:	None.
Best months:	April–November.
Maps:	Loy Butte, Wilson Mountain USGS; Coconino National Forest.
Permit:	None.
For more information:	Coconino National Forest, Sedona Ranger District.

Secret Mountain Trail

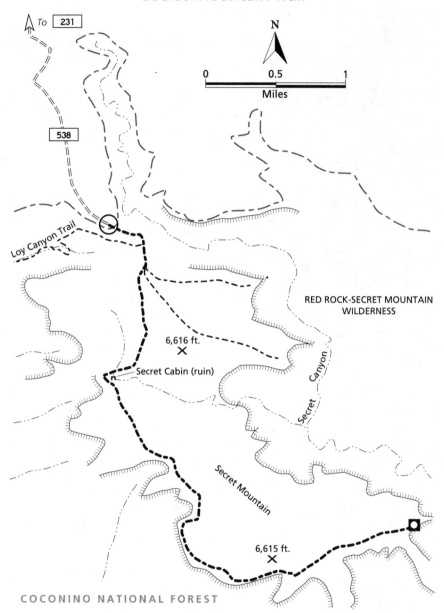

To 231

N

0   0.5   1
Miles

538

Loy Canyon Trail

RED ROCK-SECRET MOUNTAIN
WILDERNESS

6,616 ft.
X

Secret Cabin (ruin)

Secret Canyon

Secret Mountain

6,615 ft.
X

COCONINO NATIONAL FOREST

Finding the trailhead: From Flagstaff, drive west on West Route 66 (Business I–40) about 2 miles, then turn left (south) on the Woody Mountain Road (Forest Road 231). This road starts out paved but soon becomes maintained dirt. Continue 13.7 miles, then turn right (west) at Phone Booth Tank onto a narrower maintained dirt road (Forest Road 538). Continue on this road 6.8 miles, passing the turnoff to Turkey Butte Lookout. (The road is unmaintained after this point but is passable to low-clearance vehicles, with care, when it is dry. After a storm or during snowmelt, the mud will be impassable.) In another 1.5 miles the road passes just west of a power line, then passes a stock tank. About 8.9 miles from Phone Booth Tank, Forest Road 538 turns left (southeast) at the junction with Forest Road 538B and crosses under the power line. Continue 2.7 miles on Forest Road 538 to the end of the road.

Key points:

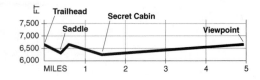

0.0	Trailhead.
0.4	Loy Canyon Trail at saddle.
0.6	Side trails.
1.4	Secret Cabin.
4.9	Viewpoint.

The hike: The trailhead is on the edge of the Mogollon Rim, but the view is mostly blocked by the bulk of Secret Mountain rising to the south. Start by following the Secret Mountain Trail along the ridge to the southeast. It drops down to the saddle between the rim and Secret Mountain, meeting the Loy Canyon Trail. (See Hike 33 for information.)

The Secret Mountain Trail climbs about 200 feet onto Secret Mountain, where there is a trail junction. These two side trails lead east to viewpoints overlooking Secret Canyon. The main trail continues south across the pine- and oak-forested plateau to the ruins of Secret Cabin. Most likely, ranchers built the cabin as a line cabin for use during roundups. Water can sometimes be found in the drainage east of the ruin.

From the cabin, continue south. Soon the trail reaches a point on the west rim of Secret Mountain with views to the southwest toward the Verde Valley and Mingus Mountain. After this point, the trail heads generally southeast and skirts the southwest rim of Secret Mountain. A large fire burned much of this area in 1996. The trail finally turns east and ends at the eastern tip of Secret Mountain. You're looking down Long Canyon and at the mass of Maroon Mountain, which divides Long and Secret Canyons.

There is unlimited camping along the trail, so it makes a pleasant, easy overnight backpack trip if one is willing to carry water for a dry camp.

—Bruce Grubbs

33 Loy Canyon Trail

Description:	A scenic hike up a red rock canyon to the Mogollon Rim in the Red Rock–Secret Mountain Wilderness.
Location:	12 miles northwest of Sedona.
Type of hike:	Out-and-back day hike.
Difficulty:	Moderate.
Total distance:	9.6 miles.
Elevation change:	1,900 feet.
Water:	None.
Best months:	All year.
Maps:	Loy Butte USGS; Coconino National Forest.
Permit:	Red Rock Permit required for parking.
For more information:	Coconino National Forest, Sedona Ranger District.

Finding the trailhead: From Sedona, drive to the west end of town on Arizona 89A; turn right at a traffic light onto the Dry Creek Road. Drive 2.8 miles, then turn left onto Boynton Canyon Road. Continue 1.6 miles and turn left onto Forest Road 152C, a maintained dirt road. After 3.0 miles, turn right onto Forest Road 525. Continue 3.7 miles to the Loy Canyon Trailhead. (If you go too far you will see the Hancock Ranch to the right.)

Key points:

- 0.0 Loy Canyon Trailhead.
- 2.1 Red rock narrows.
- 3.0 End of narrows.
- 4.4 Turn left on the Secret Mountain Trail.
- 4.8 Secret Mountain Trailhead.

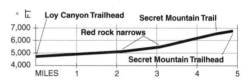

Sandstone formations along Loy Canyon, Red Rock–Secret Mountain Wilderness.

Loy Canyon Trail

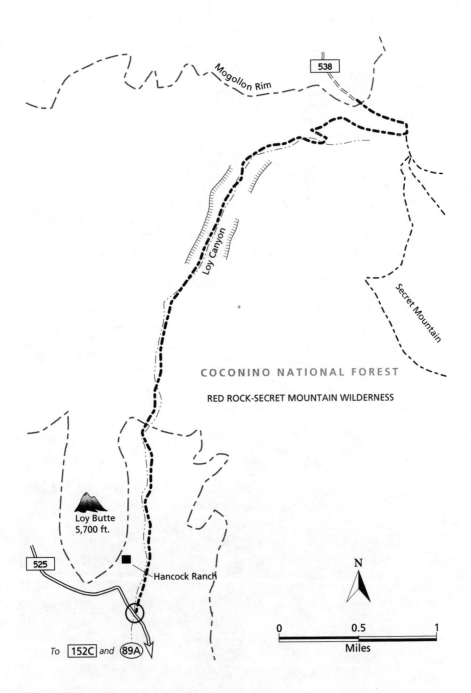

538

Mogollon Rim

Loy Canyon

Secret Mountain

COCONINO NATIONAL FOREST

RED ROCK-SECRET MOUNTAIN WILDERNESS

Loy Butte
5,700 ft.

525

Hancock Ranch

N

To 152C and 89A

0	0.5	1

Miles

The hike: Initially the trail skirts the Hancock Ranch along its east boundary, then joins the dry creekbed which it follows northward through the open pinyon pine, juniper, and Arizona cypress forest. Conical Loy Butte looms to the west, and the cliffs of Secret Mountain tower over Loy Canyon on the east. After 2.1 miles, the canyon becomes narrower, and the trail turns slightly toward the northeast. In another mile the trail turns toward the east as the canyon opens up a bit. The buff-colored Coconino sandstone cliffs of the Mogollon Rim tower above the trail to the north, and matching cliffs form the north end of Secret Mountain. Watch carefully for the point where the trail leaves the canyon bottom and begins climbing the north side of the canyon in a series of switchbacks. Alhough it is a steep climb, the reward is an expanding view of Loy Canyon. Notice the contrast between the brushy vegetation on this dry south-facing slope and the cool, moist pine and fir forest across the canyon to the south.

The Loy Canyon Trail ends where it joins the Secret Mountain Trail in the saddle between Secret Mountain and the Mogollon Rim. Turn left here and climb the short distance to the rim and the Secret Mountain Trailhead. Views are limited here, but if you walk a few hundred yards along the road there is a great view down Loy Canyon.

As an option, you could combine the Loy Canyon and Secret Mountain Trails for a longer hike. See Hike 32, Secret Mountain Trail, for information.

—Bruce Grubbs

34 Secret Canyon

Description:	This is an exceptionally fine hike up the longest canyon in the Red Rock-Secret Mountain Wilderness. Its length keeps the crowds away.
Location:	5 miles northwest of Sedona.
Type of hike:	Out-and-back day hike.
Difficulty:	Moderate.
Total distance:	7.8 miles.
Elevation change:	480 feet.
Water:	Upper Secret Canyon.
Best months:	All year.
Maps:	Wilson Mountain USGS; Coconino National Forest.
Permit:	Red Rock Pass required for parking.
For more information:	Coconino National Forest, Sedona Ranger District.

Finding the trailhead: From Sedona, drive to the west end of town on Arizona 89A; turn right at a traffic light onto the Dry Creek Road. After 2.0 miles, turn right on dirt Forest Road 152 (also called Dry Creek Road). Although this road is maintained, it receives a lot of traffic, and its condition varies. Drive 3.2 miles to the Secret Canyon Trailhead on the left side of the road. The parking area is small, but there are other parking spots nearby.

Secret Canyon • Bear Sign Canyon

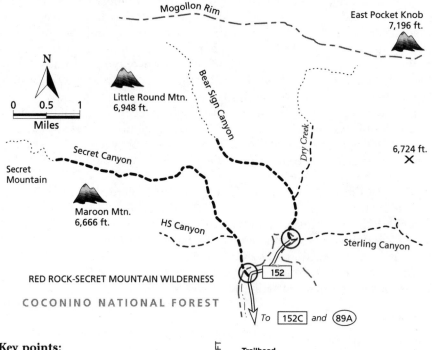

Key points:

  0.0   Secret Canyon Trailhead.
  1.8   End of old jeep road.
  3.9   End of trail in
       Secret Canyon.

The hike: Secret Canyon is the
longest and most remote canyon in the Dry Creek Basin, and is nearly as long
as its more famous neighbor, Oak Creek. It also has permanent water in the
upper section, a rarity in the red rock area.

The Secret Canyon Trail crosses Dry Creek and enters the Red Rock–Secret Mountain Wilderness only a few yards from the road. You'll cross Secret Canyon wash several times; if either it or Dry Creek is flooding, then
this hike will be impossible. Normally, however, Secret Canyon is dry in the
lower section, and the hike is easy through the pinyon-juniper-cypress forest. About 0.5 mile from the trailhead, the HS Canyon Trail branches left.
At 1.8 miles, the trail passes through a small clearing, giving you good views
into upper Secret Canyon.

Now the trail contours along the north side of the drainage for a short
distance before dropping back into the bed. The canyon walls become narrower here, and are formed by the Mogollon Rim on the north and Maroon
Mountain on the south. There is normally water in this section. Watch for
poison ivy, a low-growing plant with shiny leaves that grow in groups of three.
Fall colors in this part of the canyon are a beautiful mix of reds, oranges,

Secret Mountain in the Red Rock–Secret Mountain Wilderness.

and violets, with most of the color provided by Arizona bigtooth maple and poison ivy.

About 4 miles from the trailhead, our hike ends as the trail fades out. Only those willing to do difficult cross-country hiking should continue beyond this point.

—Bruce Grubbs

35 Bear Sign Canyon

See Map on Page 116

Description:	A very easy hike into a red rock canyon in the Red Rock–Secret Mountain Wilderness.
Location:	6 miles northwest of Sedona.
Type of hike:	Out-and-back day hike.
Difficulty:	Easy.
Total distance:	3.2 miles.
Elevation change:	280 feet.
Water:	Seasonal in Bear Sign Canyon.
Best months:	All year.
Maps:	Wilson Mountain USGS; Coconino National Forest
Permit:	Red Rock Pass required for parking.
For more information:	Coconino National Forest, Sedona Ranger District.

Finding the trailhead: From Sedona, drive to the west end of town on Arizona 89A; turn right at a traffic light onto the Dry Creek Road. After 2.0 miles, turn right on dirt Forest Road 152 (also called Dry Creek Road). Although

Along the Bear Sign Trail under the Mogollon Rim.

this road is maintained, it receives a lot of traffic, and its condition varies. Drive 4.0 miles to the end of the road at the Dry Creek Trailhead.

Key points:
- 0.0 Dry Creek Trailhead.
- 0.6 Turn left onto Bear Sign Canyon Trail.
- 1.6 End of trail.

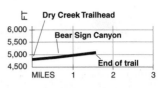

The hike: Two trails begin at this trailhead. The Dry Creek Trail goes north, and the Vultee Arch Trail goes east. Start out on the Dry Creek Trail, hike 0.6 mile north, and then turn left (northwest) at Bear Sign Canyon, the first side canyon on the left. The trail continues about a mile up Bear Sign Canyon before fading out. It is possible to go farther, but the canyon becomes much rougher. There are great views of the cliffs of the Mogollon Rim, and after wet periods the creek will be running. The vegetation is the usual but still delightful mix of Arizona cypress, pinyon pine, juniper trees, and chaparral brush.

—Bruce Grubbs

---

36 Thomas Point Trail

Description:	This hike is a great alternative to the crowded West Fork Trail, and is right across the highway. There are excellent views of the West Fork of Oak Creek and of Oak Creek Canyon itself.
Location:	11 miles north of Sedona.
Type of hike:	Out-and-back day hike.
Difficulty:	Moderate.
Total distance:	2.0 miles.
Elevation change:	970 feet.
Water:	None.
Best months:	April–November.
Maps:	Munds Park USGS; Coconino National Forest.
Permit:	Red Rock Pass required for parking, in addition to parking lot fee.
For more information:	Coconino National Forest, Sedona Ranger District.

Finding the trailhead: From Sedona, drive about 11 miles north on Arizona 89A, then turn left into the West Fork parking area. You'll have to pay a fee to park here.

Key points:
- 0.0 Trailhead.
- 0.4 Viewpoint.
- 1.0 East rim of Oak Creek Canyon.

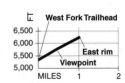

Thomas Point Trail • West Fork Trail • AB Young Trail

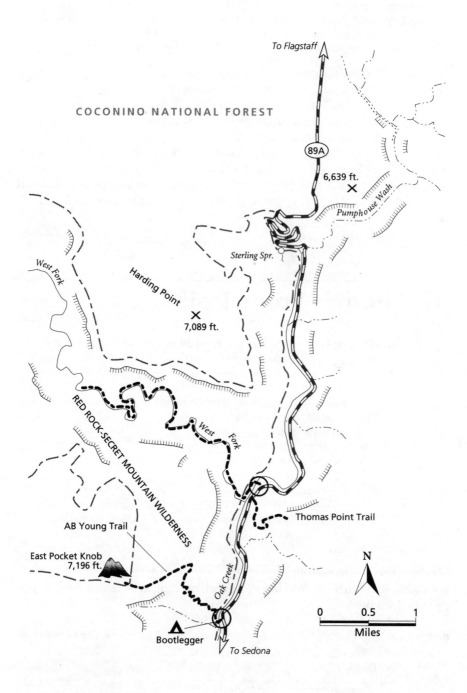

To Flagstaff

COCONINO NATIONAL FOREST

89A

6,639 ft.
✕

Pumphouse Wash

Sterling Spr.

West Fork

Harding Point

✕
7,089 ft.

RED ROCK-SECRET MOUNTAIN WILDERNESS

West Fork

Thomas Point Trail

AB Young Trail

East Pocket Knob
7,196 ft.

Oak Creek

N

Bootlegger

To Sedona

0   0.5   1
Miles

Looking up West Fork of Oak Creek from the Thomas Point Trail.

The hike: Like most of the old trails in Oak Creek Canyon, this trail is not shown on the topographic map. From the parking area, follow the trail south through the old orchard for about 100 yards, then cross the highway to a trail sign. The trail climbs south through shady ponderosa pine–Gambel oak forest, and then turns a corner onto a much drier south-facing slope. Here, because of the increased temperature and evaporation, the chaparral plants dominate: scrub oak, mountain mahogany, and manzanita. There are fine views down the canyon to the flat-topped mesa of Wilson Mountain.

A switchback leads to a point overlooking the mouth of the West Fork, and then the trail turns east again and climbs into a pine saddle. The trail finishes by following the ridge east 100 yards to the rim, where views are limited because of the thick forest. You'll find a better viewpoint by walking about 100 yards west from the saddle, onto a rock outcrop. Here you're looking up the West Fork of Oak Creek.

—Bruce Grubbs

37 West Fork Trail

Description:	An easy, very popular hike through the spectacular West Fork of Oak Creek, in the Red Rock-Secret Mountain Wilderness.
Location:	11 miles north of Sedona.
Type of hike:	Out-and-back day hike.
Difficulty:	Easy.
Total distance:	6.0 miles.
Elevation change:	300 feet.
Water:	West Fork.
Best months:	April–November.
Maps:	Dutton Hill, Wilson Mountain, Munds Park USGS; Coconino National Forest.
Permit:	The lower 6 miles of the West Fork require a special permit for camping. A Red Rock Pass is required for parking, in addition to the parking lot fee.
For more information:	Coconino National Forest, Sedona Ranger District.

See Map on Page 120

Finding the trailhead: From Sedona, drive about 11 miles north on Arizona 89A, then turn left into the West Fork Trailhead parking area. You'll have to pay to park here.

Key points:
- 0.0 Trailhead.
- 0.4 Mouth of the West Fork.
- 3.0 Trail ends.

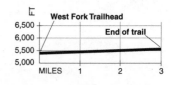

The hike: The West Fork is an easy but extremely popular hike. It is not the place to go to escape crowds, especially on weekends. For solitude, try the Thomas Point Trail on the opposite side of Oak Creek (see Hike 36). Note that the Forest Service restricts camping in the lower West Fork due to heavy use. Stay on the trail and do not pick flowers or otherwise disturb this fragile environment. Watch for poison ivy, which is common along the trail.

Follow the trail, which is not shown on the topographic map, across Oak Creek. The trail goes south along the creek, and then turns right (west) into the West Fork. Soon you'll leave the sounds of the busy highway behind and be able to hear the pleasant murmur of the creek and the whisper of the wind in the trees. Buttresses of Coconino sandstone tower on the left, while

Along the popular, scenic West Fork Trail in Oak Creek Canyon.

the canyon floor is filled with a tall ponderosa pine and Douglas fir forest. The trail crosses the creek several times, and ends about 3 miles up the canyon. Walking is very easy to this point, which is the end of the hike.

Options: Experienced canyon hikers may continue up the West Fork to its head near Forest Road 231. This hike requires wading in the creek and occasional swimming to cross deep pools. There is a serious danger of flash flooding; do not continue unless you have a stable weather forecast and are prepared to handle the deep, often cold pools.

Another possible hike for the adventurous, experienced canyon hiker is to climb to the south rim of the canyon, then hike to East Pocket Knob and use the AB Young Trail (see Hike 38) to descend back into Oak Creek Canyon. There is a route up the nameless canyon that is just west of West Buzzard Point.

—Bruce Grubbs

38 AB Young Trail

See Map on Page 120

Description:	This is a good trail to the west rim of Oak Creek Canyon in the Red Rock–Secret Mountain Wilderness. It offers the best views of Oak Creek Canyon from any of the rim trails.
Location:	9 miles north of Sedona.
Type of hike:	Out and back day hike.
Difficulty:	Moderate.
Total distance:	4.4 miles.
Elevation change:	2,000 feet.
Water:	None.
Best months:	April–November.
Maps:	Munds Park, Wilson Mountain USGS; Coconino National Forest.
Permit:	Red Rock Pass required for parking.
For more information:	Coconino National Forest, Sedona Ranger District.

Finding the trailhead: From Sedona, drive about 9 miles north on Arizona 89A to the Bootlegger Campground. Do not block the campground entrance; park in the highway pullout just to the north.

Key points:

0.0 Trailhead at Bootlegger Campground.
1.4 West Rim of Oak Creek Canyon.
1.8 Trail leaves rim.
2.2 East Pocket Lookout.

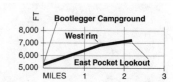

The hike: Walk through the campground and cross Oak Creek. Turn left (south) on the trail, which parallels the creek, and watch for the signed junction with

The AB Young Trail was built by a pioneer rancher to move stock to the Mogollon Rim.

the AB Young Trail. It is a good, maintained trail, which turns sharply right and starts climbing to the northwest. The broad-leaved trees in the riparian habitat along the creek are soon left behind as the trail climbs through ponderosa pine forest. After a short distance, the trail begins switchbacking directly up the steep slope. The dry southwest exposure supports dense chaparral brush, and the view opens up as you climb. Just below the rim, the trail veers north in a long final switchback.

At the rim, the trail enters pine forest again. Turn southwest and follow the cairned trail, which is fainter, along the pine-forested rim to the crest of an east-west ridge. Here the trail turns west and follows the flat-topped ridge to East Pocket Knob and the end of the trail at the U.S. Forest Service fire tower. Get permission from the lookout before climbing the tower for a panoramic view of the Mogollon Rim and Oak Creek Canyon.

The AB Young Trail was originally built to move cattle to and from the rim country, and then improved by the Civilian Conservation Corps in the 1930s. The CCC, along with several other conservation agencies, built thousands of miles of trails in the national forests and parks during this period.

– Bruce Grubbs

39 North Wilson Mountain Trail

Description:	This is a good hike on a hot day, as much of the trail is in a north-facing, shady canyon in the Red Rock–Secret Mountain Wilderness. You'll have excellent views of Oak Creek Canyon, the Dry Creek basin, and the Mogollon Rim.
Location:	5 miles north of Sedona.
Type of hike:	Out-and-back day hike.
Difficulty:	Difficult.
Total distance:	7.6 miles.
Elevation change:	2,200 feet.
Water:	None.
Best months:	April–November.
Maps:	Munds Park, Wilson Mountain USGS; Coconino National Forest.
Permit:	Red Rock Pass required for parking.
For more information:	Coconino National Forest, Sedona Ranger District.

Finding the trailhead: From Sedona, drive about 5 miles north on Arizona 89A to the Encinosa Picnic Area. Park in the trailhead parking area at the entrance to the picnic area.

Key points:

0.0 North Wilson Mountain Trailhead.

1.4 First Bench of Wilson Mountain.

1.8 Turn right on the Wilson Mountain Trail.

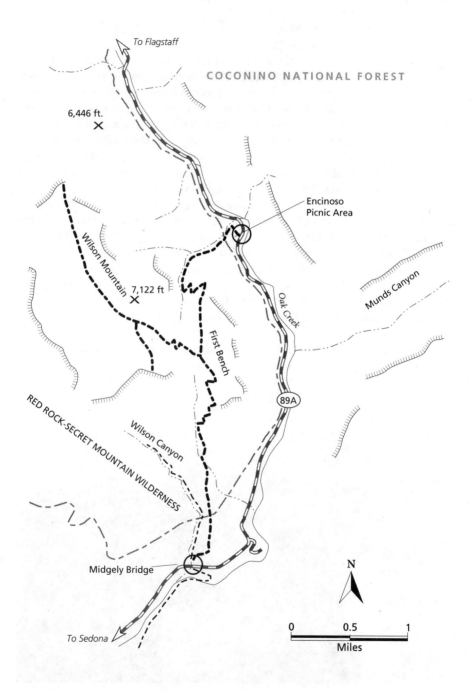

To Flagstaff

COCONINO NATIONAL FOREST

6,446 ft.

Wilson Mountain

Encinoso
Picnic Area

7,122 ft

Munds Canyon

Oak Creek

First Bench

89A

RED ROCK-SECRET MOUNTAIN WILDERNESS

Wilson Canyon

Midgely Bridge

To Sedona

N

0   0.5   1
Miles

| 2.4 | Summit trail junction. |
| 3.8 | North rim of Wilson Mountain. |

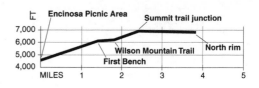

The hike: The trailhead is signed, although the North Wilson Mountain Trail is not shown on the topographic map. The trail starts climbing immediately through mixed chaparral, ponderosa pine, and oak forest. When the trail reaches the ridge above the picnic area, it turns to the south and follows the ridge a short distance, giving you good views of Oak Creek Canyon. After leaving the ridge, the trail climbs southwest up a heavily wooded drainage. The shade of the large ponderosa pines is a welcome relief on hot days. As the trail nears the base of the massive, buff-colored Coconino sandstone cliffs, it crosses the drainage and begins to switchback up the slope to the east. There are more fine views when the trail reaches the ridge at the top of this slope.

Now the trail turns to the south again and follows the ridge onto the First Bench of Wilson Mountain, a gently sloping volcanic plateau level with the east rim of Oak Creek Canyon. Near the south end of the bench, the North Wilson Mountain Trail meets the Wilson Mountain Trail at a signed junction. This trail is shown on the topographic map. Turn right (west) here and follow the Wilson Mountain Trail as it climbs Wilson Mountain itself. Several switchbacks lead through the basalt cliffs near the rim. The trail swings left into a drainage, which it follows to reach a gentle saddle on the wooded summit plateau.

There is a signed trail junction in the saddle. The actual summit is a small knob with limited views, located 0.2 mile north of this junction. A better option is to walk 0.4 mile to the south rim of the mountain.

Rim of Wilson Mountain.

Continue straight ahead and follow the trail northwest about 1.4 miles to the north end of Wilson Mountain. The topographic map shows the trail ending just west of the point marked 7,076 on the map, but actually it continues to the rim. Here you are overlooking Sterling Pass, upper Dry Creek, Oak Creek, the Mogollon Rim, and the San Francisco Peaks. The view of the maze of red, buff, and gray cliffs is well worth the long hike.

—Bruce Grubbs

40 Wilson Mountain Trail

See Map on Page 127

Description:	This popular trail climbs the south slopes of Wilson Mountain in the Red Rock–Secret Mountain Wilderness. Your reward for the effort is one of the best views of the Sedona area.
Location:	2 miles north of Sedona.
Type of hike:	Out-and-back day hike.
Difficulty:	Difficult.
Total distance:	6.4 miles.
Elevation change:	2,440 feet.
Water:	None. The trail faces south and is hot in summer; bring plenty of water.
Best months:	All year.
Maps:	Wilson Mountain, Munds Park USGS; Coconino National Forest.
Permit:	Red Rock Pass required for parking.
For more information:	Coconino National Forest, Sedona Ranger District.

Finding the trailhead: From Sedona, drive 1.6 miles north on Arizona 89. Cross Midgely Bridge, then turn left into the Wilson Canyon Trailhead and viewpoint.

Key points:

0.0   Wilson Canyon Trailhead.
2.2   First Bench of Wilson Mountain.
2.8   Saddle.
3.2   South rim of Wilson Mountain.

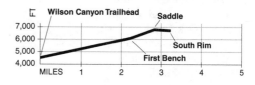

The hike: The Wilson Mountain Trail starts climbing immediately, but then the climb moderates for a bit as the trail goes north through open pinyon-juniper forest. The climb starts in earnest as the trail starts switchbacking up the steep south-facing slopes. The view opens out as the chaparral brush that favors this sun-baked slope replaces the pygmy forest.

The trail reaches the First Bench of Wilson Mountain, then continues north past the junction with the North Wilson Mountain Trail. Stay left here, and continue as the trail swings west and climbs onto the summit plateau. At a trail junction in a saddle, turn left and walk 0.4 mile to the south rim of Wilson Mountain. This great spot has a sweeping view of the Sedona area.

—Bruce Grubbs

41 Huckaby Trail

Description:	A fine day hike on a new trail in the Coconino National Forest that follows Oak Creek for part of the way.
Location:	2 miles east of Sedona.
Type of hike:	Out-and-back day hike (can be done one-way with a shuttle).
Difficulty:	Easy.
Total distance:	5.0 miles.
Elevation change:	260 feet.
Water:	Oak Creek.
Best months:	All year.
Maps:	Munds Park, Munds Mountain, Sedona USGS; Coconino National Forest.
Permit:	Red Rock Pass required for parking.
For more information:	Coconino National Forest, Sedona Ranger District.

Finding the trailhead: From the junction of Arizona 89A and Arizona 179 in Sedona, go south 0.4 mile on Arizona 179, cross Oak Creek Bridge, then turn left on Schnebly Hill Road. Drive 1.9 mile, and turn left into Margs Draw/Huckaby Trailhead. To reach the north trailhead from Arizona 179 in Sedona, drive 1.6 miles north on Arizona 89A, cross Midgely Bridge, and park on the left at the Wilson Canyon Trailhead and viewpoint

Key points:

0.0 Trailhead.
0.3 Bear Wallow Canyon.
1.5 Oak Creek.
2.1 Cross Oak Creek.
2.5 Wilson Mountain trailhead.

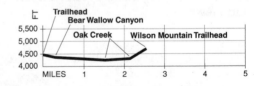

The hike: At first, the trail goes west through a confusing area of rehabilitated jeep trails. After the Margs Draw Trail junction, the Huckaby Trail turns right and follows an old road down into Bear Wallow Canyon. This is the canyon north of the trailhead. With time, the route should become more distinct. Once you've found the old road, the rest of the trail is easy to follow.

Follow the old road across normally dry Bear Wallow Canyon and out the north side. Here the newly constructed foot trail leaves the old road and contours northeast above the canyon. Soon a switchback takes you to the north as the trail begins to work its way toward Oak Creek. This is a delightful

130

Huckaby Trail • Munds Mountain

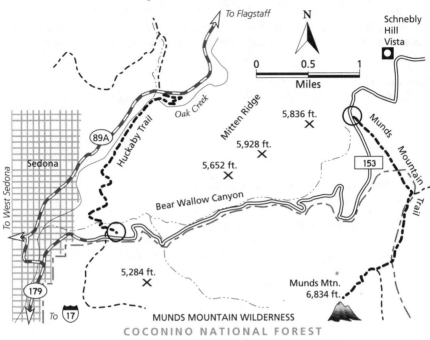

traverse through pinyon-juniper forest, although it would be hot on a summer afternoon. Soon you'll start to descend, and the trail finally switchbacks down to Oak Creek.

Wilson Mountain from the Huckaby Trail.

For more than a half mile, the trail stays on the east side of the creek, then crosses to the west side below Midgely Bridge, the impressive structure spanning Wilson Canyon on Arizona 89A. Now it follows an old wagon road that climbs steeply out of the canyon and switchbacks up to the north end of the bridge. Follow the trail past the viewpoint, under the bridge, and up to the Wilson Mountain Trailhead.

Options: This hike can be done one-way with a shuttle. Another option is to hike farther on the Wilson Mountain Trail; see Hike 40 for details.

—Bruce Grubbs

42 Munds Mountain

See Map on Page 131

Description:	This hike in the Munds Mountain Wilderness takes you up a historic road, and offers excellent views of Mitten Ridge, Bear Wallow Canyon, Munds Mountain, and Sedona.
Location:	4 miles east of Sedona.
Type of hike:	Out-and-back day hike.
Difficulty:	Moderate.
Total distance:	4.2 miles.
Elevation change:	1,200 feet.
Water:	None.
Best months:	April–November.
Maps:	Munds Park, Munds Mountain USGS; Coconino National Forest.
Permit:	Red Rock Pass required for parking.
For more information:	Coconino National Forest, Sedona Ranger District.

Finding the trailhead: From the junction of Arizona 89A and Arizona 179 in Sedona, go south 0.4 mile on Arizona 179. Cross Oak Creek Bridge, then turn left on Schnebly Hill Road. Drive 4.3 miles, and park at the unsigned trailhead where the road passes through a saddle between the red buttes to the west and the brushy slope on the right.

Key points:
0.0 Trailhead.
0.9 Foot trail.
1.8 Saddle.
2.1 Munds Mountain.

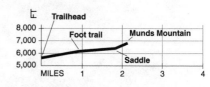

The hike: From the parking area, look across the road and up. You will see an old road descending the slopes from the left (southeast). It comes down almost to the present road then does a switchback to the right and parallels the road just above it. Walk south down the main road about 100 yards until you can climb up to reach the old road.

Follow it back to the left (north), around the switchback, and then southward. This is the old Schnebly Hill Road, which was originally built as a wagon road from Sedona to the Mogollon Rim and on to Flagstaff. It is now closed to motorized vehicles and makes a fine hiking trail with a panoramic view. Because of the west-facing slope, the dominant vegetation is chaparral brush. Near the top, there is a dense stand of Gambel oak, a small, slender deciduous tree about 20 to 30 feet high. Gambel oaks often favor the slopes just below escarpments or rims.

The trail reaches the Mogollon Rim after 0.9 mile, and the old road turns sharply north. Take the foot trail, which continues south along the rim through tall ponderosa pines, climbing gradually. About 0.7 mile from the old road, the trail reaches a high point along the rim and crosses a grassy section with scattered juniper trees where the view opens out to the southeast. The long ridge of Munds Mountain dominates the view ahead to the southwest. The trail drops down a short ridge to a saddle where there is a signed junction with the Hot Loop Trail to the left. Continue straight ahead about 50 yards to another saddle, where there is a signed junction with the Jacks Canyon Trail.

Stay right and follow the Munds Mountain Trail as it climbs steeply up the northeast slopes. Several switchbacks lead to a ridge where the grade moderates. This section is interesting for the extreme contrast in vegetation on the two sides of the ridge. Douglas firs growing on the north slopes meet pinyon, juniper, and Arizona cypress growing on the south slopes. The trail reaches the rim of Munds Mountain about 0.4 mile from the junction at the saddle. According to the map, the actual high point is about 100 yards south along the east edge of the clearing. But it's more rewarding to walk about 200 yards west to the rim for a sweeping view of Sedona and the red rock country. You can also walk about 100 yards to the north rim for a superb view of lower Oak Creek Canyon, and nearly all of the trail you just came up.

—Bruce Grubbs

43 Bell Trail

Description:	This is a popular summer hike along Wet Beaver Creek in the Wet Beaver Wilderness. The trail climbs to the Mogollon Rim for some good views.
Location:	16 miles southeast of Sedona.
Type of hike:	Out-and-back day hike.
Difficulty:	Moderate.
Total distance:	8.6 miles.
Elevation change:	1,320 feet.
Water:	Wet Beaver Creek.
Best months:	All year.
Maps:	Casner Butte USGS; Coconino National Forest.
Permit:	None.
For more information:	Coconino National Forest, Beaver Creek Ranger District.

Finding the trailhead: From Sedona, drive about 14 miles southeast on Arizona 179 and go under the Interstate 17 interchange. Continue 2.1 miles on the Beaver Creek Road (Forest Road 618), then turn left into the Wet Beaver Creek trailhead.

Key points:

0.0 Wet Beaver Creek Trailhead.
2.1 Apache Maid Trail.
3.1 Wet Beaver Creek.
4.3 Mogollon Rim.

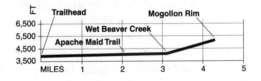

The hike: The trail stays along the north side of Wet Beaver Creek. Stands of Fremont cottonwood and other riparian vegetation crowd the creek, but there are several short side trails down to the water. One of several permanent streams flowing through the canyons below the Mogollon Rim, Wet Beaver Creek is very popular during the summer. As you continue up the canyon, notice how the slope to the left, which is sunnier and drier, features a nearly pure stand of juniper trees. On the other hand, the slope to the right faces north and is cooler and moister; it supports a mixed stand of juniper and pinyon. Evidently the pinyon pines require just a bit more moisture, and possibly cooler temperatures, than the junipers. Very slight changes in climate can have a dramatic effect on plant and animal communities.

At 2.1 miles you'll pass the Apache Maid Trail. Continue east along the canyon on the Bell Trail. There are a number of good swimming holes along the creek, just below the trail. After another mile, the trail crosses the creek and climbs up a steep ridge to the Mogollon Rim. Although the trail continues to Forest Road 214, this scenic spot makes a good turnaround point for the hike.

Bell Trail

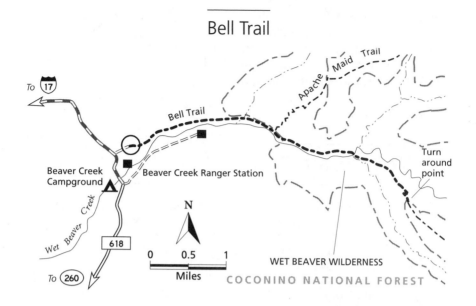

Option: You can also reach the rim via the Apache Maid Trail, which climbs the north slope of the canyon. The juniper forest is open, and the first section of the trail provides good views down Wet Beaver Creek. A series of switchbacks leads up to the base of Casner Butte, and then the trail crosses the drainage to the north and angles up to the Mogollon Rim. Here the view

All birds have keen eyesight, but turkey vultures are one of the few with a good sense of smell. After a hearty meal of carrion, vultures may have considerable difficulty taking off, but once in the air they search out rising thermals on which to soar effortlessly. From a distance, vultures can be distinguished from hawks by the way they hold their wings—hawks tend to hold their wings flat while gliding; vultures hold their wings at a slight angle or dihedral.

encompasses the San Francisco Peaks to the north and the Verde Valley to the west and southwest. Originally built for access to the Apache Maid fire tower, the remainder of the trail is faint and difficult to follow, so this is a good place to turn around. This optional side hike adds 2.8 miles and 1,050 feet of elevation gain to the main hike.

—Bruce Grubbs

44 Tramway Trail

Description:	This short trail in the West Clear Creek Wilderness is an enjoyable hike, and it provides access to spectacular West Clear Creek.
Location:	58 miles southeast of Flagstaff.
Type of hike:	Out-and-back day hike.
Difficulty:	Moderate.
Total distance:	0.8 miles.
Elevation change:	840 feet.
Water:	West Clear Creek.
Best months:	April–November.
Maps:	Calloway Butte USGS; Coconino National Forest.
Permit:	None.
For more information:	Coconino National Forest, Sedona Ranger District.

Finding the trailhead: From Flagstaff, drive about 50 miles southeast on the Lake Mary Road (Forest Highway 3), then turn right (west) on Forest Road 81. Stay on this maintained dirt road 3.0 miles, and then turn left on Forest Road 81E. After 3.6 miles, turn right on Forest Road 693. Go 1.2 miles on this unmaintained road, then turn left at a fork and continue 0.3 mile to the end of the road. The last 1.5 miles of road may be impassable during wet weather, and a high-clearance vehicle is recommended.

You may also reach Forest Road 81 from Camp Verde by driving about 30 miles east on the General Crook Trail (Arizona 260). Turn left (north) on Arizona 87 and continue 11 miles, then turn left (northwest) on the Lake Mary Road (FH 3). Go 7.0 miles, and then turn left on Forest Road 81.

Key points:

0.0   Trailhead.
0.4   West Clear Creek.

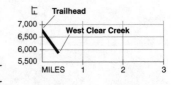

The hike: The short but spectacular trail descends into the gorge of West Clear Creek, affording fine views both up and down the canyon. It follows the route of an old aerial tramway. Kaibab limestone, a fossil-rich layer that was deposited in a shallow ocean, forms the edge of the Mogollon Rim in this area. Below the Kaibab limestone, the cross-bedded Coconino sandstone appears, with its layers of overlapping petrified sand dunes.

Tramway Trail

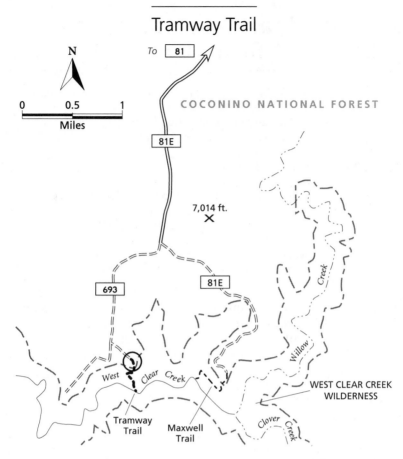

N

0   0.5   1
Miles

To 81

COCONINO NATIONAL FOREST

81E

7,014 ft.
✕

81E

693

West Clear Creek

Willow Creek

WEST CLEAR CREEK
WILDERNESS

Tramway
Trail

Maxwell
Trail

Clover Creek

The trail ends at the bottom of the canyon. One option is to hike cross-country 0.8 mile upstream and climb out via the Maxwell Trail. Another is to hike and swim the entire 25-mile length of West Clear Creek downstream to the Bull Pen Ranch trailhead. This is a difficult, multiday backpack trip that requires swimming and floating your pack across numerous pools. It should be attempted only in warm, stable weather by experienced canyon hikers.

—Bruce Grubbs

45 West Clear Creek and Blodgett Basin Loop

Description:	A very long day hike or overnight backpack into the West Clear Creek Wilderness.
Location:	20 miles east of Camp Verde.
Type of hike:	Loop day hike or backpack.
Difficulty:	Moderate.
Total distance:	13.2 miles.
Elevation change:	1,800 feet.
Water:	West Clear Creek; purify before drinking.
Best months:	March–May, September–November.
Maps:	Walker Mountain, Buckhorn Mountain USGS; Coconino National Forest.
Permit:	None.
For more information:	Coconino National Forest, Beaver Creek Ranger District.

Finding the trailhead: From Interstate 17, take exit 298 and drive east toward Beaver Creek. Cross Beaver Creek at 2.5 miles and continue on the main road. At about 10 miles from Interstate 17, turn left onto the Cedar Flat Road (Forest Road 214). Drive another 4.3 miles and park at the Blodgett Trailhead sign.

Key points:
   0.0   Bald Hill Trailhead.
   2.7   Bald Hill Trailhead.
   4.6   West Clear Creek.
 10.7   Bull Pen Ranch.
 13.2   Blodgett Trailhead.

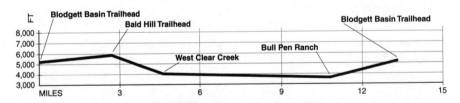

The hike: From the Bald Hill Trailhead, walk along Forest Road 214 for 1.2 miles. The road will make a fairly sharp left bend; just a little farther, a poor vehicle track takes off to the right. Follow this track, which is Forest Road 214A, and may or may not be signed. There are several forks, but continue on the most obvious road. After about 1.5 miles on Forest Road 214A, the track ends at the signed Bald Hill Trailhead.

West Clear Creek Trail starts in pinyon-juniper woodland. In a few hundred yards, the trail begins to descend into an unnamed side canyon to West Clear Creek. Yucca, agave, mountain mahogany, prickly pear cactus, and other

West Clear Creek and Blodgett Basin Loop

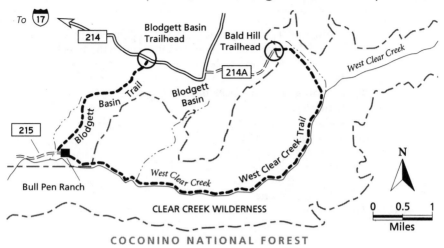

COCONINO NATIONAL FOREST

hardy shrubs cling to the rocky slopes composed of volcanic tuff and basalt. Other plants along the trail include Mormon tea, snakeweed, and nolina. Look for both white-tailed and mule deer and javelina.

The West Clear Creek Trail drops quickly in 2 miles to West Clear Creek. Here grow Arizona sycamores, Fremont cottonwoods, and velvet ash trees. During the spring and summer, birding can be quite rewarding in this relatively lush riparian habitat. Expect kingbirds, orioles, tanagers, warblers, and wrens, and possibly the rare yellow-billed cuckoo or Southwestern willow flycatcher. Anglers try their luck fishing for catfish.

The trail continues downstream 6 miles to a fence and gate. On the far side of the gate is Forest Road 215. Walk along this road a few yards and look to your right for the Blodgett Basin Trail sign. Take this trail back to the rim, Forest Road 214, and your vehicle.

—Stewart Aitchison

46 Fossil Springs Trail

Description:	This trail takes you to Fossil Springs and a historic diversion dam on Fossil Creek in the Fossil Springs Wilderness.
Location:	5 miles east of Strawberry.
Type of hike:	Out-and-back day hike.
Difficulty:	Moderate.
Total distance:	6.8 miles.
Elevation change:	860 feet.
Water:	Fossil Springs.
Best months:	April–November.
Maps:	Strawberry USGS; Tonto National Forest.
Permit:	None.
For more information:	Tonto National Forest, Payson Ranger District; Coconino National Forest, Beaver Creek Ranger District.

Finding the trailhead: From Strawberry on Arizona 87, go west 4.7 miles on the main road through town. This becomes Forest Road 708, a maintained dirt road. Turn right after 4.7 miles and go another 0.4 mile to the Fossil Springs Trailhead.

Key points:

0.0 Fossil Springs Trailhead.
2.8 Fossil Creek.
3.4 Dam.

The hike: The trail follows the route of an old jeep trail, and descends northeast below the rim of the canyon. It soon turns northwest and continues its descent for more than a mile through pinyon-juniper woodland. When you reach Fossil Creek, turn left and hike downstream. Although upper Fossil Creek often flows, there's no mistaking the added volume when you reach Fossil Springs. These warm springs gush from the right bank of the creek.

A short distance below the springs, you'll leave the wilderness area and reach an old concrete dam, the destination for our hike. The dam, which was constructed in 1916, diverts water into a flume. Several miles downstream, the water spins the turbines at the Irving Power Plant. Another power plant at the mouth of Fossil Creek on the Verde River harnesses the power of Fossil Creek a second time. These facilities were among Arizona's first hydroelectric generators, and are still producing power.

Option 1: Hike the access road to the dam, Forest Road 154. It's closed to private vehicles but open to hikers to its end at the Irving Power Plant and Forest Road 708.

Rock formations along the Mogollon Rim, Fossil Creek Wilderness.

Fossil Springs Trail

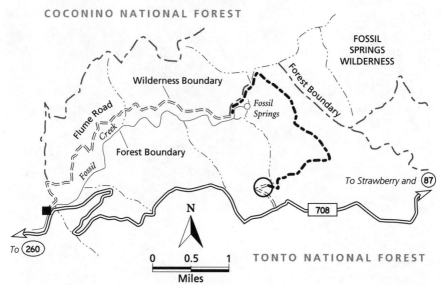

COCONINO NATIONAL FOREST

FOSSIL SPRINGS WILDERNESS

Wilderness Boundary

Fossil Springs

Forest Boundary

Flume Road

Creek

Fossil

Forest Boundary

To Strawberry and (87)

708

N

To (260)

0   0.5   1

Miles

TONTO NATIONAL FOREST

Option 2: Hike upstream, cross-country, in Fossil Creek, from the point where the trail first reached the canyon bottom. The bulk of the wilderness lies upstream and encompasses two major side canyons, Calf Pen and Sandrock Canyons.

—Bruce Grubbs

47 Kinder Crossing Trail

Description:	This is a short, historic trail providing access to East Clear Creek. You can explore up- or down-stream from the foot of the trail. East Clear Creek runs year-round, and the deep, clear pools are a delight in the hot days of summer.
Location:	70 miles southeast of Flagstaff.
Type of hike:	Out-and-back day hike.
Difficulty:	Easy.
Total distance:	1.2 miles.
Elevation change:	500 feet.
Water:	East Clear Creek.
Best months:	April–November.
Maps:	Blue Ridge Reservoir USGS; Coconino National Forest.
Permit:	None.
For more information:	Coconino National Forest, Blue Ridge Ranger District.

Kinder Crossing Trail

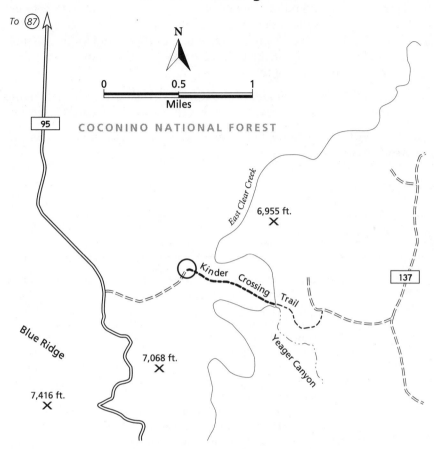

Finding the trailhead: From Flagstaff, drive about 55 miles southeast on Lake Mary Road (Forest Highway 3) to Clints Well. Turn left on Arizona 87, drive 9 miles, and turn right on Forest Road 95. Continue 4.2 miles on this maintained road, then turn left (east) on the unmaintained road to the Kinder Crossing Trail. Continue 0.6 mile to trailhead at the end of the road.

Clints Well can also be reached from Camp Verde by driving 30 miles east on the General Crook Trail (Arizona 260), then turning left (north) on Arizona 87 and continuing 11 miles to Clints Well.

Key points:

  0.0   Kinder Crossing Trailhead.
  0.6   East Clear Creek.

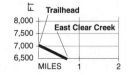

The hike: The Kinder Crossing Trail descends into East Clear Creek by following the ridge to the east, reaching the creek at the confluence of East Clear Creek and Yeager Canyon. There is a large and very inviting swimming hole at the confluence. After cooling off, it's fun to explore the canyon, in either direction.

This trail is one of several historical trails that cross East Clear Creek and other canyons on the forested Mogollon Plateau north of the Mogollon Rim. During the settlement and ranching days, before the present road network was built, the primary access to the area was via pack trails. Canyons like East Clear Creek created formidable barriers to travel and were crossable by trail at only a few points. Even today, the forest road system is constrained by the crossing points along the deep canyons.

Option 1: Follow the remainder of the Kinder Crossing Trail, which climbs 0.5 mile out the west side of the canyon to a spur road from Forest Road 137.

Option 2: With a car shuttle, hike cross-country downstream about 3 miles to Horse Crossing.

—Bruce Grubbs

48 Cabin Loop

Description:	A loop hike on a series of historic trails that connect several historic cabins south of the Mogollon Rim. The entire loop makes an enjoyable backpack trip, or you can do shorter segments as day hikes.
Location:	80 miles southeast of Flagstaff.
Type of hike:	Loop backpack.
Difficulty:	Moderate.
Total distance:	17.6 miles.
Elevation change:	620 feet.
Water:	Seasonally at Barbershop Canyon, Dane Canyon, Dane Spring, Coyote Spring, Barbershop Spring, Houston Draw, and Aspen Spring.
Best months:	April–November.
Maps:	Blue Ridge Reservoir, Dane Canyon USGS; Coconino National Forest.
Permit:	None.
For more information:	Coconino National Forest, Blue Ridge Ranger District.

Finding the trailhead: From Flagstaff, drive about 55 miles southeast on Lake Mary Road (Forest Highway 3) to Clints Well. Turn left on Arizona 87, go north 9 miles, then turn right on Forest Road 95. Continue 11.1 miles on this maintained road, and then turn left (south) on Forest Road 139A. After just over 0.1 mile, turn left onto an unsigned rough road (park low-clearance vehicles here). The road drops into Houston Draw and ends at Pinchot Cabin, the trailhead, in 0.5 mile.

Clints Well can also be reached from Camp Verde by driving 30 miles east on the General Crook Trail (Arizona 260), then turning left on Arizona 87 and continuing 11 miles to Clints Well.

Cabin Loop

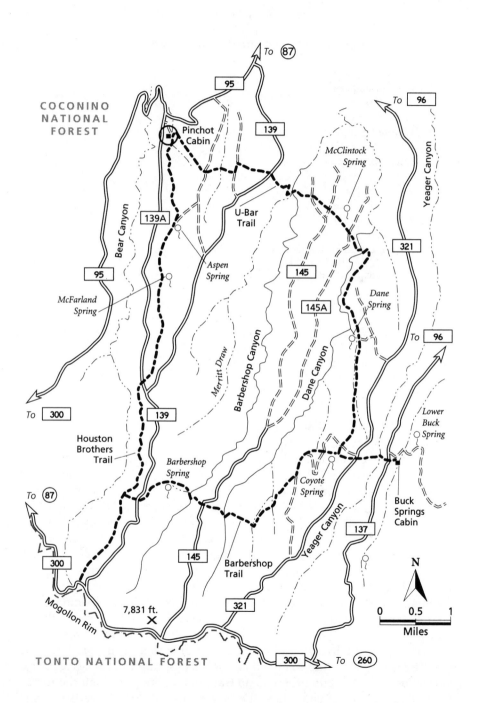

To ⑧⑦

95

COCONINO NATIONAL FOREST

139

To ⑨⑥

Pinchot Cabin

McClintock Spring

Bear Canyon

139A

U-Bar Trail

Yeager Canyon

95

Aspen Spring

145

321

McFarland Spring

145A

Dane Spring

To ⑨⑥

Merritt Draw

Barbershop Canyon

Dane Canyon

Lower Buck Spring

To 300

139

Houston Brothers Trail

Barbershop Spring

Coyote Spring

Buck Springs Cabin

To ⑧⑦

Yeager Canyon

To ⑧⑦

137

300

145

Barbershop Trail

Mogollon Rim

7,831 ft.
X

321

300

To ②⑥⓪

TONTO NATIONAL FOREST

N

0   0.5   1
Miles

Key points:

0.0	Pinchot Cabin Trailhead.
0.8	Turn right on a road.
1.0	T intersection; cross the road and follow the blazed trees east.
1.6	Turn left (north) along an old road.
1.8	Pass a steel water tank, then turn right and follow the blazed trail east.
2.3	Cross Forest Road 139.
2.8	Barbershop Canyon.
3.5	McClintock Spring.
4.0	Dane Canyon.
5.6	Dane Spring.
7.2	Coyote Spring.
7.6	Cross Yeager Canyon.
7.9	Buck Springs Cabin.
8.6	Coyote Spring.
10.6	Dane Canyon.
11.2	Barbershop Canyon.
11.6	Barbershop Spring.
12.2	Cross Forest Road 139.
12.4	Turn right on Houston Brothers Trail.
13.8	Cross Forest Road 139A.
15.4	McFarland Spring.
16.2	Aspen Spring.
17.6	Pinchot Cabin Trailhead.

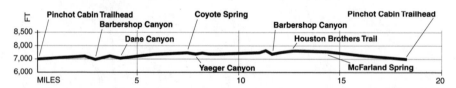

The hike: This hike follows the historic U-Bar, Barbershop, and Houston Brothers Trails, which are part of the Cabin Loop Trail System that connects several historic cabins in the Mogollon Rim country. (The trails in this system are not shown on the topographic maps.) Pinchot Cabin is named for Gifford Pinchot, the first Chief of the U.S. Forest Service. It was used for many years as a fire guard station. The trail system provided the main transportation routes through this remote country during the early days of ranching and forestry. Most of the trails were lost during the development of the forest road system, but several, including these three trails, have recently been relocated and restored. Sections of the trail are cross-country, but are well marked by recent tree blazes.

Initially, the U-Bar Trail route follows the road past the cabin and up the hill to the east. Note the fresh tree blazes. The entire trail is blazed with the same style blazes. After 0.8 mile, turn right (south) onto another road (note the blaze and right arrow), and continue 0.2 mile to a third road intersection. The trail crosses the road and continues east into the forest, ignoring both roads. In this section there is no trail, but walking through the forest is easy and pleasant if you follow the blazes carefully. The trick is to walk from blaze to blaze, always keeping the last blaze in sight. If the route is lost, return to the last known blaze and locate the next one before continuing.

The route crosses Dick Hart Draw, and then meets another road in 0.6 mile. Turn left (north) and follow the old road past a large steel water tank. After about 0.3 mile the route turns sharply right (east) and leaves the road. After another 0.5 mile the blazed trail crosses a maintained dirt road (Forest Road 139), and a sign points out the U-Bar Trail. The route veers somewhat left as it crosses the road; follow the blazes carefully. The U-Bar route goes to the southeast out onto a point then descends through a gate.

Past the gate, the trail becomes obvious as it descends into Barbershop Canyon, which is 0.5 mile from Forest Road 139. Serious trail construction was done on this section. Barbershop Canyon has a fine little permanent stream, and this would make a good goal for hikers wanting an easy day. There is very limited camping in the canyon bottom. For those on a backpack trip, it would be better to carry water about 0.2 mile up to the east rim, where there is unlimited camping.

The trail, still distinct, climbs the east wall of the canyon and crosses a faint road. After this, the trail becomes a blazed route again. About 0.7 mile from Barbershop Canyon, the route crosses a road at a right angle, and a sign marks the U-Bar Trail. On the east side of the main road, the U-Bar Trail follows an unmaintained road past a fine little meadow bordered by pines and aspens. The road passes McClintock Spring, then joins another road; the route continues across the road and descends into Dane Canyon. The historic trail is distinct again in this section. Dane Canyon has a permanent stream and offers plentiful campsites on grassy meadows. A lush forest of Douglas fir and ponderosa pine covers the canyon walls, spiced by an occasional aspen, limber pine, or white fir.

Lightweight camping equipment lets you be safe and comfortable while leaving zero impact.

After crossing the creek, the trail climbs east out of the canyon then turns south along the east rim. This is one of the prettiest sections of the trail, as it stays below the heavily logged ridge top. About 1.6 miles from Dane Canyon, the U-Bar Trail reaches Dane Spring and the ruins of an old cabin. This is an excellent goal for a more ambitious day hike.

The trail continues south along the east side of a shallow drainage, then crosses the drainage and climbs to cross a road on a ridge top. It descends into the next drainage to end at the junction with the Barbershop Trail, 1.5 miles from Dane Spring. Turn left (east) on the Barbershop Trail to reach the trailhead at Buck Springs Cabin in an additional 0.5 mile.

From the Buck Springs Cabin Trailhead, retrace your steps to the U-Bar Trail, then continue straight on the Barbershop Trail, which follows the drainage west to Bill McClintock Draw, then climbs southwest to cross a low ridge. For the next 1.5 miles or so, the trail crosses several drainages and follows several roads for short distances. Follow the blazes carefully so that you don't miss the places where the trail leaves the road.

About 2.0 miles from the junction with the U-Bar Trail, the Barbershop Trail crosses Dane Canyon at a sign. It climbs up a drainage to the west, crosses a maintained road, then drops into Barbershop Canyon, which usually has flowing water. The trail climbs steeply for a couple hundred yards then contours into a meadow at Barbershop Spring. After the spring, the trail goes up the bed of a shallow drainage to the west, and then climbs out on the right to cross Forest Road 139, a maintained dirt road. The Barbershop Trail ends about 0.2 mile west of the road, at the signed junction with the Houston Brothers Trail.

Turn right and follow the Houston Brothers Trail north along Dick Hart Ridge. Very little of the original trail remains along this section; follow the

Historic Buck Springs Cabin on the Cabin Loop trail system.

Shades and a hat are essential when hiking with the hot Arizona sun beating down.

tree blazes carefully. If you lose the trail, it's always possible to walk east to Forest Road 139, which is never more than 0.2 mile away. Eventually, the trail crosses Forest Road 139A and descends into Houston Draw, where it becomes a distinct footpath. The forest at the head of Houston Draw is a delightful mix of Douglas fir, white fir, and ponderosa pine. Soon the trail emerges into a series of fine alpine meadows bordered with quaking aspen. You'll pass McFarland Spring and then Aspen Spring. There is also an intermittent flow in the creek. All too soon, the trail ends at the Pinchot Trailhead, completing the loop.

Option: From the junction of the Barbershop and Houston Brothers Trails, turn left and head south 1.4 miles on the Houston Brothers Trail to reach Forest Road 300. Cross the road to the edge of the Mogollon Rim. The view of the rim country and the central mountains to the south is a treat, marred only slightly by the carnage wreaked on the forest by the Dude Fire in 1990. This side hike adds 2.8 miles to the hike, and 150 feet of elevation gain.

—Bruce Grubbs

49 Chevelon Canyon

Description:	This is a backpack into a little-visited canyon with a trout stream coursing through it.
Location:	40 miles south of Winslow.
Type of hike:	Out-and-back backpack.
Difficulty:	Moderate.
Total distance:	About 16.8 miles.
Elevation change:	220 feet.
Water:	Chevelon Creek; purify before drinking.
Best months:	May–October.
Maps:	Chevelon Crossing USGS; Apache-Sitgreaves National Forest USFS.
Permit:	None.
For more information:	Apache-Sitgreaves National Forest, Black Mesa Ranger District.

Finding the trailhead: Drive south from Winslow on Arizona 99 for approximately 38 miles to Chevelon Crossing and campground.

Key points:
0.0 Trailhead.
3.5 Power line crosses canyon overhead.
8.4 Chevelon Canyon Dam.

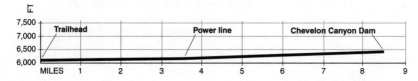

Chevelon Canyon

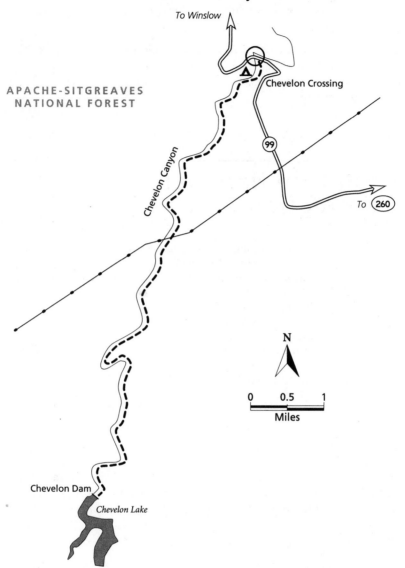

To Winslow

APACHE-SITGREAVES
NATIONAL FOREST

Chevelon Canyon

Chevelon Crossing

99

To 260

N

0   0.5   1
Miles

Chevelon Dam

Chevelon Lake

The hike: This backpack is an 8.4-mile hike upstream to Chevelon Canyon Lake, a man-made reservoir. There is no formal trail, but fisherman, day hikers, and wildlife have made paths that follow the course of the creek. A few stream crossings are necessary, so this hike would not be possible during periods of high water.

The easy route passes beaver ponds, swimming holes, and grassy campsites amid ponderosa pine, Fremont cottonwood, New Mexican locust, and other riparian species. Be wary of poison ivy. Elk and mule deer are common, and at night it's not unusual to hear a beaver slapping its tail on the water.

In 1851, Captain Lorenzo Sitgreaves wrote that the stream received its name from a trapper called Chevelon, who died after eating some poisonous root along its banks. Poison hemlock does grow along the creek and may have been the culprit.

Option: Exploration downstream from Chevelon Crossing is possible but somewhat more challenging. The canyon narrows and more time is needed to make deep-water crossings. Sometimes swimming is necessary to make progress downstream.

—Stewart Aitchison

50 Highline National Recreation Trail

Description:	A long, scenic trail near the southern edge of the Colorado Plateau.
Location:	Pine trailhead is about 10 miles northwest of Payson.
Type of hike:	Shuttle backpack.
Difficulty:	Moderate.
Total distance:	About 50 miles.
Elevation change:	1,200 feet.
Water:	Several creeks and springs are located along the trail, but check with forest rangers about reliability.
Best months:	March–November.
Maps:	Pine, Buckhead Mesa, Kehl Ridge, Dane Canyon, Diamond Point, Promontory Butte, Knoll Lake, Woods Canyon USGS; Tonto National Forest.
Permit:	None.
For more information:	Tonto National Forest, Payson Ranger District.

Finding the trailhead: The Pine Trailhead is located about 1 mile south of Pine on Arizona 87 and is signed. The 260 Trailhead is on Arizona 260, not quite 4 miles from the top of the Mogollon Rim, and is also signed.

Key points:
- 0.0 Pine Trailhead.
- 11.0 Forest Road 440.
- 20.0 Forest Road 32A.
- 28.5 Forest Road 430.
- 33.5 Forest Road 289.

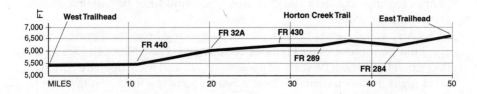

Highline National Recreation Trail

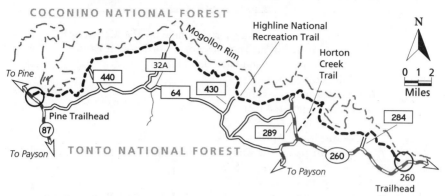

37.0 Junction with Horton Creek Trail.
43.0 Forest Road 284.
49.5 260 Trailhead.

The hike: Because fifteen side trails intersect, the Highline National Recreation Trail can be done as a series of day hikes or as a loop. This highly scenic trail travels about 50 miles just under the Mogollon Rim in central Arizona. The trail is well maintained and easy to follow, although intersections with other trails may cause confusion. Be sure to check the map often. Although the trail profile suggests a steady uphill climb going from west to east, the scale does not reveal the many ups and downs. The trail is rocky in places but well marked with small trail signs, tree blazes, and rock cairns. The section from Forest Road 284 to the 260 trailhead is very popular with mountain bikers and horseback riders; however, it also has some of the finest views of the Mogollon Run.

Allow at least five days for traversing the entire route one-way. (Or sign up for the annual Zane Grey Ultramarathon and run, walk, or crawl the entire trail in one day! The current record is less than 9 hours.) Most of the route traverses forest consisting of an interesting mixture of ponderosa and pinyon pine, several species of juniper, Arizona cypress, and various oaks. Near water sources, deciduous trees become more dominant. The trail also passes through part of the forest burned in the Dude Fire of 1990 that destroyed western writer Zane Grey's cabin on Tonto Creek. Settlers built much of the original trail in the 1800s to link their ranches together.

—Stewart Aitchison

51 Tunnel Trail

Description:	This is a short day hike off the Mogollon Rim.
Location:	About 15 miles north-northeast of Payson.
Type of hike:	Out-and-back day hike.
Difficulty:	Easy.
Total distance:	1.5 miles.
Elevation change:	464 feet.
Water:	None.
Best months:	April–October.
Maps:	Dane Canyon, Kehl Ridge USGS; Tonto National Forest USFS.
Permit:	None.
For more information:	Tonto National Forest, Payson Ranger District.

Finding the trailhead: Take Arizona 87 about 13 miles north of the tiny community of Strawberry and turn right onto Forest Road 300 (Rim Road). About 14 miles later, you will come to a historical marker for the Battle of Big Dry Wash on the left (north) side of the road. Park here.

Key points:
- 0.0 Trailhead.
- 0.4 Turnoff to tunnel.
- 0.75 Tunnel.

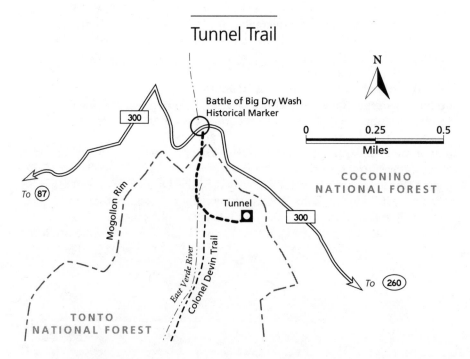

The hike: To the south of the historical marker, toward the Mogollon Rim, is a sign marking the Colonel Devin Trail. Take this trail about 0.5 mile to a signed turnoff for the Tunnel Trail on the left. Follow the trail as it winds uphill a short distance to the uncompleted railroad tunnel and the ruins of a building.

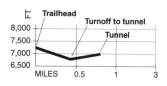

In 1883, developers proposed a trans–Mogollon Rim rail line to connect Flagstaff and the Union Pacific Railroad with the rich mineral district of Morenci. Several years passed before financing became available. Thirty-five miles of track were laid heading southeast out of Flagstaff. At the same time, a tunnel was begun under the Rim, but the Arizona Mineral Belt Railroad went bankrupt before the planned 3,100-foot tunnel was completed.

—Stewart Aitchison

52 Horton Creek Trail

Description:	This is a pleasant day hike along a trout stream.
Location:	15 miles northeast of Payson.
Type of hike:	Out-and-back day hike.
Difficulty:	Easy.
Total distance:	6.8 miles.
Elevation change:	1,170 feet.
Water:	Horton Spring; purify before using.
Best months:	All year.
Maps:	Promontory Butte USGS; Tonto National Forest USFS.
Permit:	None.
For more information:	Tonto National Forest, Payson Ranger District.

Finding the trailhead: From Payson, drive about 15 miles east on Arizona 260. Turn left (north) onto Tonto Creek Road (Forest Road 289). Travel 1 mile to the Horton (Upper Tonto) Campground. Park below the entrance gate to the campground but do not block the road. The trail begins about 150 feet up the campground road.

Key points:
- 0.0 Trailhead.
- 3.0 Junction with Highline Trail.
- 3.4 Horton Spring.

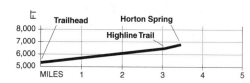

The hike: The trail follows an old logging road that parallels Horton Creek. The trail is within sight of the creek for the first 1.2 miles and no more than 300 yards away the rest of the

Horton Creek Trail

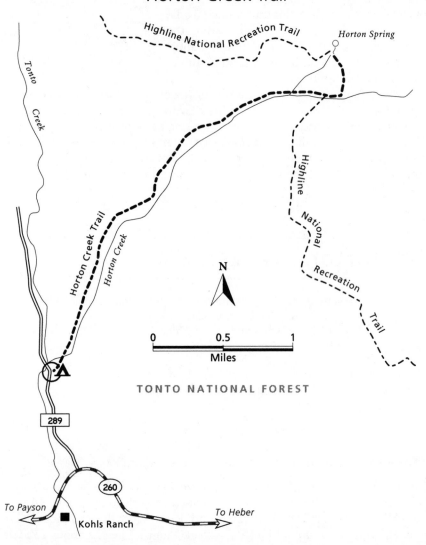

way. After 3 miles, this trail joins the Highline Trail. Turn left onto the High-line and go another 0.5 mile to the large, beautiful Horton Spring, which gushes out the side of the mountain.

—Stewart Aitchison

53 Hells Gate Trail

Description:	This hike takes you to the confluence of Tonto and Haigler Creeks in the Hellsgate Wilderness, a spot noted for its spectacular canyon narrows.
Location:	11 miles east of Payson.
Type of hike:	Out-and-back day hike or backpack.
Difficulty:	Difficult.
Total distance:	16.2 miles.
Elevation change:	2,080 feet.
Water:	Seasonally in Tonto Creek.
Best months:	March–May, October–November.
Maps:	McDonald Mountain, Diamond Butte, Diamond Point, Promontory Butte USGS, Tonto National Forest.
Permit:	Groups are limited to fifteen, and pack stock is limited to fifteen animals.
For more information:	Tonto National Forest, Payson Ranger District.

Finding the trailhead: From Payson, drive 11.2 miles east on Arizona 260, then turn right into the signed Hells Gate Trailhead.

Key points:
- 0.0   Hells Gate Trailhead.
- 1.3   Head of Salt Lick Canyon.
- 3.4   High point on ridge.
- 6.0   Start descent from Apache Ridge.
- 7.4   El Grande Tank.
- 8.1   Hells Gate.

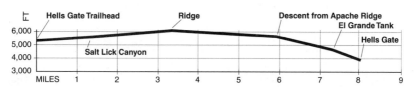

The hike: The Hells Gate Trail wanders south over a low pass, then crosses Little Green Valley and climbs up a ravine through ponderosa pine forest. It crosses a flat for a short distance before passing the head of Salt Lick Canyon. A short climb leads onto the Green Valley Hills, then the trail passes through a saddle and turns east. It works its way along a ridge, and then turns south onto Apache Ridge.

Hells Gate Trail

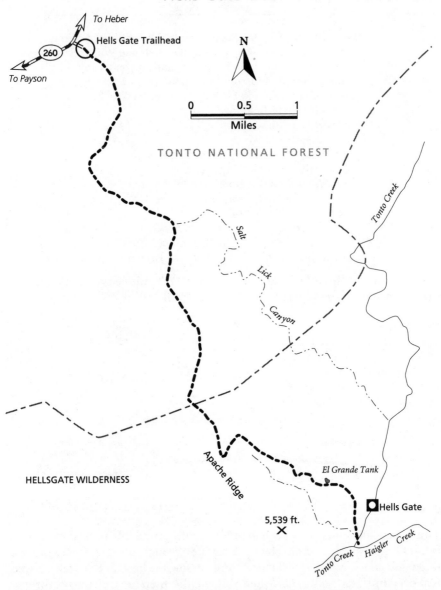

To Heber

Hells Gate Trailhead

260

To Payson

N

0   0.5   1

Miles

TONTO NATIONAL FOREST

Salt

Lick

Canyon

Tonto Creek

Apache Ridge

HELLSGATE WILDERNESS

El Grande Tank

Hells Gate

5,539 ft.
X

Tonto Creek   Haigler Creek

A new foot trail has been constructed that bypasses the old jeep trail. Generally, this trail contours around the hilltops instead of going over them. After 6 miles, the trail starts a steep descent off the east side of the ridge, passes El Grande Tank, and drops steeply into Tonto Creek. Just over 2 miles from the ridge, the trail reaches the creek bed a short distance downstream of Hells Gate, and ends at the confluence of Tonto and Haigler Creeks. There is seasonal water in both creeks, and limited camping at the confluence.

—Bruce Grubbs

Tonto Creek in the Hellsgate Wilderness.

Central Highlands

In the transition zone between the layer cake–like geology of the Colorado Plateau to the somewhat regular block-faulted mountains and valleys of the Basin and Range Country, Arizona's "middle" was broken and twisted into very rugged, steep mountains cut by precipitous canyons. The Sierra Prietas, Bradshaws, Sierra Anchas, Mazatzals, and Superstition Mountains offer some of the most challenging hiking in the state.

---

54 Yaeger Canyon Loop

Description:	This is an enjoyable loop hike on Mingus Mountain, with views of Prescott Valley.
Location:	20 miles east of Prescott.
Type of hike:	Loop day hike.
Difficulty:	Moderate.
Total distance:	6.0 miles.
Elevation change:	980 feet.
Water:	None.
Best months:	April–November.
Maps:	Hickey Mountain USGS; Prescott National Forest.
Permit:	None.
For more information:	Prescott National Forest, Verde Ranger District.

Finding the trailhead: From Prescott, 5 miles north on U.S. 89, then turn right on Arizona 89A and drive 15.3 miles to the unmarked trailhead. Turn right onto the dirt road, and park on either side of the normally dry creek.

Key points:

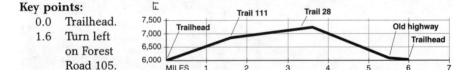

0.0	Trailhead.
1.6	Turn left on Forest Road 105.
1.8	Turn left on Yaeger Cabin Trail (Trail 111).
3.6	Turn left at an unsigned trail junction.
3.7	Turn left on Yaeger Canyon Trail (Trail 28).
5.5	Turn left at old highway.
6.0	Trailhead.

The hike: The hike starts on the Little Yaeger Canyon Trail, which is signed and begins from the southeast side of the parking area. Several switchbacks through pinyon-juniper forest lead to the top of a gentle ridge, where ponderosa pines begin to take over. The trail climbs more gradually through a small saddle, and then ends at Forest Road 105. Turn left and walk down

Yaeger Canyon Loop

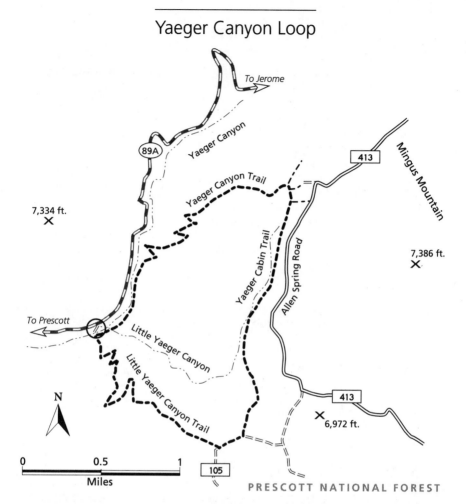

To Jerome

89A

Yaeger Canyon

Yaeger Canyon Trail

413

Mingus Mountain

7,334 ft.
×

Yaeger Cabin Trail

Allen Spring Road

7,386 ft.
×

To Prescott

Little Yaeger Canyon

Little Yaeger Canyon Trail

413

×
6,972 ft.

N

0   0.5   1
Miles

105

PRESCOTT NATIONAL FOREST

the road 0.2 mile to the Yaeger Cabin Trail (Forest Trail 111), and turn left.

Still in pine-oak forest, the Yaeger Cabin Trail drops slightly as it traverses a side canyon of Little Yaeger Canyon, then begins to work its way up the head of the canyon. There is sometimes water in the bed of the canyon near its head. The trail comes out onto a pine flat on the southwest ridge of Mingus Mountain and closely parallels Forest Road 413 for a short distance. Several spur trails branch right; stay left. Continue 0.1 mile to the end of the Yaeger Cabin Trail at a junction near Forest Road 413.

Turn left (west), and follow the Yaeger Canyon Trail (Trail 28) to the rim; there is a good view of Little Yaeger Canyon and the rim of Mingus Mountain. The trail descends to the southwest in a series of switchbacks, and the trailhead is visible next to the highway. When the trail reaches the bottom of Yaeger Canyon, it turns left on the old highway roadbed. It stays on the left (east) side of the creek and doesn't cross on the old highway bridge. Continue down the canyon to your vehicle.

—Bruce Grubbs

55 Woodchute Trail

Description:	This easy trail goes to the north end of Woodchute Mountain in the Woodchute Wilderness. You'll have some panoramic views of the western Mogollon Rim and Sycamore Canyon.
Location:	7 miles south of Jerome.
Type of hike:	Out-and-back day hike.
Difficulty:	Easy.
Total distance:	7.4 miles.
Elevation change:	640 feet.
Water:	None.
Best months:	April–November.
Maps:	Hickey Mountain, Munds Draw USGS; Prescott National Forest.
Permit:	None.
For more information:	Prescott National Forest, Verde Ranger District.

Alligator juniper along the Woodchute Trail.

Woodchute Trail

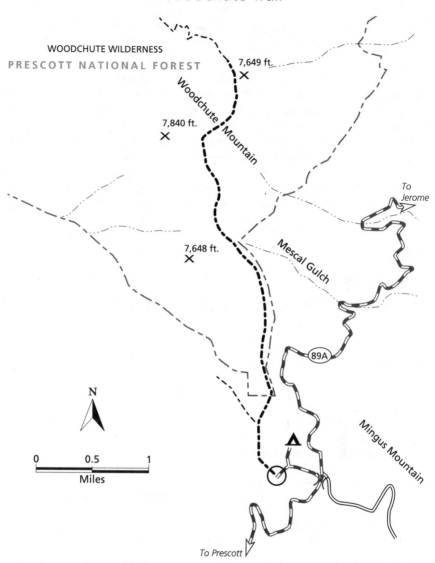

WOODCHUTE WILDERNESS
PRESCOTT NATIONAL FOREST

7,649 ft.
X

Woodchute Mountain

7,840 ft.
X

7,648 ft.
X

Mescal Gulch

To Jerome

89A

Mingus Mountain

N

0   0.5   1
Miles

To Prescott

Finding the trailhead: From Jerome, drive about 7 miles west on Arizona 89A. At the highway pass on Mingus Mountain, turn right at Potato Patch Campground. Go about 0.4 mile, then turn left into the Woodchute Trailhead.

Key points:

- 0.0   Woodchute Trailhead.
- 0.4   Turn right on the Woodchute Trail.
- 1.7   Ridge top.
- 2.2   Mescal Gulch.
- 2.7   South rim of Woodchute Mountain.
- 3.7   North rim of Woodchute Mountain.

The hike: From the trailhead, hike north on an old road for 0.4 mile through ponderosa pine woodland. Notice the large alligator junipers, the trees with, appropriately enough, bark that looks like alligator hide.

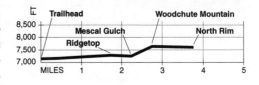

The Woodchute Trail forks right then climbs another half mile onto the main crest of the mountain. After crossing several dips in the ridge, it contours into the head of Mescal Gulch, then climbs to the south rim of Woodchute Mountain.

The trail continues north across the flat summit area, and finally reaches the north rim of Woodchute, our destination. (From here, the trail descends the north slopes of Woodchute Mountain and ends at Forest Road 318A after another 2.6 miles. This section of the trail is seldom used.) From the north rim, you have a panoramic view of the headwaters of the Verde River, the western Mogollon Rim, and Sycamore Canyon Wilderness.

—Bruce Grubbs

56 Granite Mountain Trail

Description:	This popular hike climbs through rugged granite terrain to a viewpoint overlooking Granite Basin and the Sierra Prieta.
Location:	8.5 miles northwest of Prescott.
Type of hike:	Out and back day hike.
Difficulty:	Moderate.
Total distance:	7.4 miles.
Elevation change:	1,560 feet.
Water:	None.
Best months:	March–November.
Maps:	Iron Springs, Jerome Canyon USGS; Prescott National Forest.
Permit:	None.
For more information:	Prescott National Forest, Bradshaw Ranger District.

Finding the trailhead: From Prescott, drive northwest about 4.5 miles on Iron Springs Road, then turn right on paved Granite Basin Road. Continue 4 miles to the Metate Trailhead, where you must pay to park.

Key points:
0.0   Metate Trailhead.
1.8   Blair Pass.
2.9   Pass.
3.7   Viewpoint.

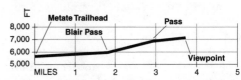

The hike: The Granite Mountain Trail crosses a wash, then follows a drainage uphill through a forest of juniper, pinyon pine, oak, and ponderosa

Granite Mountain Trail

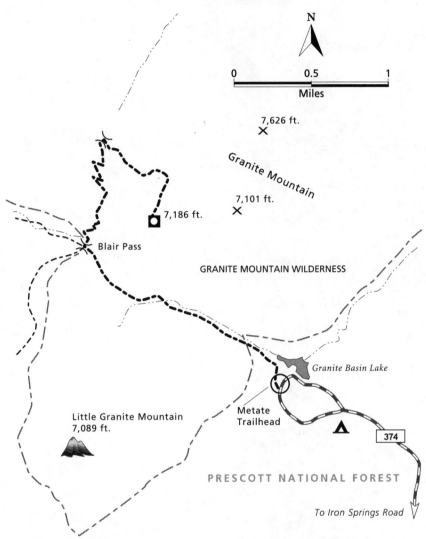

N

```
0              0.5              1
■■■■■■■■■■■■■■■■■■■■■■■■■■■■
              Miles
```

7,626 ft.
✕

Granite Mountain

7,101 ft.
✕

◻ 7,186 ft.

✕ Blair Pass

GRANITE MOUNTAIN WILDERNESS

Granite Basin Lake

Ⓥ

Little Granite Mountain
7,089 ft.

Metate
Trailhead

▲

374

PRESCOTT NATIONAL FOREST

To Iron Springs Road ⬇

pine. To the right there are occasional views of Granite Mountain, the destination for this hike. After 1.8 miles, you meet the junction with the Cedar Spring and Little Granite Mountain Trails at Blair Pass. Turn right to continue on the Granite Mountain Trail. After following a broad ridge a short distance, the trail begins to ascend the rocky slopes in a series of switchbacks. You may see rock climbers taking an unmarked turnoff toward the prominent granite cliff above. Granite Mountain Wall offers some of the best technical climbing in the state.

The terrain faces south here and the increased heat and dryness cause the pines to give way to chaparral and juniper. Chaparral is not a single plant, but an association of three shrubs that commonly grow together in the

Granite Mountain from near Blair Pass.

upper Sonoran life zone. It provides vital cover and habitat for wildlife. The red-barked bush is manzanita, the brush with the oaklike prickly leaves is scrub oak, and the plant with longish leaves, curled under at the edges and fuzzy underneath, is mountain mahogany.

The reward for the steady climb is expanding views. Little Granite Mountain forms a conspicuous landmark to the south; beyond are the pine-forested slopes of the Sierra Prieta Mountains. A little more than a mile from Blair Pass, you'll reach another pass. Here the trail turns east and climbs the beautiful west ridge of Granite Mountain, passing through stately groves of ponderosa pines and winding around granite slabs. Some of the slabs look almost glacial in origin. When the trail reaches the summit plateau, it turns south and ends at a viewpoint above the Granite Mountain Wall. Granite Basin Lake, Prescott, and the northern Bradshaw Mountains are all visible. Although this is not the true summit of the mountain, the views are excellent.

—Bruce Grubbs

57 Pine Mountain

Description:	This is an enjoyable loop over the summit of Pine Mountain, on the Verde Rim in the Pine Mountain Wilderness.
Location:	93 miles north of Phoenix.
Type of hike:	Loop day hike or backpack.
Difficulty:	Moderate.
Total distance:	13.3 miles.
Elevation change:	1,730 feet.
Water:	Seasonal at Nelson Place, Beehouse, Bishop, Pine, and Willow Springs.
Best months:	April–November.
Maps:	Tule Mesa USGS; Prescott National Forest.
Permit:	None.
For more information:	Prescott National Forest, Verde Ranger District.

Finding the trailhead: From Phoenix, drive north about 75 miles on Interstate 17 to the Dugas Interchange, then turn east on County Road 171, which becomes Forest Road 68. After 10.9 miles, Forest Road 68G continues straight ahead; be sure to turn right here to remain on Forest Road 68. Continue another 6.6 miles to the end of the road and the trailhead. There is limited camping at the trailhead.

Key points:
- 0.0   Pine Mountain Trailhead.
- 0.8   Turn right on Beehouse Canyon Trail.
- 1.8   Pine Flat; turn left on the Pine Flat Trail.
- 3.7   Turn left on the Verde Rim Trail.
- 5.4   Bishop Creek Trail forks left; stay right.
- 8.3   Bishop Creek Trail again joins from the left; stay right.

Pine Mountain

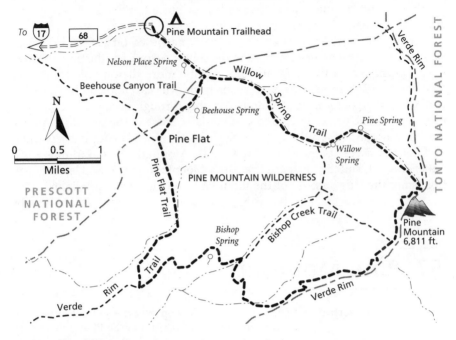

8.9   Pine Mountain.
9.3   Turn left on the Willow Spring Trail.
10.8   Bishop Creek Trail joins from the left.
12.6   Beehouse Canyon Trail joins from the left.
13.3   Pine Mountain Trailhead.

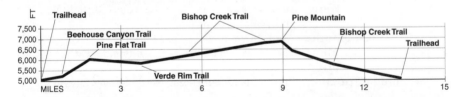

The hike: Pine Mountain is a small wilderness area astride the Verde Rim. It offers super views of the Mazatzal Wilderness and the wild Verde River country south of Camp Verde. A power line corridor is the only nonwilderness feature separating the two areas. This loop hike circumnavigates the higher western portion of the Pine Mountain Wilderness. Numerous wildfires have burned parts of the backcountry over the years, and you will encounter evidence of these fires on most of the trails. Expect to see downed trees across the trail periodically.

The trail heads southeast, and follows Sycamore Creek past Nelson Place Spring. This was the site of an old homestead and ranch; remains of the fruit orchard and building foundations can still be seen. After 0.8 mile, turn right (south) onto the Beehouse Canyon Trail, which follows its namesake canyon

South along the Verde Rim from the summit of Pine Mountain.

past Beehouse Spring and up to a saddle at Pine Flat. Turn left here, onto the Pine Flat Trail, and cross Pine Flat itself, which features a fine stand of ponderosa pines. Now the trail drops into the South Prong of Sycamore Creek, crosses the drainage, and works its way along the east side of the canyon to meet the Verde Rim Trail in a saddle about 2 miles from Pine Flat. Turn left here and follow the trail northeast into Bishop Canyon. The Verde Rim Trail passes Bishop Spring in a side canyon, and then contours into the main arm of Bishop Creek. Here, the Bishop Creek Trail forks left; stay right.

After passing through a shallow saddle, the trail finally reaches the Verde Rim itself. As promised, the views of the Verde River and Mazatzal Mountains are expansive. The trail now climbs along the Verde Rim to the northeast, heading toward Pine Mountain. Another trail goes left from a shallow saddle before you reach Pine Mountain. The Bishop Creek Trail skirts Pine Mountain on the west, but a short spur trail makes it an easy walk to the summit, which is the highest point on the Verde Rim.

Continuing north on the Verde Rim Trail, descend steeply into a saddle, and then turn left on the Willow Spring Trail (the Verde Rim Trail continues straight ahead). This trail descends into the headwaters of Sycamore Creek through another fine stand of ponderosa pine and Gambel oak. There are several possible campsites as the grade levels out, and there is seasonal water at Pine and Willow Springs. After passing Willow Spring, the Bishop Creek Trail again joins from the left. Continue down Sycamore Creek past Beehouse Canyon Trail, which completes the loop, and on past Nelson Place Spring to the trailhead.

—Bruce Grubbs

58 Y Bar Basin– Barnhardt Canyon Loop

Description:	This classic route takes you around the range's highest peak and through a remarkable variety of terrain in the Mazatzal Wilderness. These trails are better maintained and easier to find than most of the trails in the wilderness.
Location:	72 miles north of Mesa.
Type of hike:	Loop day hike or backpack.
Difficulty:	Difficult.
Total distance:	11.6 miles.
Elevation change:	2,400 feet.
Water:	Seasonal at Y Bar Tanks and Windsor Spring
Best season:	October–April.
Maps:	Mazatzal Peak USGS; Mazatzal Wilderness, Tonto National Forest USFS.
Permit:	Group size is limited to fifteen, and the stay limit is fourteen days.
For more information:	Tonto National Forest, Tonto Basin and Payson Ranger Districts.

Y Bar Basin–Barnhardt Canyon Loop

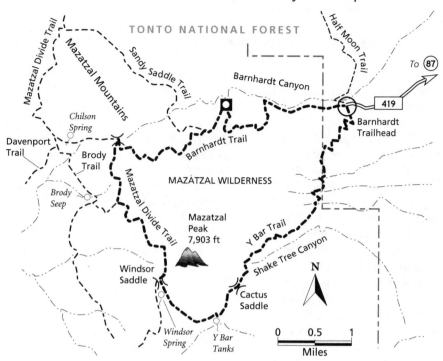

Finding the trailhead: From Mesa, drive about 67 miles north on Arizona 87, then turn left on the Barnhardt Road, Forest Road 419 (this turnoff is just south of the Gisela turnoff). Continue 5 miles to the end of the maintained dirt road at the trailhead.

Key points:

0.0	Barnhardt Trailhead.
4.2	Cactus Saddle.
4.8	Y Bar Tanks.
5.7	Windsor Saddle; turn right on the Mazatal Divide Trail.
6.9	Stay right at junction with Brody Trail.
8.3	Turn right on the Barnhardt Trail.
10.4	Viewpoint.
11.6	Barnhardt Trailhead.

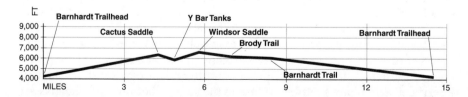

The hike: Start on the Barnhardt Trail, then, just a dozen yards from the trailhead, turn left on the Y Bar Trail (sometimes called the Shake Tree Trail).

The Barnhardt Trail will be our return. The Y Bar Trail climbs up a broad ridge in a series of rocky switchbacks, heading generally southwest through pinyon pine and juniper forest. When the trail passes the wilderness boundary, it turns more to the south and climbs along the east slopes of Mazatzal Peak, crossing numerous small canyons. After about a mile of this, it crosses into Shake Tree Canyon and climbs along the west slopes. Below to the east, Shake Tree Canyon cuts through a spectacular area of cliffs and rock fins.

The trail continues up Shake Tree Canyon, entering a pine-forested northeast-facing slope, then works its way across the slopes west of the canyon's bed. The climb ends as the trail reaches the saddle between Mazatzal Peak and Cactus Ridge. It's possible to camp here, but the nearest water is more than a half mile away at Y Bar Tanks. The Y Bar Trail descends southwest from the saddle, then levels out and contours across a small drainage. A small seep spring here, Y Bar Tanks, often has water. If not, follow the drainage downstream a hundred yards, where you may find large pools.

After the seep, the trail contours westward, then turns northwest and climbs to Windsor Saddle. Windsor Spring, a small pool next to the trail about 0.1 mile south of the saddle, sometimes goes dry. There is limited camping in Windsor Saddle itself.

Turn right onto the Mazatzal Divide Trail, which heads north and contours the west slopes of Mazatzal Peak. You'll have fine views of the rocky summit, as well as the head of the South Fork of Deadman Creek to the west. The well-constructed trail (also the route of the Arizona Trail) descends gradually northwest as it works its way around ridges and ravines. You'll pass the junction with Brody Trail (Brody Seep is 0.7 mile west and there are several campsites nearby); stay right on the Mazatzal Divide Trail. You'll turn northward again, and pass through several small stands of ponderosa pine as the trail contours to the saddle at the head of Barnhardt Canyon.

Turn right at the saddle onto the Barnhardt Trail. This popular trail is well constructed and easy to find. It heads generally east, contouring the south slopes of the broad basin at the head of Barnhardt Canyon. The trail passes through several stands of ponderosa pine, but much of the basin is covered with dense chaparral brush. Stay right at the junction with the Sandy Saddle Trail (Casterson Seep, shown on the maps where the Sandy Saddle Trail crosses Barnhardt Creek, is not reliable). The Barnhardt Trail swings around a ridge, where you can leave the trail momentarily and walk a few yards north to a viewpoint overlooking the impressive gorge of Barnhardt Canyon.

The trail swings south after this point, and crosses a drainage where there may be seasonal pools a short distance upstream from the trail. In cold weather the waterfall above the upper pool is often graced with a beautiful tapestry of icicles. Now the trail descends eastward along the south slopes of Barnhardt Canyon, skirting some impressive cliffs. Note the bent and twisted layers of metamorphic rock, mute testimony to the inconceivable forces that created these mountains. The trail turns north and descends a steep ridge in a series of switchbacks until it is close to the canyon bottom, then heads east again and stays just above the bed all the way to the Barnhardt Trailhead.

—Bruce Grubbs

59 Deer Creek

Description:	This loop hike takes you through several deep canyons in the eastern portion of the Mazatzal Wilderness, and has several options for exploring the several forks of Deer Creek. This hike also starts from one of the few trailheads located next to a paved highway.
Location:	63 miles north of Mesa.
Type of hike:	Loop backpack.
Difficulty:	Difficult.
Total distance:	14.9 miles.
Elevation change:	2,800 feet.
Water:	Seasonal in Deer Creek and at Maple and Pigeon Springs.
Best months:	October–November, March–April.
Maps:	Mazatzal Peak USGS; Mazatzal Wilderness, Tonto National Forest USFS.
Permit:	Group size is limited to fifteen, and the stay limit is fourteen days.
For more information:	Tonto National Forest, Tonto Basin Ranger District.

Finding the trailhead: From Mesa, drive about 63 miles north on Arizona 87. Turn left into the Deer Creek Trailhead which is just south of the junction with Arizona 188.

Key points:

0.0	Deer Creek Trailhead.
0.1	Stay right at Gold Ridge Trail.
0.3	Stay right at South Fork Trail.
1.0	Deer Creek.
7.0	Turn left onto the Davey Gowan Trail.
8.6	Turn left on the Mount Peeley Road.
9.2	Pass the South Fork Trail.
9.5	Turn left on the old road to the Gold Ridge Trail.
9.7	Pass the road closure and start the descent.
14.8	Turn right onto Deer Creek Trail.
14.9	Deer Creek Trailhead.

The hike: From the trailhead, start northwest on the Deer Creek Trail (Forest Trail 45) as it climbs onto a low ridge. Within a short distance, both the Gold Ridge Trail (which will be our return) and the South Fork Trail branch

Deer Creek

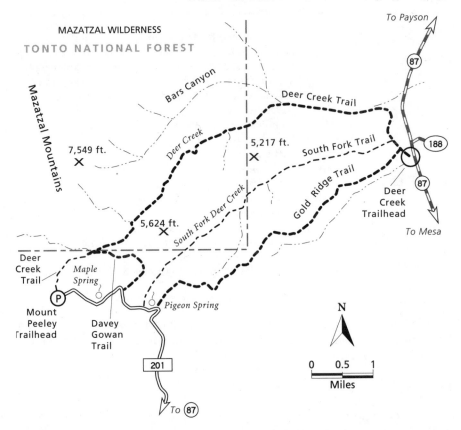

left; stay right at both junctions. After a mile, the Deer Creek Trail crosses the South Fork of Deer Creek then swings into Deer Creek just upstream of a ranch located on private land. Now the trail follows the creek west toward the mountains. Although the stream flow is seasonal, depending on recent rain and snow, the canyon bottom is still delightfully shaded by Arizona sycamores and other streamside trees. When Deer Creek starts a turn toward the southwest, Bars Canyon joins from the right.

As you continue upstream along Deer Creek, the trail becomes fainter, but always stays near the bottom of the canyon. The appearance of the first ponderosa pines along the north-facing slopes signal that you're reaching the head of the canyon. After an unnamed tributary canyon comes in from the northwest, Deer Creek swings to the south briefly before resuming its southwesterly direction. You'll hike through a brushy meadow, and then meet the Davey Gowan Trail (Forest Trail 48).

Turn left here and follow the Davey Gowan Trail as it climbs east out of the canyon, then swings south onto a ridge and climbs to meet the Mount Peeley Road (Forest Road 201). This entire section is covered with a fine ponderosa pine and Douglas fir forest. Turn left on the road, and hike east about

0.9 mile to a spur road branching left and downhill. Follow this road northeast about 0.2 mile to the road closure and the start of the Gold Ridge Trail (Forest Trail 47). The trail, an old jeep road, drops off the northwest side of the ridge, then swings east to follow the general ridge system.

You'll leave the pine forest behind as the trail descends onto lower, drier slopes. Watch for the point where the old jeep road veers north, and the Gold Ridge Trail becomes a foot trail, heading east for a short distance before turning northeast again. It descends a ridge, which gives you great views to the northeast, then finally emerges onto gentler slopes, which are covered with high desert grasses. Continue about 1 more mile to the Deer Creek Trailhead.

Option 1: Instead of leaving Deer Creek on the Davey Gowan Trail, stay right and follow the Deer Creek Trail southwest as it climbs through a dense forest of pine and fir to the Mount Peeley Trailhead. Turn left and walk the Mount Peeley Road 1.4 miles to the Davey Gowan Trail junction (Forest Trail 48), then continue 0.9 mile east to the Gold Ridge Trail. This option gets you into the head of Deer Creek, though it involves a little more road walking. It adds 0.7 mile and less than an hour to the loop.

Option 2: From the Mount Peeley Road, return via the South Fork Trail (Forest Trail 46). This little-used trail leaves the road 0.6 mile east of the Davey Gowan Trail, and passes Maple Spring before dropping into the South Fork of Deer Creek. This option is 0.2 mile shorter.

—Bruce Grubbs

60 Browns Peak

Description:	A trail and cross-country hike to the top of the highest of the Four Peaks, and the highest in the southern Mazatzal Mountains. Although the craggy peak looks impressive, it's actually easy to climb and you'll only need your hands in a few places.
Location:	50 miles northeast of Mesa.
Type of hike:	Out-and-back day hike.
Difficulty:	Difficult.
Total distance:	4.6 miles.
Elevation change:	1,960 feet.
Water:	None.
Best months:	April–November.
Maps:	Four Peaks USGS; Tonto National Forest USFS.
Permit:	Group size is limited to fifteen, and the stay limit is fourteen days.
For more information:	Tonto National Forest, Mesa Ranger District.

Finding the trailhead: From Mesa, drive northeast on Arizona 87. At Shea Boulevard, note your mileage, and continue 14 miles to Forest Road 143. Turn right onto this maintained dirt road, which becomes unmaintained and

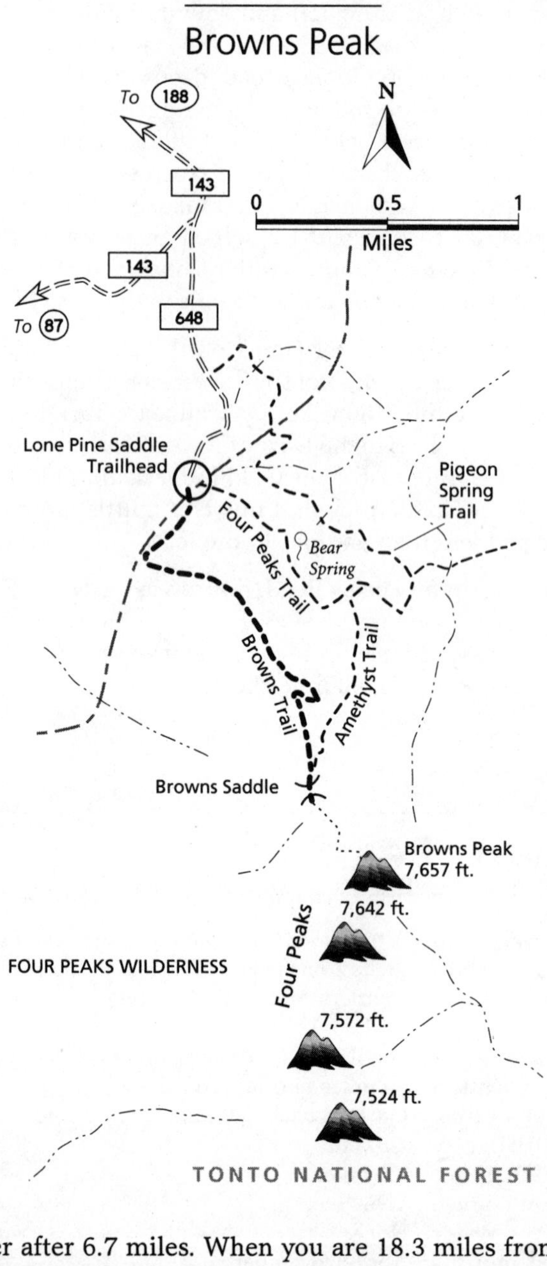

Browns Peak

N

To (188)

[143]

[143]

To (87)

[648]

0   0.5   1
Miles

Lone Pine Saddle
Trailhead

Pigeon
Spring
Trail

Four Peaks Trail

Bear
Spring

Browns Trail

Amethyst Trail

Browns Saddle

Browns Peak
7,657 ft.

7,642 ft.

Four Peaks

FOUR PEAKS WILDERNESS

7,572 ft.

7,524 ft.

TONTO NATIONAL FOREST

much rougher after 6.7 miles. When you are 18.3 miles from the highway, turn right onto Forest Road 648 and continue 1.0 mile south to the Lone Pine Saddle Trailhead at the end of the road.

Key points:
- 0.0   Lone Pine Saddle Trailhead.
- 1.7   Turn right on the Amethyst Trail.
- 1.9   Browns Saddle.
- 2.3   Browns Peak.

Browns Peak, on the left in this aerial view, is the highest summit of the Four Peaks.

The hike: The trail climbs south from the trailhead through a fine stand of ponderosa pine and Gambel oak that was nearly untouched by the Lone Fire of 1996. It swings southwest and passes through a broad saddle, then turns south-

east, back toward the main ridge, and enters an area where the fire killed nearly all of the trees. Be alert for falling trees, which can topple at any time but are especially likely to fall during windy or wet weather. The view is much better without the trees, or at least it will be until the chaparral brush gets reestablished. After crossing the main ridge, the trail works its way up the northeast slopes, switchbacking occasionally. Finally, it meets the Amethyst Trail. Turn right and continue 0.2 mile to Browns Saddle.

Leave the trail and continue cross-country up the ridge toward Browns Peak, heading south. Note the prominent ravine that splits the north face of the peak. This is your goal, but you won't be able to see it when you get closer. Although several different routes can reach the summit, the following method is one of the easiest. When you reach the first rock outcrops, turn right and work your way into the main gully that drains the ravine. If you stay high, right at the base of the rock, you'll avoid the worst of the brush. Then head directly up the ravine; there's one spot where you'll need your hands. The ravine tops out on the west shoulder of the peak, and it's then a short scramble to the left (east) to reach the summit.

From this lofty vantage point you can see much of the country covered by this guidebook. Although the bulk of the other three peaks blocks some of the view to the south, you can still see much of the Superstition Mountains. To the west lies the Valley of the Sun, containing Phoenix and its sister cities. The desert plain is dotted with low mountain ranges that seem to recede into the distance. On a clear day you can see the McDowell Mountains, and far to the west, the Harquahala Mountains. To the northwest, the bulk of the Bradshaw Mountains looms above the lower elevation New River Mountains. The Mazatzal Mountains run north-northwest from your perch; the rounded summit of Mount Ord, crowned with radio towers and a fire lookout, is clearly visible. The rugged peaks of the Mazatzal Wilderness form the backdrop for Mount Ord. North and eastward, the clean line of the Mogollon Rim slices across the horizon near Payson, and to the east the wide bulk of the Sierra Ancha dominate the skyline. To the southeast, you can see Pinal Peak, rising above the town of Globe.

—Bruce Grubbs

61 Hells Hole

Description:	An overnight backpack into the Salome Wilderness Area.
Location:	20 miles south of Young.
Type of hike:	Out-and-back backpack.
Difficulty:	Difficult.
Total distance:	10.6 miles.
Elevation change:	1,200 feet.
Water:	Workman Creek.
Best months:	March–November.
Maps:	Aztec Peak, Armor Mountain, Copper Mountain USGS; Tonto National Forest USFS.
Permit:	None.
For more information:	Tonto National Forest, Pleasant Valley Ranger District.

Finding the trailhead: From Globe drive 3 miles west on U.S. 60, then turn right on Arizona 88. Go 14.8 miles, then turn right on Arizona 288. Continue 23.4 miles to the Reynolds Creek Group Campsite. There is a turnout to the south just before entering the campground, which is the parking area for this trail.

Hells Hole

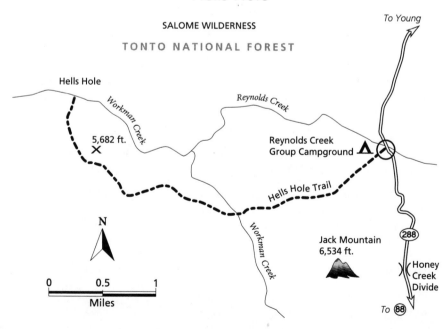

Key points:

0.0 Trailhead.
0.8 First pass.
1.6 Workman Creek.
3.0 Far rim.
4.6 Hells Hole.

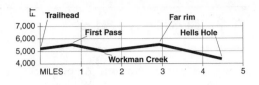

The hike: The trail starts in ponderosa pine forest and climbs southwesterly to the pass between Jack Mountain and an unnamed peak to the north. Beyond the pass, the trail drops into Workman Creek, crosses it, and then climbs about 600 vertical feet to the top of the far rim. The trail then passes south of a knoll and descends steeply into Hells Hole, a particularly dramatic section of Workman Creek. The trail may be overgrown in places. Finding the route can be challenging. Camping is possible along the creek.

The determined angler can try his or her luck at Workman Creek for German brown and rainbow trout. Other wildlife in the area includes mule deer, white-tailed deer, javelina, mountain lion, coyote, black bear, and wild turkey.

—Stewart Aitchison

62 Barks Canyon

Description: This hike takes you up popular, scenic Peralta Canyon and returns cross-country via scenic Barks Canyon.
Location: 16 miles east of Apache Junction.
Type of hike: Loop day hike.
Difficulty: Moderate.
Total distance: 5.2 miles.
Elevation change: 1,360 feet.
Water: None.
Best months: October–April.
Maps: Weavers Needle USGS; Superstition Wilderness USFS.
Permit: None.
For more information: Tonto National Forest, Mesa Ranger District.

Finding the trailhead: From Apache Junction, drive about 8.5 miles east on U.S. 60, then turn left onto Peralta Road (Forest Road 77), which is maintained dirt. Continue 8 miles to the end of the road at Peralta Trailhead.

Key points:

0.0 Peralta Trailhead.
1.9 Fremont Saddle.
2.4 Weavers Needle view.
2.6 Barks Canyon; turn right.
3.4 Bluff Spring Trail; turn right.
5.2 Peralta Trailhead.

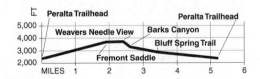

Barks Canyon • Dutchmans Loop

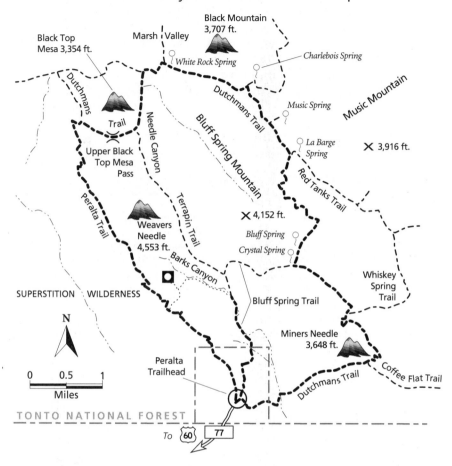

The hike: Start the loop on the well-graded Peralta Trail, which heads north-west up Peralta Canyon, climbing steadily. The trail generally stays near the bed of the canyon, occasionally crossing it. Numerous stone pinnacles, known locally as "stone ghosts," are scattered along the canyon and its rims. The pinnacles are mostly carved from rhyolite, a volcanic rock. The mountains eroded along cracks in the rock, carving out odd-looking fins and pinnacles. The trail steepens somewhat near the head of the canyon, and a few short switchbacks lead to Fremont Saddle at the head of Peralta Canyon.

Fremont Saddle, at 1.9 miles, is one of many places throughout the American West named for John C. Fremont, the noted American explorer who led several government-sponsored survey trips. The Peralta Trail continues north from the saddle, but our loop heads cross-country onto the broken plateau northeast of the saddle. You'll need the topographic map and skill in cross-country route finding to follow this route. Continue northeast, then north across the plateau to its northern rim, and a panoramic view of Weavers Needle.

Pick your way off the rim (it's easier to the south, along the east rim). The exact point at which you start the descent is not critical, because the entire eastern rim drains into Barks Canyon. Follow the drainage northeast into Barks Canyon, then turn right and follow Barks Canyon downstream. Volcanic pinnacles and stone grottoes line both sides of the shallow canyon, and it's an interesting area to explore. After a major tributary joins from the left, watch for the Bluff Spring Trail, which descends the eastern slopes into Barks Canyon. Turn right, and follow this good trail back to the Peralta Trailhead.

—Bruce Grubbs

63 Dutchmans Loop

See Map on Page 181

Description: This popular loop through the western Superstitions takes in a lot of interesting country, following well-graded, easy trails. The hike is a good one for newcomers to the sport of backpacking.

Location: 16 miles east of Apache Junction.

Type of hike: Loop backpack.

Difficulty: Moderate.

Total distance: 14.8 miles.

Elevation change: 1,340 feet.

Water: Crystal Spring, Bluff Spring, La Barge Spring, Music Spring, Charlebois Spring, White Rock Spring.

Best months: October–March.

Maps: Weavers Needle USGS; Superstition Wilderness, Tonto National Forest USFS.

Permit: Group size is limited to fifteen, and the stay limit is fourteen days.

For more information: Tonto National Forest, Mesa Ranger District.

Finding the trailhead: From Apache Junction, drive about 8.5 miles east on U.S. 60, then turn left onto Peralta Road, which is maintained dirt. Continue 8 miles to the end of the road at Peralta Trailhead.

Key points:

0.0   Peralta Trailhead.
2.2   Coffee Flat Trail.
2.6   Miners Summit and Whiskey Spring Trail.
3.8   Bluff Spring Trail; turn right to stay on the Dutchmans Trail.
5.0   Red Tanks Trail junction and La Barge Spring; stay left.
6.1   Peters Trail and Charlebois Spring; stay left.
7.4   Marsh Valley, White Rock Spring, and the Cavalry Trail; stay left.
7.8   Bull Pass Trail; stay left on the Dutchmans Trail.
8.6   Terrapin Trail; stay right on the Dutchmans Trail.
9.4   Turn left on the Peralta Trail in East Boulder Canyon.
13.0   Fremont Saddle.
14.8   Peralta Trailhead.

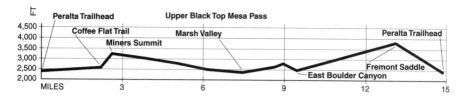

The hike: Hike east on the Dutchmans Trail over a low ridge. The trail loops around the base of Miners Needle, climbing to Miners Summit via a couple of switchbacks. It then descends northwest to Crystal Spring at the base of Bluff Springs Mountain. Turning northeast, the good trail descends Bluff Spring Canyon, passing the spur trail to Bluff Spring, and then turns more to the north and works its way down to La Barge Canyon and the junction with the Red Tanks Trail. La Barge Spring is located just east of this junction, on the north side of the canyon. There are several campsites in the area.

Stay left on the Dutchmans Trail and follow it down La Barge Canyon to the northwest. A spur trail leads to Music Spring. At the junction with the Peters Trail, you can reach Charlebois Spring by following the Peters Trail a short distance into the side canyon. There are several popular campsites near this spring. The main trail continues down La Barge Canyon to Marsh Valley and the junction with the Cavalry Trail. White Rock Spring usually has water, and there is limited camping nearby.

Again, stay left on the Dutchmans Trail and climb west to a low saddle. Here, at the junction with the Bull Pass Trail, the Dutchmans Trail turns south and drops into Needle Canyon. After following Needle Canyon for a while, turn right at the junction with the Terrapin Trail and follow the Dutchmans Trail up an unnamed drainage south of Black Top Mesa. The trail reaches Black Top Mesa Pass then descends northwest into East Boulder Canyon to meet the Peralta Trail. There are campsites in this scenic basin, which is dominated by towering Weavers Needle to the south. There is seasonal water in the bed of the wash.

Turn left onto the Peralta Trail, which climbs west in well-graded switchbacks to the ridge south of Palomino Mountain, then heads south on the slopes above a tributary of Little Boulder Canyon. A few switchbacks take the trail over a saddle next to a rock outcrop, and then the trail descends back into East Boulder Canyon below triple-summited Weavers Needle. It then works its way up the scenic head of East Boulder Canyon, past heavily used Pinyon Camp, which is marked by its namesake pinyon pines. Water can sometimes be found in the creekbed near the camp. The Peralta Trail climbs to Fremont Saddle in a couple of switchbacks, and then descends scenic Peralta Canyon to the Peralta Trailhead.

—Bruce Grubbs

64 Fireline Loop

Description:	A most enjoyable hike through the high country in the eastern Superstitions. You'll have a chance to climb the highest peak in the range, visit the site of historic Reavis Ranch, and hike along beautiful Campaign Creek.
Location:	56 miles northeast of Apache Junction.
Type of hike:	Loop backpack.
Difficulty:	Difficult.
Total distance:	14.5 miles.
Elevation change:	2,200 feet.
Water:	Campaign Creek near the trailhead, Walnut Spring, Whiskey Spring, Black Jack Spring, Brushy Spring; seasonal in Pine Creek, Reavis Creek, and upper Campaign Creek.
Best months:	October–November, March–April.
Maps:	Pinyon Mountain, Two Bar Mountain, Haunted Canyon, Iron Mountain USGS; Superstition Wilderness, Tonto National Forest USFS.
Permit:	Group size is limited to fifteen, and the stay limit is fourteen days.
For more information:	Tonto National Forest, Tonto Basin Ranger District.

Finding the trailhead: From Apache Junction, drive 20 miles east on Arizona 88 to the end of the pavement. Continue another 20 miles on the gravel road to Roosevelt Dam, and then turn right to remain on Arizona 88, which is now paved. Continue 8.6 miles, and then turn right on Forest Road 449, the Campaign Creek Road, which is maintained dirt. Go 1.9 miles, turn left at a fork onto Forest Road 449A, and continue 5.2 miles to the end of the road at the Reavis Mountain School. Forest Road 449A follows Campaign Creek and crosses it numerous times. This route requires a high-clearance vehicle, and may be washed out and impassable after major storms. The trailhead is on private land; please park in the signed trailhead parking. There is no camping at the trailhead.

You can also reach Forest Road 449 from Globe by driving about 20 miles west on Arizona 88, which is paved.

Key points:
0.0	Campaign Trailhead (old Upper Horrell Place).
0.7	Turn right on Reavis Gap Trail.
3.0	Reavis Gap and junction with Two Bar Ridge Trail.
3.3	Pine Creek.
6.1	Turn left on Reavis Ranch Trail.
6.5	Reavis Ranch site.
6.8	Turn left on the Fireline Trail.
8.0	Reavis Creek–Pine Creek divide.
8.9	The trail leaves Pine Creek.
10.0	Turn left on the Pinto Peak Trail in Campaign Creek.

Fireline Loop

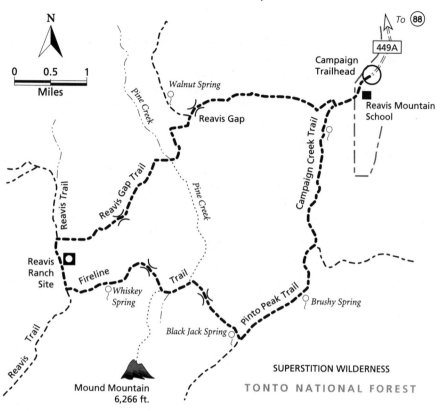

11.8 Turn left onto the Campaign Creek Trail.
13.9 Pass the junction with the Reavis Gap Trail.
14.5 Campaign Trailhead.

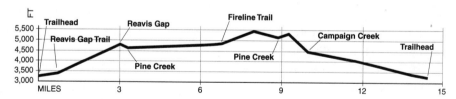

The hike: Hike through the Reavis Mountain School and continue southwest along Campaign Creek. This section of the creek has a permanent flow of water from several nearby springs. Just after a side canyon comes in from the right, turn right on the Reavis Gap Trail. This trail is not shown on the USGS maps and sections can be difficult to follow. The trail first climbs over a low ridge, then heads west up an unnamed canyon system, climbing steadily. After it crosses the normally dry wash, the grade steepens as it heads for Reavis Gap, a saddle on Two Bar Ridge. Just after passing through Reavis Gap, the Two Bar Ridge Trail branches right. (Walnut Spring is about 0.5

mile north on the Two Bar Ridge Trail.) Stay on the Reavis Gap Trail as it passes through another saddle, then swings south and drops into Pine Creek. There is seasonal water in Pine Creek and several campsites scattered in the pinyon pine–juniper forest along the creek.

After crossing Pine Creek, the trail again heads southwest and climbs gradually toward another saddle. It then drops gradually west down a tributary of Reavis Creek, and ends at the Reavis Trail on the west side of Reavis Creek. Turn left on the Reavis Trail. The trail passes an apple orchard, and then emerges into a meadow next to Reavis Creek. This was the site of the old ranch house. There's plenty of camping both up- and downstream from the former ranch site, and you can usually find flowing water in the creek upstream for about 0.7 mile.

When the ranch was sold to the Forest Service in the 1960s, the historic ranch house was still intact and usable as an emergency shelter. Unfortunately, years of weather and vandalism took their toll, and careless campers finally burned the building to the ground. Although the ruins of the house were cleaned up and removed, you may find artifacts from the old ranching days; please leave everything as you find it.

Continue the hike by heading south on the Reavis Trail. Turn left (east) on the Fireline Trail before reaching the first major drainage that comes in on the left. Parts of this trail follow an old bulldozer track made by the U.S. Forest Service while fighting a forest fire in 1966. Wildfires are common in this remote country and difficult to fight. In the early days of this wilderness, it was thought that all wildfires should be aggressively suppressed, and bulldozers were used to build access roads and construct fire lines, leaving scars that are still visible. The U.S. Forest Service now recognizes that lightning-caused fires are part of the natural forest cycle and are necessary to keep the wilderness wild. Such natural fires are allowed to burn uncontrolled, except for monitoring and containment efforts to keep the fire from threatening developed areas outside the wilderness. Another fire burned the area in the 1980s, but because these new fire-fighting techniques were used, there was much less impact on the wilderness.

You'll mostly be in a mixed chaparral brush and pinyon-juniper forest along the first part of the Fireline Trail. After passing Whiskey Spring, the trail turns more to the northeast and climbs up a drainage to the divide between Reavis Creek and Pine Creek. It then heads southeast and descends gradually into the head of Pine Creek. There are pockets of tall ponderosa pines growing in favored locations, hence the name of the creek. The old dozer trail suddenly turns east and drops steeply into the bed of Pine Creek, following the drainage for a short distance before climbing out to the east and crossing the divide between Pine and Campaign Creeks. It plunges steeply into Campaign Creek, passing Black Jack Spring just before ending at the Pinto Peak Trail in Campaign Creek. There are several good campsites, graced by more pines, at this trail junction.

Now turn left again and follow the Pinto Peak Trail down Campaign Creek. After the rugged country you've just crossed, it's a joy to wander down the scenic canyon bottom. There's seasonal water in the creekbed. The

Pinto Peak Trail veers right and climbs out of Campaign Creek at a trail junction; go left here onto the Campaign Creek Trail and continue north down Campaign Creek. Finally, the trail climbs over a low saddle to avoid a narrow, rough section of the canyon bottom, and then meets the Reavis Gap Trail. Stay right to return to the Campaign Trailhead.

Option 1: At Reavis Gap, turn right onto the Two Bar Ridge Trail, and hike 1.2 miles north, past Walnut Spring, to the point where the trail starts to drop into a tributary of Pine Creek. This point is a fine overlook of lower Pine Creek and Two Bar Ridge. This option adds 2.4 miles and 200 feet of elevation change to the hike.

Option 2: Where the Reavis Gap Trail crosses Pine Creek, turn left and hike cross-country up Pine Creek to the Fireline Trail. Sections of upper Pine Creek are rough and slow because of large boulders and dense brush. It's 1.8 miles to the Fireline Trail and you'll climb about 620 feet. This option shortens the loop by 5.6 miles, but is much more difficult than staying on the trails.

Option 3: When the Fireline Trail starts down into Pine Creek, leave the trail and hike cross-country south along the pinyon-juniper covered ridge. Although the upper part of this ridge is brushy, with some route finding you can find a reasonably brush-free route to the top of Mound Mountain. At 6,266 feet, this round summit is the highest point in the Superstition Mountains, and has an appropriately commanding view of the range. This option adds 2.6 miles and 800 feet of elevation change to the trip.

Option 4: At the junction of the Fireline Trail and Pinto Peak Trail, turn right and hike up the Pinto Peak Trail to the saddle at the head of Campaign Creek. You'll get good views of upper Pinto Creek and the rugged country around Iron Mountain and Pinto Peak in the southeast corner of the Superstition Mountains. This hike adds 3.2 miles to the trip, and 690 feet of elevation gain.

—Bruce Grubbs

The White Mountains

The White Mountains in east-central Arizona offer a respite from the desert lowlands. This area averages 8,000 feet above sea level and has a long, snowy winter season. The region is cloaked by spruce, fir, and pine forest and is the source for several of the Southwest's major rivers, such as the Salt and the Little Colorado.

65 Escudilla Mountain

Description:	This alpine hike takes you to the summit of Arizona's third highest mountain, Escudilla Mountain in the Escudilla Wilderness.
Location:	11 miles north of Alpine.
Type of hike:	Out-and-back day hike.
Difficulty:	Moderate.
Total distance:	5.8 miles.
Elevation change:	1,200 feet.
Water:	None.
Best months:	June–October.
Maps:	Escudilla Mountain USGS; Apache National Forest.
Permit:	None, but camping is discouraged.
or more information:	Apache-Sitgreaves National Forest, Alpine Ranger District.

Finding the trailhead: From Alpine, drive about 6.0 miles north on U.S. 180, then turn right on Forest Road 56. Continue about 4.6 miles to the Terry Flat Road; stay left, and go another 0.3 mile to the Escudilla Mountain Trailhead.

Key points:

0.0 Escudilla Mountain Trailhead.
1.5 Profanity Ridge.
2.9 Escudilla Fire Lookout.

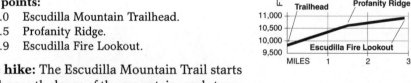

The hike: The Escudilla Mountain Trail starts up the south slopes of the mountain, and steepens as it begins to switchback through stands of quaking aspen. The final switchbacks lead into an alpine meadow with excellent views of Terry Flat to the south. At the north side of this meadow, the trail crosses Profanity Ridge, and then descends slightly into another beautiful meadow. Here, the Government Trail joins from the left (west). Our trail continues north and climbs through fir and spruce forest to reach the fire lookout. Be sure to ask permission of the lookout personnel before climbing the tower. The highest point of the mountain is actually 0.6 miles to the north.

Aspens along the Escudilla Mountain Trail.

Escudilla Mountain

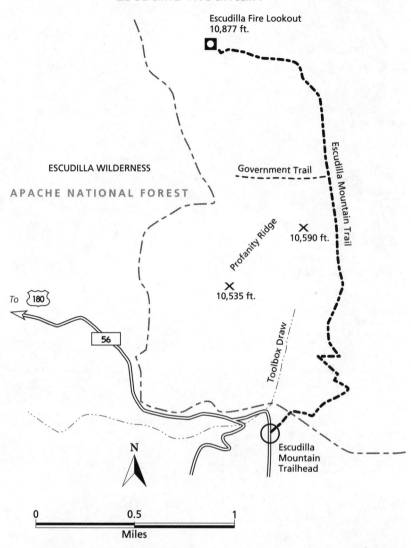

Escudilla Fire Lookout
10,877 ft.

ESCUDILLA WILDERNESS

APACHE NATIONAL FOREST

Government Trail

Escudilla Mountain Trail

Profanity Ridge

×
10,590 ft.

×
10,535 ft.

To 〔180〕

56

Toolbox Draw

N

Escudilla
Mountain
Trailhead

| 0 | 0.5 | 1 |
Miles

Escudilla Mountain was one of the favorite places of Aldo Leopold, a U.S. Forest Service employee. In the 1930s, Leopold and others began to promote the idea of preserving roadless areas within the national forests. This resulted in the first National Forest Wilderness Areas, and then the Wilderness Act of 1964, in which the U.S. Congress created the National Wilderness Preservation System.

—Bruce Grubbs

66 Apache Railroad Trail

Description:	This hike follows the old Apache Railroad grade through the scenic high country of the White Mountains. The trail is open to hikers, horses, and bicycles but closed to motor vehicles.
Location:	36 miles east of Show Low.
Type of hike:	Shuttle, either a long day hike or an easy overnight backpack.
Difficulty:	Moderate.
Total distance:	19.1 miles.
Elevation change:	400 feet.
Water:	The West Fork of the Little Colorado River is the only reliable water that's easy to reach. Seasonally, there's water in several reservoirs and small lakes that you'll pass, but the shores are usually swampy and the water hard to reach.
Best months:	June–October.
Maps:	Big Lake North, Mount Baldy, Greer, Greens Peak USGS; Apache-Sitgreaves National Forest.
Permit:	None.
For more information:	Apache-Sitgreaves National Forest, Springerville Ranger District.

Finding the trailhead: To reach the Highway 260 Trailhead from Show Low, drive about 36 miles east on Arizona 260, passing the Arizona 273 junction. The trailhead is about 1.5 miles east of the Arizona 273 turnoff, just after leaving the White Mountain Apache Reservation. If you plan to do the entire hike one-way, you'll need to leave a shuttle vehicle here.

To reach the Sheep Crossing Trailhead, drive 8.7 miles south on Arizona 273, and then turn right into the trailhead parking area. This trailhead can be used to hike either the north or south portion of the trail, for a shorter hike.

To reach the Big Lake Trailhead and the start of the hike, continue on Arizona 273 another 5.6 miles, then turn right on Forest Road 116. Continue 2.6 miles, and then turn left on Forest Road 249E. Go 2.1 miles, then turn left and continue 0.4 mile to the trailhead.

Key points:
- 0.0   Big Lake Trailhead.
- 2.6   Pass Basin Lake.
- 3.0   Cross Arizona 273.
- 5.2   High point of the hike.
- 6.5   Coulter Reservoir.
- 9.2   West Fork of the Little Colorado River.
- 10.0 Sheep Crossing Trailhead.
- 12.2 Benny Creek.
- 13.7 White Mountain Reservoir.
- 19.1 Highway 260 Trailhead.

Apache Railroad Trail

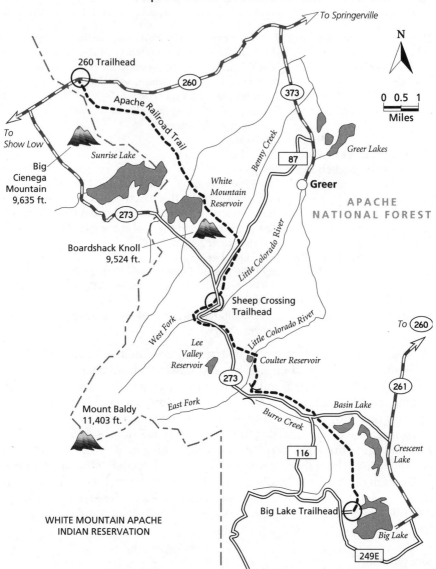

To Springerville

N

260 Trailhead

260

Apache Railroad Trail

To Show Low

Big Cienega Mountain 9,635 ft.

Sunrise Lake

273

Boardshack Knoll 9,524 ft.

West Fork

Lee Valley Reservoir

273

Mount Baldy 11,403 ft.

East Fork

WHITE MOUNTAIN APACHE INDIAN RESERVATION

373

Benny Creek

White Mountain Reservoir

87

Greer Lakes

Greer

APACHE NATIONAL FOREST

Little Colorado River

Sheep Crossing Trailhead

Little Colorado River

Coulter Reservoir

Burro Creek

116

To 260

261

Basin Lake

Crescent Lake

Big Lake Trailhead

Big Lake

249E

0 0.5 1
Miles

The hike: Follow the old railroad grade north as it cuts through the rolling alpine meadow northwest of Big Lake. This high plateau is formed from basalt lava flows, and the volcanic origins of the White Mountains are evidenced

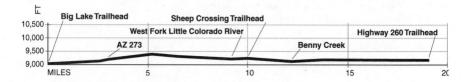

Big Lake Trailhead

Sheep Crossing Trailhead

West Fork Little Colorado River

Highway 260 Trailhead

AZ 273

Benny Creek

10,500
10,000
9,500
9,000

MILES   5   10   15   20

192

Big Lake, near the southern end of the Apache Railroad Trail, in the White Mountains.

by the cinders underfoot. All of the hills and mountains in this area are old volcanoes.

As the trail turns more to the northwest, you'll pass Basin Lake, and then cross Arizona 273. The trail closely parallels Arizona 273 for a time, as it enters mixed fir-aspen-spruce forest along Burro Creek. Just after the trail emerges into a small meadow at the head of the creek, it crosses the divide between Burro Creek and the East Fork of the Little Colorado River, which is the high point of this nearly level hike.

Now the old railroad grade swings around the base of a hill, leaving Arizona 273 behind as it parallels the East Fork. It crosses the East Fork on the dam below Coulter Reservoir, and then heads generally northwest again. A sharp (for a railroad) right then left turn marks the approach to the West Fork of the Little Colorado River at Sheep Crossing.

After crossing the river, the trail closely parallels Arizona 273 again. It passes the Sheep Crossing Trailhead, then crosses Arizona 273 a final time and heads northeast through alternating meadows and forest. For a while the trail parallels Forest Road 87, then crosses the road. It crosses Benny Creek on a bridge, then heads northwest along the northeast slopes of Boardshack Knoll. After passing White Mountain Reservoir, the trail is in open meadow with only a few stands of trees nearby. It finally approaches the eastern side of Big Cienega Mountain, and reaches the Arizona 260 Trailhead at the north end of this large hill, which is marked by a prominent red and white microwave tower.

—Bruce Grubbs

67 Mount Baldy

Description:	A day hike to the top of the White Mountains.
Location:	25 miles southwest of Springerville.
Type of hike:	Out-and-back day hike.
Difficulty:	Moderate.
Total distance:	12 miles.
Elevation change:	2,220 feet.
Water:	West Fork; purify before using.
Best months:	June–October.
Maps:	Mount Baldy USGS; Mount Baldy Wilderness Map USFS.
Permit:	None, but Baldy Peak on the White Mountain Apache Reservation is closed to entry.
For more information:	Apache-Sitgreaves National Forest, Springerville Ranger District.

Finding the trailhead: From Greer, take Forest Road 87 6 miles to its junction with Arizona 273. Turn left and drive about 2 miles to Sheep Crossing on the West Fork of the Little Colorado River. The trailhead is signed on the right side of the road above Sheep Crossing.

Key points:
- 0.0 Trailhead.
- 3.0 Cross tributary.
- 4.4 Ridge.
- 5.3 Reservation boundary.

Alpine meadows below Mount Baldy.

Mount Baldy

N

0   0.5   1
Miles

WHITE MOUNTAIN APACHE
INDIAN RESERVATION

Sheep
Crossing
Trailhead

113

To Greer

West Fork Trail

West Fork Little Colorado River

MOUNT BALDY WILDERNESS

APACHE-SITGREAVES
NATIONAL FOREST

Mount Baldy

X 11,420 ft.

WHITE MOUNTAIN APACHE
INDIAN RESERVATION

Baldy Peak
11,403 ft.

5.4   Junction with East Fork Trail.
5.6   Saddle just north of Baldy Peak.
6.0   True unnamed summit.

The hike: This popular trail begins along the bank of the West Fork of the Little Colorado River and climbs through lovely blue spruce forest and alpine meadows. During the short summer

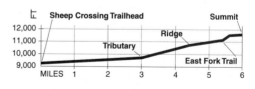

months, aster, fleabane, penstemon, cinquefoil, and iris bloom. There is evidence of past glacial activity; glacial erratics, large boulders deposited by flowing ice, lie along the valley floor.

Fishermen try their luck in West Fork which contains brook, rainbow, and cutthroat trout. About 3 miles in, the trail crosses a tributary to West Fork. In another 1.4 miles, the trail reaches the ridge leading to Baldy Peak. The

East Fork Trail joins the route 0.6 mile from the peak. This is an alternate way back down the mountain, but it will put you about 4 miles from where you left your vehicle.

As you near Baldy Peak, you are treated to spectacular vistas of the White Mountain region. Within 0.3 mile of Baldy Peak, you reach the White Mountain Apache Reservation Boundary. The Apaches have closed the last section of trail that ascends Baldy Peak. Trespassers have had their packs confiscated and have been fined for trying to sneak to the top of Baldy.

For "summit baggers" though, all is not lost. Study the topo map closely, and you will see that the highest part of the ridge is not the conical summit of Baldy Peak (11,403 feet) but rather the unnamed area on Forest Service land to the north at about 11,420 feet.

—Stewart Aitchison

68 KP Creek

Description:	A backpack trip along the Mogollon Rim and alpine creeks in the Blue Range Primitive Area.
Location:	24 miles south of Alpine.
Type of hike:	Loop backpack.
Difficulty:	Difficult.
Total distance:	20.6 miles.
Elevation change:	2,620 feet.
Water:	Grant Creek, KP Creek, seasonally at Willow and Mud Springs.
Best months:	May–October.
Maps:	Strayhorse, Hannagan Meadow, and Bear Mountain USGS; Blue Range Primitive Area.
Permit:	None.
For more information:	Apache-Sitgreaves National Forest, Alpine Ranger District.

Finding the trailhead: From Alpine, drive 24 miles south on U.S. 191, past Hannagan Meadow, then turn left into the KP Rim Trailhead.

Key points:
- 0.0 KP Rim Trailhead.
- 2.0 Turn left on Trail 73.
- 3.8 Grant Creek.
- 5.0 Turn right on Trail 76.
- 8.3 P Bar Lake; turn right on Trail 75.
- 9.3 Turn right on Trail 306.
- 10.2 Grant Creek and Trails 305 and 65; turn left on Trail 65.
- 10.7 Turn right on Trail 74.
- 10.9 Moonshine Park.
- 12.3 Steeple Creek; turn left on Trail 73.
- 12.8 Turn right on Trail 70.

KP Creek

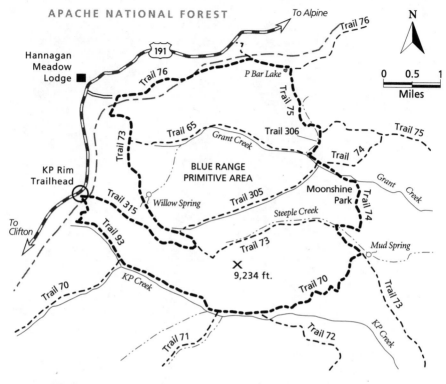

APACHE NATIONAL FOREST

To Alpine

Trail 76

191

N

Hannagan
Meadow
Lodge ■

Trail 76

P Bar Lake

Trail 75

0   0.5   1

Miles

Trail 73

Trail 65

Grant Creek

Trail 306

Trail 75

KP Rim
Trailhead

BLUE RANGE
PRIMITIVE AREA

Trail 74

Grant Creek

To
Clifton

Trail 315

Willow Spring

Trail 305

Moonshine
Park

Trail 74

Steeple Creek

Mud Spring

Trail 93

Trail 73

×
9,234 ft.

Trail 70

Trail 73

Trail 70

KP Creek

Trail 71

Trail 72

KP Creek

15.8   KP Creek and Trail 72.
16.5   Trail 71.
18.5   Turn right on Trail 93.
20.0   Mogollon Rim.
20.6   KP Rim Trailhead.

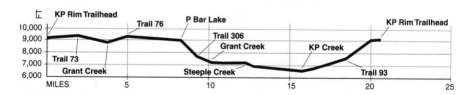

The hike: Start the loop hike on Trail 315, which heads east along the north rim of KP Creek. (Trail 93, which comes in from the south, will be our return.) Although the trail closely follows the rim of the deep canyon containing KP Creek, views are limited in the dense spruce-fir-aspen forest. At 2.0 miles, turn left on Trail 73. A short descent to the northwest leads through a meadow at the head of an unnamed tributary of Grant Creek. After a short climb to a saddle, the trail turns more to the north and crosses two more tributaries; the second of these contains another nice meadow and Willow Spring. The trail drops down another tributary, crosses Grant Creek at 3.8

Falls along KP Creek, Blue Range Primitive Area.

miles, and then climbs out via a tributary to the north. After the trail regains the Mogollon Rim at 5.0 miles, turn right on Trail 76.

This trail works its way east along the forested ridge south of Hannagan Creek, passing Trail 326 (a short spur to Arizona 191), and then meeting Trail 75 at P Bar Lake, at 8.3 miles. Turn right on Trail 75 and follow it down a steep descent in a side canyon to the south. The descent moderates at 9.3 miles; turn right on Trail 306 and follow it south and down to Grant Creek. Notice how ponderosa pines are now the dominant trees, at this lower and drier elevation.

Here at 10.2 miles, Trail 65 heads up Grant Creek, and Trail 305 goes up an unnamed tributary, but our route turns left on Trail 65. This trail follows Grant Creek downstream for 0.5 mile to Trail 74; turn right and follow this trail southeast past Moonshine Park and then west into Steeple Creek at 12.3 miles. Turn left here on Trail 73, which descends southeast along Steeple Creek to Mud Spring at 12.8 miles. Now turn right on Trail 70, which contours southwest into KP Creek. This southeast-facing slope at just under 7,000 feet is quite a bit warmer and drier than the depths of Steeple Creek canyon that we just left.

At 15.8 miles, the trail crosses the creek and passes Trail 72. Continue west up KP Creek past Trail 71. KP Creek is a beautiful alpine stream set in a forested, 2,000-foot-deep canyon, and the climb is steady but not too steep. At 18.5 miles, stay right on Trail 93. You may want to make a side trip of about 100 yards on Trail 71 to a small waterfall on KP Creek.

The grade steepens as Trail 93 climbs up an unnamed tributary of KP Creek and turns more to the northwest. A couple of switchbacks lead to the top of the ascent at 20.0 miles. Now the trail follows the rim northwest 0.6 mile to KP Rim Trailhead.

—Bruce Grubbs

69 Bear Mountain

Description: A fine backpack trip through two scenic canyons and along a portion of the Mogollon Rim in the Blue Range Primitive Area.

Location: 23 miles south of Alpine.

Type of hike: Loop backpack.

Difficulty: Moderate.

Total distance: 15.5 miles.

Elevation change: 2,300 feet.

Water: Seasonally in lower Lanphier Canyon and at Cashier, Maple, and Dutch Oven Springs.

Best months: May–November.

Maps: Bear Mountain, Blue USGS, Apache-Sitgreaves National Forest.

Permit: None.

For more information: Apache-Sitgreaves National Forest, Alpine and Clifton Ranger Districts.

Finding the trailhead: From Alpine, drive about 2 miles east on U.S. 180, then turn south on Forest Road 281. Continue about 21 miles to the Largo Creek–Lanphier Creek Trailhead at the Blue Administrative Site.

Key points:

0.0 Largo Creek–Lanphier Creek Trailhead.
0.7 Largo Creek Trail; stay left.
3.1 Trail leaves Lanphier Creek.
4.5 Trail rejoins the creek.
5.4 Turn right onto Forest Trail 55.
7.6 Campbell Flat; turn right onto Forest Trail 54.
10.3 Turn right onto the Largo Creek Trail.
12.3 Maple Spring.
14.9 Lanphier Creek Trail joins from the right.
15.5 Largo Creek–Lanphier Creek Trailhead.

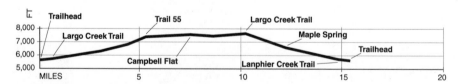

The hike: Many of the trails in the Blue Range Primitive Area are faint and little used. They are shown accurately on the USGS topo maps; you should have these maps and be comfortable with map reading and route finding before attempting this hike.

The trail first crosses the Blue River—like most rivers in Arizona, it's creek-size except when flooding—and skirts some private land before heading up Lanphier Canyon. For a while, the trail stays a short distance above the creek; where it descends to meet the creek, you'll pass the junction with the Largo

Bear Mountain

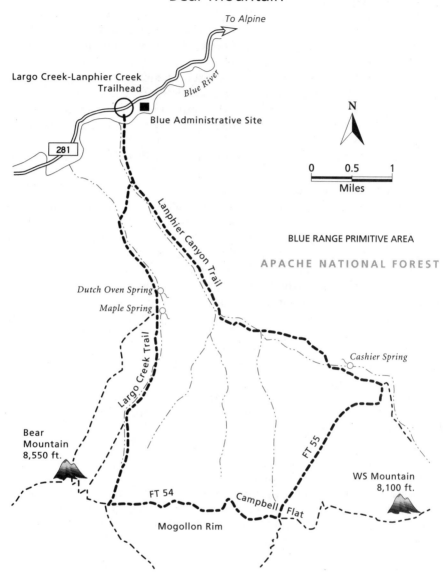

Creek Trail. This is our return route, but for now, stay left. The trail stays close to the creek as the canyon climbs gradually south-southeast through ponderosa pine and Gambel oak forest. There is usually water in the creek. During late summer, water can be a problem on the southern part of this loop, so keep your bottles full.

Where the creek turns east, the trail leaves the creek side and climbs steeply onto a bench, where it parallels the creek for about a mile. At the point where the trail again descends to meet the creek, there is limited camping. A short distance upstream, the trail passes Cashier Spring and climbs out of the canyon to the southeast. After climbing over a low ridge, it meets Forest Trail 55, where you'll turn right.

This trail heads generally southwest, first climbing a short tributary of Lanphier Creek before swinging around a ridge and climbing over a broad saddle. Open pine forest offers plenty of camping, but there is no water. At Campbell Flat, where the trail reaches the Mogollon Rim, turn right on Forest Trail 54. Burned trees in this area attest to the many wildfires that have burned in the Blue Range. At present, most lightning-caused fires are considered natural fires, and are allowed to burn under close monitoring. If you hike the Blue Range in late summer, you may see smoke from some of these fires.

Forest Trail 54 heads west along the Mogollon Rim. It climbs over several low hills and dips through several broad saddles before reaching the Largo Creek Trail at the base of Bear Mountain. By continuing straight ahead you can do a short and easy side trip to the top of Bear Mountain. A fire lookout here is manned during periods of high fire danger. There's plenty of camping in the saddle and to the north, and possible water at an unnamed spring about 0.5 mile north.

Back at the trail junction, continue the loop by turning right (north) on the Largo Creek Trail, which heads down the gentle headwaters of this drainage. After a mile or so the drainage starts to deepen into a canyon, and fir trees are mixed with the pines on the north-facing slopes. At Maple Spring, the Telephone Ridge Trail joins from the left, and there are several campsites in the area between Maple and Dutch Oven Springs. Below the springs, the trail follows the creek for a while, and then leaves it to the east, climbs over a ridge, and drops into Lanphier Creek, completing the loop. Turn left here on the Lanphier Creek Trail, and return to the trailhead.

The U.S. Forest Service, which led the way in protecting roadless areas administratively, designated the Blue Range as a Primitive Area. Under the Wilderness Act of 1964, many primitive areas were protected as permanent wilderness areas. Since that time, the remaining primitive areas have been added to the National Wilderness System, until only the Blue Range Primitive Area remains. Even the portion of the primitive area lying in New Mexico is now the Blue Range Wilderness. Conservation groups are showing renewed interest in wilderness area protection, and perhaps this time the Blue Range will be protected. The area certainly deserves wilderness status.

—Bruce Grubbs

70 Bear Wallow Trail

Description: An overnight backpack into the Bear
Wallow Wilderness.
Location: 25 miles south of Alpine.
Type of hike: Out-and-back backpack.
Difficulty: Moderate.
Total distance: 15.2 miles.
Elevation change: 2,050 feet.
Water: Bear Wallow Creek; purify before using.
Best months: June–October.
Maps: Hoodoo Knob, Baldy Bill Point USGS; Apache-
Sitgreaves National Forest.
Permit: None.
For more information: Apache-Sitgreaves National Forest, Alpine
Ranger District.

Finding the trailhead: From Hannagan Meadow, drive about 6 miles south
on U.S. 191 and turn right (west) onto Forest Road 25. Go another 3.3 miles
to the signed trailhead on your left. Park here.

Key points:
0.0 Trailhead.
1.3 North Fork Bear Wallow Creek.
2.5 Junction with Reno Trail.
3.4 Junction with main Bear Wallow Creek.
7.1 Junction with Gobbler Point Trail.
7.6 San Carlos Apache Indian Reservation.

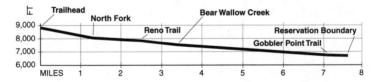

The hike: The Bear Wallow Trail starts directly behind the trailhead sign following a shallow drainage. Don't take the old logging road (Forest Road 8316)
running to your left. The trail is a bit gullied and can be muddy but is fairly
easy walking. In about a mile you will intersect with the North Fork of Bear
Wallow Creek. The creek meanders and splashes its way through virgin old-
growth forest of Douglas fir, spruce, and ponderosa pine. Along the trail grow
wild strawberries, wild geraniums, New Mexican locust, limber pine, and poison ivy—beware. Red squirrels and chipmunks are common.

At mile 2.5 the trail meets the Reno Trail (#62) and at 7.1 meets the Gobbler Point Trail (#59). At about mile 7.6, a fence marks the National Forest
boundary with the San Carlos Apache Indian Reservation. To go any farther
downstream requires a permit from the Apaches.

Mogollon Rim, Bear Wallow Wilderness.

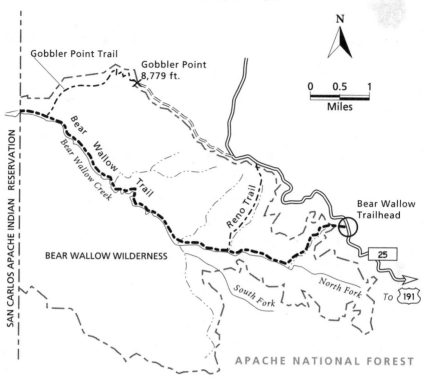

Bear Wallow is one of the few creeks in Arizona where native Apache trout have been reintroduced. This trout was almost wiped out by overfishing, the introduction of nonnative fish, and dam projects.

In 1884, rancher Pete Slaughter drove cattle into this valley and reported seeing numerous bear wallows along the creek where bruins had come to ward off pesky flies. Black bears still roam the area, as do elk, mule deer, and mountain lion. Also, the howl of a Mexican wolf might break the evening quiet. In 1998 Mexican wolves were released into the Apache-Sitgreaves National Forest after having been eliminated from Arizona by 1970.

—Stewart Aitchison

Phoenix Area

The sprawling city of Phoenix lies in the Sonoran Desert. Parks within the city and desert mountains surrounding Phoenix offer a variety of hikes. Summers can be brutally hot, so hikes at that time of year are usually limited to early morning jaunts.

71 Cave Creek Trail

Description:	A desert day hike along a flowing stream.
Location:	About 12 miles north of Carefree.
Type of hike:	Loop day hike.
Difficulty:	Moderate.
Total distance:	About 10 miles.
Elevation change:	1,040 feet.
Water:	Cave Creek; purify before drinking.
Best months:	All year.
Maps:	New River Mesa, Humboldt Mountain USGS; Tonto National Forest.
Permit:	Parking fee at Cave Creek Trailhead.
For more information:	Tonto National Forest, Cave Creek Ranger District.

Finding the trailhead: From Carefree, drive east on the Cave Creek Road until it becomes Forest Road 24. Drive 9 miles, past the Seven Springs and CCC campgrounds. Cross the creek twice to the Cave Creek trailhead parking area.

Key points:
- 0.0   Trailhead.
- 4.0   Junction with Skunk Creek Trail.
- 6.75 High point on trail.
- 9.0   Junction with Forest Trail 247.
- 10.0 Trailhead.

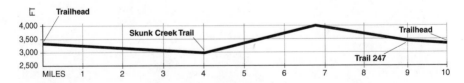

The hike: Start on the easy Cave Creek Trail (Forest Trail 4). The trail follows the creek, crossing it a few times. After about 4 miles, turn left onto the Skunk Creek Trail. A steep 1,000-foot climb over the next 1.5 miles will make you break into a sweat. After another 5 miles, turn left onto Forest Trail 247, an old mining road, to return to the trailhead.

Cave Creek Trail

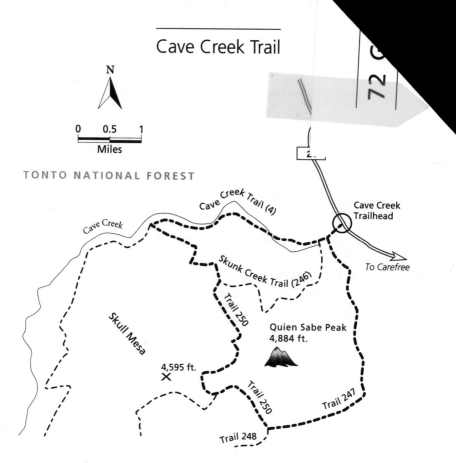

N

0 0.5 1
Miles

TONTO NATIONAL FOREST

Cave Creek Trail (4)

Cave Creek

Cave Creek Trailhead

To Carefree

Skunk Creek Trail (246)

Trail 250

Skull Mesa

Quien Sabe Peak
4,884 ft.

4,595 ft.
X

Trail 250

Trail 247

Trail 248

Along Cave Creek is a lovely riparian habitat with Fremont cotton-woods, ash, alder, walnut, and Arizona sycamores. This is a great birding area, especially in late spring and early summer. Once you leave the creek, the route enters typical Sonoran desert. Saguaro, cholla, ocatillo, and palo verde are common.

On your way to the trailhead, just inside the forest boundary, is a half-mile side trip to Sears-Kay Ruin, the remains of a thousand-year-old Hohokam settlement. A self-guided tour includes signs explaining the site.

—Stewart Aitchison

Description:	A gorgeous loop through the desert north of Phoenix.
Location:	Immediately west of Cave Creek.
Type of hike:	Loop day hike.
Difficulty:	Easy.
Total distance:	4.8 miles.
Elevation change:	300 feet.
Water:	None.
Best months:	October–April.
Maps:	Cave Creek USGS.
Permit:	Park entrance fee must be paid.
For more information:	Maricopa County Parks and Recreation.

Finding the trailhead: From I-17, drive east on the Carefree Highway to 32nd Street. Turn north and go into the Cave Creek Recreation Area. Pass

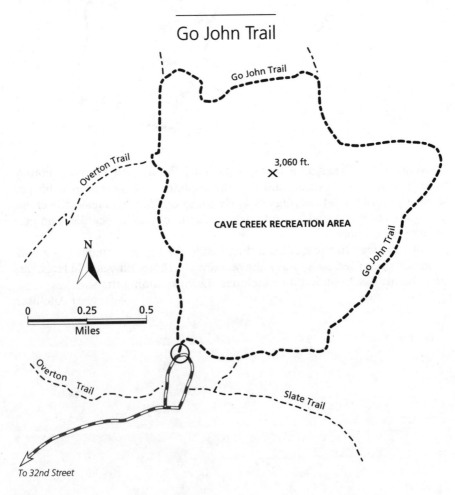

Go John Trail

the horse rental and picnic areas and then turn left at the second trailhead sign. The Go John Trail is signed.

Key points:
   0.0   Trailhead.
   4.8   Trailhead.

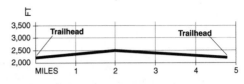

The hike: This pleasant loop gives hikers a good introduction to the Sonoran Desert. The abundance and diversity of plant life surprise most first-time visitors. One factor that allows the Sonoran Desert to contain so many different kinds of plants—from cacti and wildflowers to small trees and shrubs—is that there are two rainy seasons. Certain plants tend to utilize the winter moisture, while other species rely upon the summer rains. Thus, not every plant is competing all the time with its neighbor for the precious rare fluid.

—Stewart Aitchison

73 Lookout Mountain

           Description: A loop hike in the Sonoran Desert.
              Location: North Phoenix.
         Type of hike: Loop day hike.
           Difficulty: Easy.
     Total distance: 2.6 miles.
 Elevation change: 40 feet on main trail; 474 feet to summit of
                               Lookout Mountain.
               Water: None.
      Best months: October–April.
              Maps: Union Hills, Sunnyslope USGS.
            Permit: None.
For more information: Phoenix Parks and Recreation.

Finding the trailhead: From Bell Road, drive south about 1 mile on 16th Street to the Lookout Mountain Park entrance. The trailhead is at the parking area.

Key points:
   0.0   Trailhead.
   0.12 Junction with Summit Trail.
   2.6   Trailhead.

The hike: The Circumference Trail goes around Lookout Mountain. Start by going west (counterclockwise). In about 0.12 mile, the 0.6-mile Summit Trail climbs to the top of Lookout Mountain, providing a 360-degree view of the Valley of the Sun. The main trail continues for 2.5 miles to return to the trailhead.

Lookout Mountain

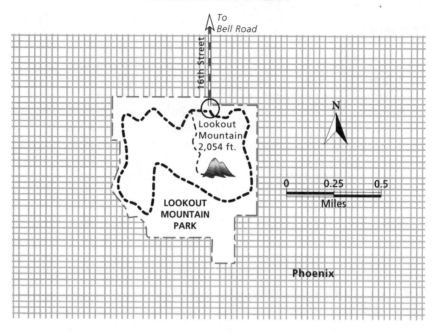

Although this park is in the heart of suburbia, it's not unusual to see a coyote or some of the typical desert birds such as roadrunners and Gila woodpeckers.

—Stewart Aitchison

74 Cholla Trail

Description:	A short hike on Camelback Mountain.
Location:	On the Phoenix-Scottsdale border.
Type of hike:	Out-and-back day hike.
Difficulty:	Easy.
Total distance:	1.5 miles.
Elevation change:	1,264 feet.
Water:	None.
Best months:	October–April.
Maps:	Paradise Valley USGS.
Permit:	None.
For more information:	Phoenix Parks and Recreation.

Finding the trailhead: From Camelback Road, turn north onto 64th Street (Invergordon Road). Drive about 0.75 mile and turn left onto Cholla Lane. There is no official parking lot. Park where you can, but watch out for no-parking areas.

Cholla Trail

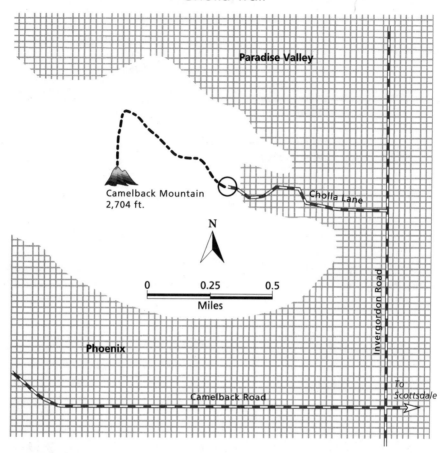

Paradise Valley

Camelback Mountain
2,704 ft.

N

Cholla Lane

Invergordon Road

0   0.25   0.5
Miles

Phoenix

Camelback Road

To
Scottsdale

Key points:
  0.0   Trailhead.
  0.75 Ridge top.

Trailhead
4,000
3,000
2,000
1,000
Ridge top

The hike: The well-marked Cholla Trail begins at the west end of Cholla Lane and climbs steeply along a ridge. Near the top, you must scramble over rocks. There are great views of the Valley of the Sun, including a peek into the "backyard" of the Phoenix Resort.

—Stewart Aitchison

75 Pass Mountain Trail

Description:	This trail loops through the western Goldfield Mountains northeast of Mesa. It offers a fine sense of remoteness, considering its location near the greater Phoenix area.
Location:	Mesa.
Type of hike:	Loop day hike.
Difficulty:	Moderate.
Total distance:	7.1 miles.
Elevation change:	580 feet.
Water:	None.
Best months:	October–April.
Maps:	Apache Junction USGS; Usery Mountain Recreation Area map, Tonto National Forest.
Permit:	None.
For more information:	Usery Mountain Recreation Area.

Finding the trailhead: From Mesa, go north on Ellsworth Road, which becomes Usery Pass Road. Turn right at the recreation area entrance and go to the horse staging area, which is the trailhead.

The bite of the giant desert centipede is painful but otherwise is not a serious injury. The tip of each of the centipede's forty-two legs is equipped with a sharp claw which may make tiny punctures, but a double pair of jaws under the head do the actual biting. Unless you make a habit of putting your bare hand under rocks or into crevices, you are unlikely to be bitten.

Pass Mountain Trail

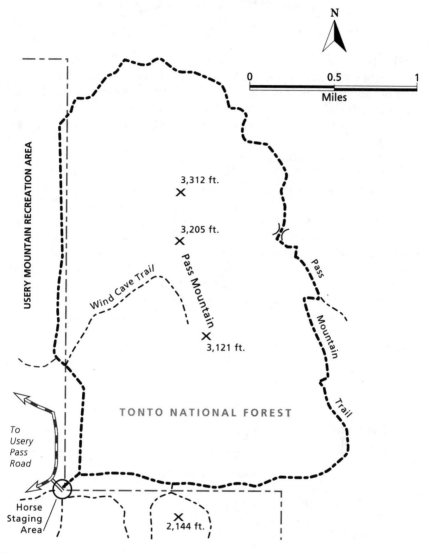

Key points:

- 0.0   Horse staging area.
- 0.7   Stay left at the junction with the Wind Cave Trail.
- 2.3   Tonto National Forest boundary.
- 4.4   Pass.
- 4.6   Old trail forks left; stay right, on the new trail.
- 6.1   Stay right at an unsigned trail junction.
- 7.1   Stay right at the junction with the Cat Peaks Trail.
- 7.6   Turn left to return to the trailhead.
- 7.7   Horse staging area.

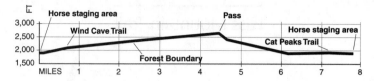

The hike: From the horse staging area, head east on the Pass Mountain Trail. After a couple of hundred yards, turn left at a T intersection to start the loop portion of the hike. The trail wanders north along the east side of the park facilities. After passing a final ramada and parking area, you'll pass the Wind Cave Trail; stay left. The trail works its way north along the west slopes of Pass Mountain.

At 2.3 miles, a fence marks the boundary of the Tonto National Forest, and the trail climbs gradually around the north side of the mountain. As it crosses a ridge, the remainder of the Goldfield Mountains becomes visible to the northeast, and beyond, the distinctive summits of Four Peaks. Continuing to climb, the trail turns south into a canyon, and climbs to a pass. This spot is the high point of the hike. With the bulk of Pass Mountain hiding the metropolitan area to the southwest, this saddle is a wild and rugged spot.

The descent is eroded and steep at first, but then a newer trail branches right and continues the descent at a more gradual rate. As you reach the mouth of the canyon and the southern foothills, the trail starts to swing west along the base of the mountain. Ignore an unsigned trail branching left, and stay right at the junction with the Cat Peaks Trail. When you reach the T intersection near the horse staging area, turn left to return to the trailhead.

—Bruce Grubbs

76 Mayors Loop Trail

Description:	An easy hike in the Sonoran Desert.
Location:	About 25 miles west of Phoenix.
Type of hike:	Loop day hike.
Difficulty:	Easy.
Total distance:	1.75 miles.
Elevation change:	200 feet.
Water:	None.
Best months:	October–April.
Maps:	Perryville, Tolleson, Avondale SE, Avondale SW USGS.
Permit:	Entrance fee must be paid at Estrella Mountain Regional Park.
For more information:	Maricopa County Parks and Recreation.

Finding the trailhead: From Phoenix, drive west on I–10 about 25 miles to the Estrella Parkway exit. Go south 7 miles then turn left onto Vineyard Avenue. Go about 2.5 miles to the Estrella Mountain Regional Park

Mayors Loop Trail

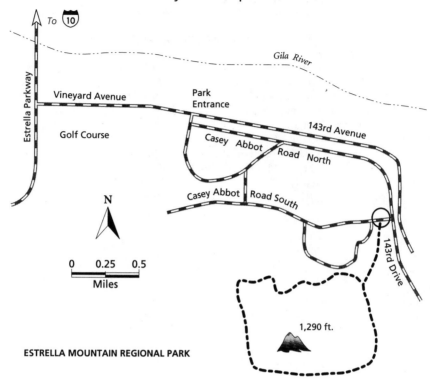

ESTRELLA MOUNTAIN REGIONAL PARK

entrance. Follow Casey Abbott Road South past the amphitheater to the trailhead parking area. The trailhead is signed.

Key points:
    0.0   Trailhead.
    1.75 Trailhead.

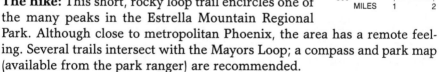

The hike: This short, rocky loop trail encircles one of the many peaks in the Estrella Mountain Regional Park. Although close to metropolitan Phoenix, the area has a remote feeling. Several trails intersect with the Mayors Loop; a compass and park map (available from the park ranger) are recommended.

This short hike is a good introduction to the flora and fauna of the Sonoran desert. Look for football-size cactus wren nests in the abundant cholla cacti. The nest's interior is accessible only through a small opening at one end. At 8 to 9 inches in length, the cactus wren is North America's largest wren. Unlike most birds, this wren can be heard singing year-round.

—Stewart Aitchison

77 Quartz Peak Trail

Description:	A rugged hike in the seldom-visited Sierra Estrella Wilderness.
Location:	20 miles south of Phoenix.
Type of hike:	Out-and-back day hike.
Difficulty:	Difficult.
Total distance:	6 miles.
Elevation change:	2,502 feet.
Water:	None.
Best months:	October–April.
Maps:	Montezuma Peak USGS.
Permit:	None.
For more information:	Lower Gila Resource Area Bureau of Land Management.

Finding the trailhead: Although distinguished as one of the closest wilderness areas to metropolitan Phoenix, four-wheel-drive vehicles are required when approaching the wilderness boundary. Primitive dirt roads near the boundary are extremely sandy or silty, and wash crossings are rugged and deep. Take Interstate 10 to exit 126 and travel 8.3 miles south to Elliot Road. Turn right and go 2.6 miles to Rainbow Valley Road. Turn left and drive 9.3 miles south until the pavement ends. Turn left onto the Riggs Road, continue 4 miles to an intersection, but go straight another 5.3 miles to a power line road. Turn right and drive 1.9 miles to a road to the left. Take it 1.9 miles east to the Quartz Peak Trailhead. Some lands around and within the wilderness are not federally administered. Please respect the property rights of the owners and do not cross or use these lands without their permission.

Key points:

   0.0   Trailhead.

   3.0   Quartz Peak.

The hike: Quartz Peak Trail, in the 14,400-acre Sierra Estrella Wilderness, leads visitors from the floor of Rainbow Valley (elevation 1,550 feet) to the summit ridge of the Sierra Estrella at Quartz Peak (elevation 4,052 feet) in just 3 miles. The trail is extremely steep and difficult to follow in places. This is a hike for experienced and well-conditioned hikers only!

From the Quartz Peak Trailhead, follow a closed four-wheel-drive track approximately 0.25 mile. Look to the left as you walk up the old road to find a narrow trail ascending the ridge to the north. The trail is poorly marked in places and does not extend to the summit; the final 0.25 mile to Quartz Peak is a scramble over boulder and talus slopes that requires careful footing. Quartz Peak is a point on the spine of the Sierra Estrella capped by an outcrop of white quartz.

Saguaro cactus in the Sierra Estrella Wilderness.

Quartz Peak Trail

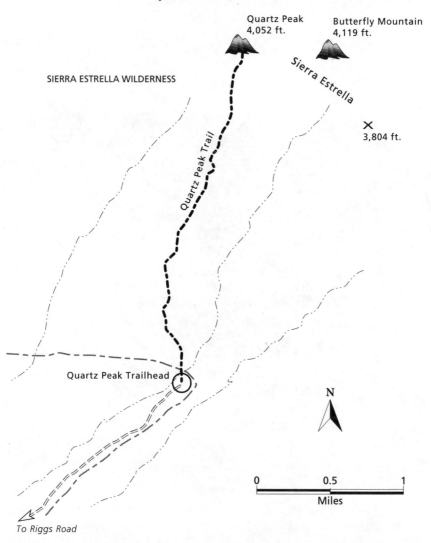

Along the way, visitors are treated to a variety of Sonoran desert plants and wildlife, scenic vistas, and evidence of the area's volcanic history. The views from the summit are spectacular; to the west is a dramatic panorama of rugged mountain ranges and desert plains and to the east metropolitan Phoenix unfolds over the valley of the lower Salt River.

—Stewart Aitchison

78 Margies Cove Trail

Description:	This hike wanders across Sonoran desert plains and into a scenic canyon in the North Maricopa Mountains Wilderness.
Location:	55 miles southwest of Phoenix.
Type of hike:	Out-and-back day hike.
Difficulty:	Moderate.
Total distance:	9.0 miles.
Elevation change:	700 feet.
Water:	None.
Best months:	October–March.
Maps:	Cotton Center SE USGS.
Permit:	None.
For more information:	Phoenix Field Office, Bureau of Land Management.

Finding the trailhead: From Phoenix, drive about 30 miles west on I-10, then turn south on Arizona 85. Continue about 20 miles, and then turn left (east) on an obscure, unmarked dirt road at an old corral. This road is unmaintained but should be passable to most vehicles if driven with care. Go through a wire gate at 3.3 miles, and at 4.0 miles turn right (south) on an unmarked road. The road ends at 5.2 miles at the Margies Cove North Trailhead.

Key points:
- 0.0 West Trailhead.
- 5.7 Brittlebush Trail.
- 9.0 East Trailhead.

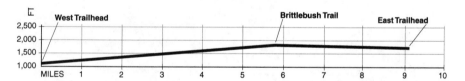

The hike: Starting from the Margies Cove North Trailhead, the trail follows a closed road and meanders up the broad, gently sloping valley. You'll pass an old windmill site in the first half mile. Gradually the mountains close in on either side. After about 3.1 miles, the trail starts following a gravelly wash as the old road veers away. Watch for rock cairns and BLM trail markers along this section. The rugged peaks and canyon walls add to the wilderness atmosphere. At 5.7 miles, you'll pass The Brittlebush Trail, which heads right (south). Our hike ends at the East Trailhead about 9.0 miles from the trailhead.

The North Maricopa Mountains are a jumble of long ridges and isolated peaks separated by extensive saguaro-studded bajadas and wide desert washes. Cholla, ocotillo, prickly pear, palo verde, ironwood, and Mexican

Cholla cactus in the Maricopa Mountains—it looks cuddly, but it's not.

Margies Cove Trail

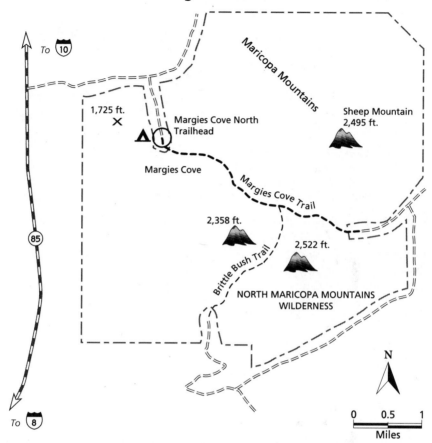

jumping bean complement the thick stands of saguaro to form classic Sonoran desert vistas. Commonly seen wildlife includes desert mule deer, javelina, desert bighorn sheep, coyote, desert tortoise, and numerous varieties of lizards and birds.

A segment of the 1850s Butterfield Stageline runs along the southern boundary of the wilderness. This stageline was the first reliable, relatively fast method of transportation between the eastern United States and California. The stage carried people, mail, and freight more than 2,700 miles in less than 25 days. In its three-year history, the stage boasted that it was late only three times.

—Bruce Grubbs and Stewart Aitchison

79 Table Top Trail

Description:	A great winter hike, this trail takes you to the top of Table Top Mountain through lush Sonoran desert.
Location:	104 miles south of Phoenix.
Type of hike:	Out-and-back day hike.
Difficulty:	Moderate.
Total distance:	7.0 miles.
Elevation change:	2,050 feet.
Water:	None.
Best months:	October–March.
Maps:	Little Table Top USGS.
Permit:	None.
For more information:	Phoenix Field Office, Bureau of Land Management.

Finding the trailhead: From Phoenix, go south about 50 miles on I-10, then turn west on I-8. Go west about 38 miles; exit at Vekol Road (exit 144). Turn south on the maintained gravel road. The maintenance ends 1.9 miles from I-8; bear right here, at the turnoff to Vekol Ranch. The rest of the road is seldom maintained; use caution for washouts, loose sand, and rocks. A high-clearance vehicle is recommended. Go straight at a fork 7.8 miles from I-8. Stay right at a fork 12.1 miles from the freeway. You'll reach the Lava Flow South Trailhead 14.9 miles from I-8. The road ends at the Table Top Trailhead at 15.7 miles. The trailhead has a small campground and day-use parking, but no water.

Key points:

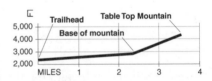

0.0   Table Top Trailhead.
2.3   Base of mountain.
3.5   Table Top Mountain.

The hike: A pleasant stroll through magnificent saguaro forest starts the hike. This section wanders up a gentle valley between rugged low hills. After crossing a dry wash, the trail follows a gentle ridge with good views of the surrounding mountains. Although the surrounding hills are covered with basalt boulders, the rock underfoot is schist. The trail crosses another wash, the rock underfoot becomes granite, and the climb becomes steeper. As the trail approaches the base of the mountain, it becomes steeper yet. It swings right and crosses two ravines, which show plain evidence of massive flooding from some past storm. Switchbacks lead up the steep southwest slopes of the mountain.

Near the summit, the trail is briefly bordered by 3- to 4-foot-high stone walls. Although the construction was skillfully done, the origin and purpose of these structures is unknown. A final meander up a ridge leads to the end of the trail. Notice that there are no saguaros on the summit plateau. Saguaros can't stand prolonged frost; the climate at the top of the mountain is evidently a little too cool for them. The summit supports an unusual forty-acre

Table Top Wilderness.

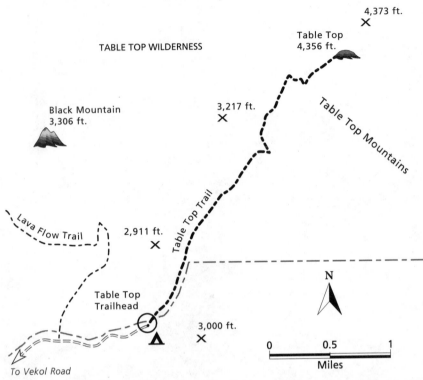

island of desert grassland, where the rare Gila spotted whiptail lizard or Ajo mountain whipsnake may be encountered.

The view is open in all directions except the northeast, where the summit plateau blocks it. The Bradshaw Mountains are visible to the north and the Santa Catalina and Santa Rita mountains to the southeast. The distinctive square tower of Baboquivari Peak is obvious to the south, and the bulk of Harquahala Mountain is visible to the distant northwest.

Visitors may see Cooper's hawk, red-tailed hawk, prairie falcon, Gambel's quail, or turkey vultures. Mule deer, javelina, desert bighorn sheep, coyote, and antelope jackrabbits are also present within this 43,400-acre wilderness.

—Bruce Grubbs and Stewart Aitchison

Tucson Area

Like Phoenix, the city of Tucson lies within the Sonoran Desert. High mountains to the north and east allow summer hiking. The lower foothills and valley are pleasant in winter. The Tucson area offers varied and year-round hiking experiences.

80 Hunter Trail

Description:	A fascinating hike to the top of Picacho Peak.
Location:	50 miles north of Tucson.
Type of hike:	Out-and-back day hike.
Difficulty:	Moderate.
Total distance:	4 miles.
Elevation change:	1,370 feet.
Water:	None.
Best months:	October–April.
Maps:	Newman Peak USGS.
Permit:	No permit, but there is a park entrance fee.
For more information:	Arizona State Parks.

Finding the trailhead: From Tucson, drive 50 miles north on I–10 to the well-marked exit for the Picacho Peak State Park. The trailhead is located in the southwest corner of the park's Barrett Loop, near the Saguaro Ramada.

Key points:

0.0	Trailhead.
1.8	Main Saddle.
2.0	Picacho Peak.

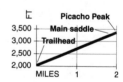

The hike: Rising 1,500 vertical feet above the surrounding desert floor, 3,374-foot Picacho Peak is an isolated 22-million-year-old volcanic mountain situated midway between the Gila River and Tucson. This is the site of Arizona's only Civil War battle. The "Battle of Picacho Pass" took place on April 15, 1862, lasted about an hour and a half, and cost the lives of four "Johnny Rebs" and three "Yanks." Petroglyphs abound in the area, testifying that the prehistoric Hohokam were here long before the white man.

In 1933, the Civilian Conservation Corps built a trail to the summit that now sees 10,000 or more hikers a year. In the early 1970s, an Explorer Scout Troop constructed a new trail to replace the lower half of the original CCC trail. Frequent trail signs and steel-cable handrails show the way over the eastern headwall to the main saddle. From the saddle, railroad-tie wooden

Hunter Trail

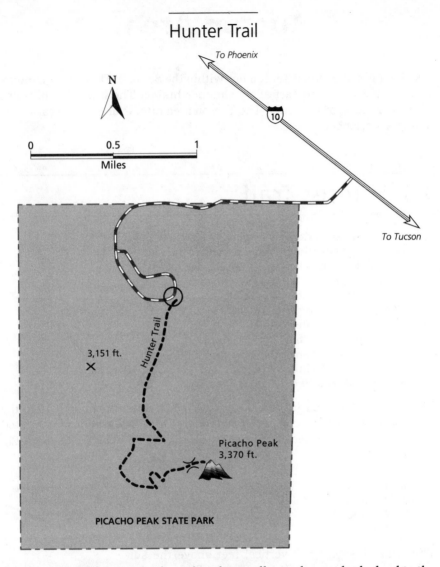

To Phoenix

N

0   0.5   1
Miles

To Tucson

Hunter Trail

3,151 ft.
×

Picacho Peak
3,370 ft.

PICACHO PEAK STATE PARK

steps, steel cables, wire-mesh-enclosed catwalks, and gangplanks lead to the summit. On a clear day, there are 100-mile views in all directions. Unfortunately, with each passing year, there is less of the natural desert landscape and more urban development surrounding the park.

—Stewart Aitchison

81 Wilderness of Rocks

Description: A hike through cool pine-fir forest to the edge of the
Wilderness of Rocks in the Santa Catalina Mountains
and the Pusch Ridge Wilderness.
Location: About 32 miles north of Tucson.
Type of hike: Loop day hike.
Difficulty: Easy.
Total distance: 3.2 miles.
Elevation change: 660 feet.
Water: None.
Best months: May–October.
Maps: Mount Lemmon USGS; Pusch Ridge
Wilderness USFS.
Permit: None.
For more information: Coronado National Forest, Santa Catalina
Ranger District.

Finding the trailhead: From I-10 in Tucson, exit at Grant Road, then drive
8.5 miles east. Turn left on Tanque Verde Road, go 3.2 miles, then turn left
onto Catalina Highway, which becomes General Hitchcock Highway (Forest Road 833) as it starts up the Santa Catalina Mountains. (There is a recreation fee, payable at the entrance station.) Continue about 32 miles, and then
turn left on Forest Road 10 into Summerhaven. Continue 1.4 miles south on
the main road, Forest Road 10, through Summerhaven to its end at the Marshall Gulch Trailhead.

Key points:

0.0   Marshall Gulch Trailhead.
1.2   Turn left on Aspen Trail.
3.2   Marshall Gulch Trailhead.

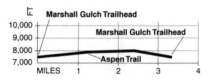

The hike: Start on the Marshall Gulch
Trail, which climbs west along the north
side of Marshall Gulch. This cool, shady ravine is densely forested with ponderosa pine, Douglas fir, and quaking aspen. At the head of the gulch, the
trail emerges onto broad pine-covered Marshall Saddle. Turn left here, at 1.2
miles, onto the Aspen Trail, which climbs gradually as it heads south along
the east slopes of Marshall Peak. At 1.7 miles, the trail passes through a broad
saddle and turns more easterly. You can leave the trail here and follow an
informal trail southwest to a rocky viewpoint overlooking the Wilderness

Wilderness of Rocks, Pusch Ridge Wilderness, Santa Catalina Mountains.

Wilderness of Rocks

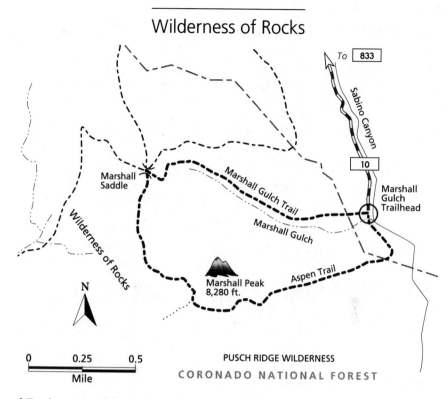

PUSCH RIDGE WILDERNESS

CORONADO NATIONAL FOREST

of Rocks, named for its granite outcrops. Back on the main trail, follow it east as it climbs gently for a half mile to the highest elevation of the hike, then descends rapidly east toward Sabino Canyon. It swings north and descends to the Marshall Gulch Trailhead, completing the loop.

—Bruce Grubbs

82 Butterfly Trail

Description:	A hike on the cool, northeast slopes of Mount Bigelow, in the Santa Catalina Mountains.
Location:	About 27 miles north of Tucson.
Type of hike:	Out-and-back or shuttle day hike.
Difficulty:	Moderate with a shuttle, difficult out and back.
Total distance:	5.2 miles one-way.
Elevation change:	1,700 feet.
Water:	Seasonal at Novio Spring.
Best months:	May–October.
Maps:	Mount Bigelow USGS; Pusch Ridge Wilderness USFS.
Permit:	None.
For more information:	Coronado National Forest, Santa Catalina Ranger District.

Finding the trailhead: From I–10 in Tucson, exit at Grant Road, then drive 8.5 miles east. Turn left on Tanque Verde Road, go 3.2 miles, then turn left onto Catalina Highway, which becomes General Hitchcock Highway (Forest Road 833) as it starts up the Santa Catalina Mountains. (There is a recreation fee, payable at the entrance station.) Continue about 27 miles to the Palisades Ranger Station. This is the end trailhead; leave a vehicle here if doing a shuttle. Drive another 2.9 miles to the Butterfly Trailhead, the start of the hike.

Key points:

0.0 Butterfly Trailhead.
1.3 Trail 17.
2.3 Novio Spring.
3.3 Ridge.
4.7 Bigelow-Kellogg Saddle.
5.2 Palisades Ranger Station.

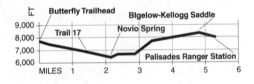

The hike: The Butterfly Trails starts out as an old jeep road, which descends rapidly to the north, but soon becomes a foot trail. Now the trail contours east, heads several drainages, then descends to the junction with Trail 17, southeast of Butterfly Peak, at 1.3 miles. Again the trail contours east, then descends sharply to the lowest elevation of the hike. There are seasonal waterfalls in the drainage below the trail. Novio Spring is located in a drainage near the trail, at 2.3 miles.

Now the trail swings north around the drainage, which is an unnamed tributary of Alder Creek. It then turns east again and starts to climb. Switchbacks lead south onto the north end of a ridge at 3.3 miles, and the climb moderates for a while. The trail climbs east across a north-facing slope, then swings south for the final climb to the Bigelow-Kellogg Saddle, at 4.7 miles. A gradual descent leads to the Palisades Ranger Station. If you didn't leave a vehicle here, return the way you came.

Butterfly Trail

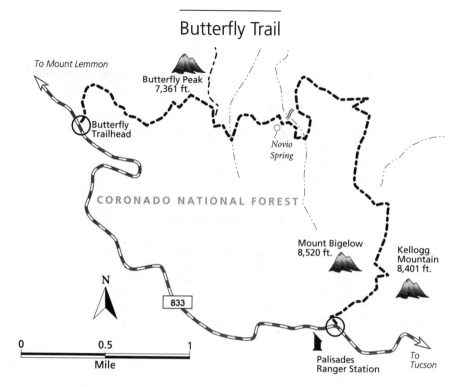

The north-facing slopes along the Butterfly Trail are mostly covered with a lush green pine–fir forest. As the trail crosses slopes with slightly different aspects, you can clearly see the effect of microclimates. West- and south-facing slopes are drier and warmer, and the tall trees give way to chaparral.

—Bruce Grubbs

83 Finger Rock Trail

Description:	A hike up a rugged, scenic canyon in the foothills of the Santa Catalina Mountains and the Pusch Ridge Wilderness.
Location:	Tucson.
Type of hike:	Out-and-back day hike or backpack.
Difficulty:	Difficult.
Total distance:	8.8 miles.
Elevation change:	4,150 feet.
Water:	Seasonal at Finger Rock Spring.
Best months:	October–November.
Maps:	Tucson North, Oro Valley USGS; Pusch Ridge Wilderness USFS.
Permit:	To protect bighorn sheep, no dogs are allowed at any time. Day hike group size limit is fifteen persons; overnight group size limit is six persons. From January 1 to April 30, no camping beyond 400 feet from system trails. No hiking on unofficial trails.
For more information:	Coronado National Forest, Santa Catalina Ranger District.

Finding the trailhead: From I–10, exit onto Orange Grove Road and go 6.7 miles east. Turn right on Skyline Road, and drive 1.8 miles. Turn left onto Alvernon Way, and continue 1.0 mile north to the end of the road and the Finger Rock Trailhead.

The Santa Catalina foothills are cut by numerous deep, rock canyons.

Finger Rock Trail

N

Mount Kimball
9,782 ft.

0   0.5   1
Mile

CORONADO NATIONAL FOREST

7,123 ft.
X

Finger Rock
6,425 ft.

Linda Vista Saddle

Finger Rock Canyon

Finger Rock Trail

PUSCH RIDGE WILDERNESS

Finger Rock Spring

Pontatoc Ridge

Finger Rock Trailhead

Alvernon Way

Tucson

To Skyline Road

Key points:

0.0   Finger Rock Trailhead.
0.9   Finger Rock Spring.
3.4   Spur trail to Linda
      Vista Saddle.
3.9   Turn left on Pima
      Canyon Trail.
4.2   Turn right on Mount
      Kimball Trail.
4.4   Mount Kimball.

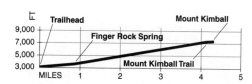

233

The hike: Start on the Finger Rock Trail, which heads north into the mouth of Finger Rock Canyon. The trail climbs gradually northeast up the canyon to Finger Rock Spring at 0.9 mile. The main trail turns right here and switchbacks up the slope to the east; it stays on this slope nearly all the way to the head of the canyon. It's a steep climb but worth it. As you ascend, the vegetation changes from saguaro-forested desert to pinyon pine–juniper forest. After about 3 miles, the trail swings east into a basin; watch for a spur trail that goes east to Linda Vista Saddle. This beautiful saddle with its sweeping view is a good destination for a shorter hike.

Continuing on the main trail, it climbs to a saddle at the head of Finger Rock Canyon, where it meets the Pima Canyon Trail at 3.9 miles. Turn left and follow this trail as it climbs onto the summit ridge of Mount Kimball. Turn right at 4.2 miles and continue 0.2 mile to the summit. It's been a long climb, but from this vantage point you can see much of the front range of the Santa Catalina.

—Bruce Grubbs

84 West Fork Sabino Canyon

Description:	A hike to fine pools in the Santa Catalina Mountains and the Pusch Ridge Wilderness.
Location:	Tucson.
Type of hike:	Out-and-back day hike.
Difficulty:	Moderate.
Total distance:	8.8 miles.
Elevation change:	1,000 feet.
Water:	Seasonal in Sabino Canyon and West Fork Sabino Canyon.
Best months:	October–November.
Maps:	Sabino Canyon, Mount Lemmon USGS; Pusch Ridge Wilderness USFS.
Permit:	None.
For more information:	Coronado National Forest, Santa Catalina Ranger District.

Finding the trailhead: From I-10 in Tucson, exit at Grant Road and go 8.5 miles east. Turn left on Tanque Verde Road, continue 0.5 mile, then turn left on Sabino Canyon Road and drive 4.4 miles to the Sabino Canyon Visitor Center. Take the Sabino Canyon Tram (fee) to the Sabino Canyon Trailhead.

Key points:

0.0	Sabino Canyon Trailhead.	2.2	Turn left on West Fork Trail.
0.4	Telephone Ridge Trail.	3.6	West Fork Sabino Canyon.
0.9	Saddle.	4.4	Pools.

West Fork Sabino Canyon

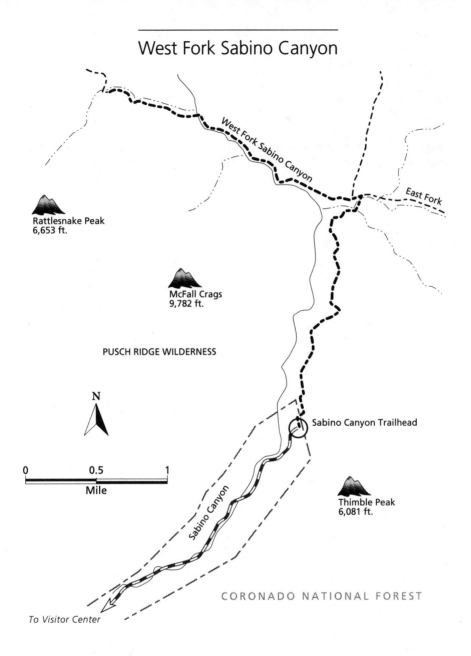

The hike: The Sabino Canyon Trail switchbacks up the slope east of Sabino Creek, then climbs more gradually. After passing through a saddle at 0.9 mile, the good trail contours along the east side of Sabino Canyon, well above the bed of the canyon. The trail crosses an unnamed drainage, and then meets the West Fork, East Fork, and Mount Lemmon Trails at 2.2 miles; turn left onto the West Fork Trail.

After crossing the East Fork of Sabino Canyon, the trail heads west along the north bank of the West Fork. At 3.6 miles, follow the trail across the West Fork and up the slope to

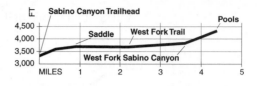

the west. Watch for several spur trails to the right. These go to several large pools along the bed of the creek, our goal for the hike.

—Bruce Grubbs

85 Mica Mountain

Description:	A hike to the highest point of the Rincon Mountains in the Saguaro Wilderness, Saguaro National Park.
Location:	Tucson.
Type of hike:	Out-and-back backpack.
Difficulty:	Difficult.
Total distance:	23.8 miles.
Elevation change:	5,900 feet.
Water:	Seasonal at Douglas Spring, Italian Spring, and Manning Camp.
Best months:	October–April.
Maps:	Tanque Verde, Mica Mountain USGS; Trails Illustrated Saguaro National Park.
Permit:	No off-trail hiking below 4,500 feet. Backcountry camping requires a permit; camping allowed only in designated wilderness campsites.
For more information:	Saguaro National Park.

Finding the trailhead: From I–10 in Tucson, exit at Speedway Boulevard and drive 17.4 miles to the Douglas Spring Trailhead at the end of the road.

Key points:
- 0.0 Douglas Spring Trailhead.
- 2.1 Three Tank Trail.
- 2.3 Bridal Wreath Falls Trail.
- 5.6 Douglas Spring.
- 7.7 Cow Head Saddle; turn left on Cow Head Saddle Trail.
- 10.8 North Slope Trail.
- 10.9 Turn left on Fire Loop Trail.
- 11.5 Trail junction near Spud Rock.
- 11.9 Mica Mountain.

The hike: This hike takes you through a wide variety of terrain from the Sonoran desert foothills to the forested summit of the Rincon Mountains.

Mica Mountain

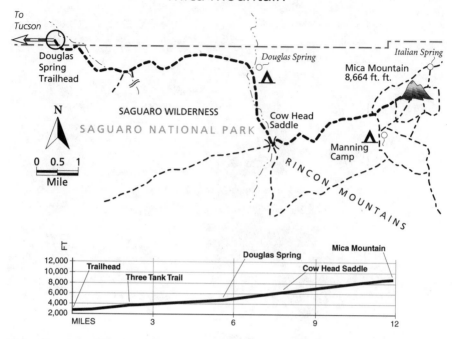

This island mountain range is the only remaining high range in southern Arizona that does not have a road to the high country.

Start on the Douglas Spring Trail, which heads eastward through classic Sonoran desert. There are several trails on the right for the first mile or so; be sure to stay left on the Douglas Spring Trail. The trail climbs steadily, then levels somewhat as you pass the Three Tank Trail at 2.1 miles. Just after this junction, watch for a spur trail to Bridal Wreath Falls, a 0.4-mile side trip. The main trail crosses the remainder of the mesquite flat, then starts to climb again. At 5.6 miles, you'll reach Douglas Spring, a seasonal water source, and designated campsite.

Now the trail turns south and begins to climb in earnest, heading up a ridge next to Canyon del Pino. After about a mile, the trail enters the forested canyon itself, and climbs to its head at Cow Head Saddle. The curious rock formation responsible for the name is visible as you approach the saddle, at 7.7 miles. Turn left on the Cow Head Saddle Trail, which heads east up a broad ridge.

Southeast of Helens Dome, at 10.8 miles, you'll pass the North Slope Trail on the left, and the trail contours southeast. Just 0.1 mile farther, turn left on the Fire Loop Trail, which climbs northeast toward Spud Rock. (The Cow Head Trail continues 0.4 mile to Manning Camp, another designated campsite with a spring.) A trail branches right near Spud Rock; continue straight ahead to Mica Mountain, the goal for our hike. The summit is marked with an old fire lookout tower, which is no longer in use.

The desert bighorn sheep is more dependent on water than many desert mammals. Therefore one of the best places to observe them is at a spring or a natural rock tank called tinajas *in southern Arizona. They try to drink at least once a day, usually in the early morning.*

Options: There are a number of trails in the Mica Mountain area. One option is to hike about 0.5 mile east on the Fire Loop Trail to a meadow with open views to the east. You could continue on the Fire Loop Trail to loop south past Manning Camp and then northwest back to the Cows Head Saddle Trail. This loop is about 1.7 miles longer than the normal return via Spud Rock.

Another loop, this time to the north, uses the North Slope Trail, which traverses the heavily forested northern slopes of Mica Mountain, and also meets the Cow Head Saddle Trail near Helens Dome. This loop is 1.9 miles longer than the direct return.

—Sid Hirsh and Bruce Grubbs

86 Tanque Verde Ridge

Description:	A hike along a scenic ridge in the Rincon Mountains and Saguaro Wilderness in Saguaro National Park.
Location:	Tucson.
Type of hike:	Out-and-back day hike or overnight backpack.
Difficulty:	Difficult.
Total distance:	12.4 miles.
Elevation change:	2,930 feet.
Water:	None.
Best months:	October–April.
Maps:	Tanque Verde Peak USGS; Trails Illustrated Saguaro National Park.
Permit:	No off-trail hiking below 4,500 feet (the 2-mile point on this hike). Backcountry camping requires a permit; camping allowed only in designated wilderness campsites.
For more information:	Saguaro National Park.

Finding the trailhead: From I-10 in Tucson, exit at Speedway Boulevard and drive 12.4 miles east to Houghton Road. Turn right, and go 2.7 miles, then turn left on Old Spanish Trail. Go another 2.7 miles, and then turn left into Saguaro National Park. Turn right at the visitor center and go about 2 miles to the Tanque Verde Ridge Trailhead.

Key points:
- 0.0   Tanque Verde Ridge Trailhead.
- 0.8   Tanque Verde Ridge.
- 6.2   Juniper Camp.

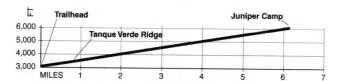

The hike: The Tanque Verde Ridge Trail first heads southeast across the desert foothills, climbing onto the west end of Tanque Verde Ridge. Here, the trail swings northeast and starts a steady climb up this long ridge. The trail dips and winds around small hills and across small drainages, but always tends to follow the main ridge. At first, you will be in the saguaro cactus "forest." The national park was established to protect this unique and beautiful desert landscape, as well as its plants and animals.

As the trail climbs along the ridge, the cactus forest gradually gives way to high desert grassland and pinyon pine–juniper forest. Saguaros are not tolerant of frost, so they disappear from the cooler north-facing slopes first. There are many points with good views of the Tucson area and its mountains along the lower portion of the ridge. As the miniature pinyon–juniper

Like many cactus, the giant saguaro displays a showy flower in the spring of wet years.

Tanque Verde Ridge

forest becomes thicker, views become limited. Below "Peak 6,300," the trail turns southeast and contours to cross a drainage, then turns east and follows another shallow drainage to Juniper Basin. This wilderness campground is a good turnaround point for a day hike, and a good goal for an overnight backpack trip.

—Bruce Grubbs

87 Hugh Norris Trail

Description:	A hike along a very scenic ridge in the Saguaro Wilderness, Saguaro National Park.
Location:	About 16 miles west of Tucson.
Type of hike:	Out-and-back day hike.
Difficulty:	Moderate.
Total distance:	8.4 miles.
Elevation change:	2,000 feet.
Water:	None.
Best months:	October–April.
Maps:	Avra USGS; Trails Illustrated Saguaro National Park.
Permit:	None.
For more information:	Saguaro National Park, Tucson Mountain District.

Finding the trailhead: From I–10 in Tucson, drive west on Speedway Boulevard, which becomes Gates Pass Road. Continue 9.5 miles, and then

Hugh Norris Trail

turn right on Kinney Road. Go 6.3 miles, turn right on Hohokam Road, and drive 0.8 mile to the Hugh Norris Trailhead.

Key points:

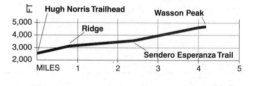

0.0   Hugh Norris Trailhead.
0.8   Ridge crest.
2.4   Sendero Esperanza Trail.
4.0   Turn left on Wasson Peak Trail.
4.2   Wasson Peak.

The hike: The trail heads southeast into a drainage, and then climbs up a ravine. A few switchbacks lead to the crest of the long ridge trending west from Wasson and Amole Peaks. After dipping through a saddle, the trail climbs gradually eastward across the north side of a peak and through another saddle. Now the trail stays near the ridge crest, generally avoiding small peaks on their north sides.

At 2.4 miles you'll cross the Sendero Esperanza Trail in a saddle. The Hugh Norris Trail continues east, climbing a bit more steeply to regain the crest, then turns slightly northeast. After passing Amole Peak on its south side, the trail climbs to meet the Wasson Peak Trail at 4.0 miles. Turn left and hike 0.2 mile to the summit of Wasson Peak.

Wasson Peak is the highest summit in the Tucson Mountains and the view is appropriately sweeping. Saguaro National Park is laid out before you, and the Tucson urban area sprawls to the east, below the massive Rincon and Santa Catalina ranges.

Saguaro cactus "forest" in the Tucson Mountains.

The Tucson Mountains contain one of the best stands of saguaro cactus in the Sonoran Desert, and Saguaro National Park was created to protect these giant cacti. Saguaros are widely used as a symbol of the American Desert, but actually they occur only in the Sonoran Desert of northwest Mexico and southwest Arizona. Young saguaros generally get their start under the protection of a nurse tree such as a palo verde. Saguaro cacti can't stand prolonged freezes, so you'll only find them where freezing temperatures are rare. Nevertheless, every few years an especially cold storm will dust the cactus forests with a few inches of snow. It quickly melts when the sun comes out.

—Bruce Grubbs

Sky Islands

The high mountains of southeastern Arizona have been called Sky Islands. The Santa Catalina, Rincon, Pinaleno, Chiricahua, and other mountain ranges rise thousands of feet above the surrounding desert. Their cool, moist forested tops are truly biological islands set within the desert sea.

88 Aravaipa Canyon

Description:	A delightful hike along one of Arizona's best desert riparian areas.
Location:	About 23 miles southeast of Winkelman.
Type of hike:	Shuttle backpack.
Difficulty:	Moderate.
Total distance:	11 miles.
Elevation change:	500 feet.
Water:	Aravaipa Creek.
Best months:	All year.
Maps:	Brandenburg Mountain, Booger Canyon USGS.
Permit:	There is a hiking fee, and a permit in advance is required.
For more information:	Safford Field Office, Bureau of Land Management.

Finding the trailhead: From Winkelman, take Arizona 77 south for 11 miles to the Aravaipa Road. Follow the Aravaipa Road 12 miles east to the trailhead. Access to the east end of the wilderness is 10 miles northwest of Klondyke on the Aravaipa Canyon Road, which requires a high-clearance vehicle. It is a 4-hour shuttle between the two trailheads. Some lands around and within the wilderness are not federally administered. Please respect the property rights of the owners, and do not cross or use these lands without their permission.

Key points:
0.0   West Trailhead.
1.3   Hells Half Acre Canyon.
3.7   Virgus Canyon.
4.1   Horse Camp Cayon.

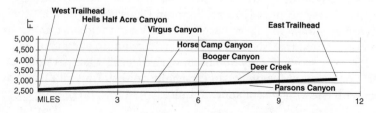

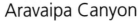

Aravaipa Canyon

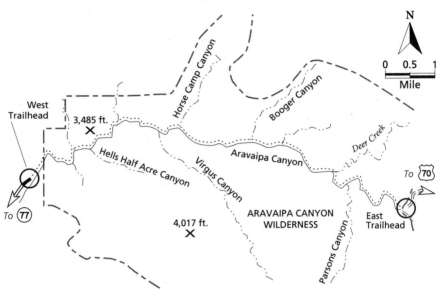

The hike: There is no established trail through Aravaipa Canyon; you simply follow the stream. Stream wading with numerous crossings (up to knee deep) and hiking through dense riparian brush can slow travel time. It takes a strong hiker about 10 hours to hike the length of the canyon. Topographic maps are handy for keeping track of your progress.

The lack of an established trail does not detract from the popularity of this hike. Aravaipa Canyon, which cuts through the northern part of the Galiuro Mountains, has long been recognized for its spectacular scenery and important wildlife habitat. A 19,410-acre designated wilderness area consists of Aravaipa Canyon, its surrounding tablelands, and nine side canyons. Thousand-foot cliffs rise above a green ribbon of rich riparian habitat found along the 11-mile segment of Aravaipa Creek that flows through the wilderness. More than 200 species of birds live among the shady cottonwoods and willows growing along the perennial waters of Aravaipa Creek. During late spring and summer, birders can expect yellow-billed cuckoos, vermilion flycatchers, northern beardless-tyrannulets, yellow warblers, yellow-breasted chats, and summer tanagers.

Two federally listed threatened fish, spikedace and loach minnow, can be found in the creek. There are an additional five species of native fish, which makes Aravaipa Creek one of the best native fisheries remaining in Arizona. The stream has been recommended for designation as a National Wild and Scenic River.

The Bureau of Land Management manages the wilderness, and a permit is required in advance to enter the area. Use is limited to fifty people per day; thirty from the west end and twenty from the east end. Maximum length of stay is three days (two nights), and party size is limited to ten people. Equestrians can have only five stock/pack animals per party and may not have animals overnight in the canyon. These regulations help ensure a desirable level of solitude for visitors and reduce the impact on the environment. An in-depth Aravaipa Canyon Wilderness brochure is available to explain permit requirements. Payment of a fee is also required. Contact the Safford Field Office for additional permit and fee information.

Adjacent to the east boundary of the wilderness area is The Nature Conservancy's Aravaipa Canyon Preserve. About 6.4 miles northwest of Klondyke, where the road goes down to cross the creek for the second crossing, is the preserve manager's house. To go off the public road, a permit is required from the preserve manager. No permit is needed if you are going straight to the wilderness trailhead.

—Stewart Aitchison

89 Powers Garden

Description:	A hike to a historic ranch in a scenic canyon in the Galiuro Wilderness.
Location:	About 51 miles southwest of Safford.
Type of hike:	Out-and-back or long day hike backpack.
Difficulty:	Moderate.
Total distance:	14.4 miles.
Elevation change:	1,600 feet.
Water:	Seasonal at Mud Spring and Powers Garden Spring.
Best months:	March–May, October–November.
Maps:	Kennedy Peak USGS; Coronado National Forest, Safford and Santa Catalina Ranger Districts.
Permit:	None.
For more information:	Coronado National Forest, Safford Ranger District.

Finding the trailhead: From Safford, drive about 15 miles west on U.S. 70, then turn left on the graded dirt Klondyke Road. Go about 24 miles to a left turn on Aravaipa Road. Continue 4.6 miles, then turn right on Forest Road 253 and go 7.4 miles to its end at the Deer Creek Trailhead and Deer Creek Cabin.

Key points:
0.0	Deer Creek Trailhead.
0.9	Oak Creek.
2.7	Sycamore Creek Trail (Trail 278).
4.5	Topout Divide.
6.9	Turn left on Rattlesnake Trail.
7.2	Powers Garden.

Powers Garden

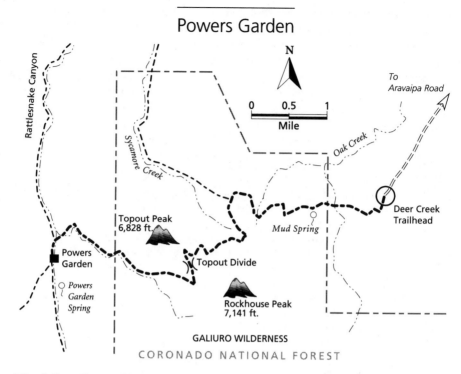

The hike: The trail heads west up a grassy hillside dotted with juniper trees, and climbs over a broad saddle. A gradual descent leads across Oak Creek at 0.9 mile. Now the trail climbs west past Mud Spring and then contours around several unnamed tributaries of Oak Creek. Note how the junipers have been joined by a few pinyon pines on this cooler north-facing slope. At 2.7 miles the trail swings south around the end of a ridge and passes the junction with the Sycamore Creek Trail. It then works its way across the headwaters of Sycamore Creek, reaching Topout Divide, a pass that marks the high point of the trail at 4.5 miles.

The trail drops south into Horse Canyon, then turns sharply northwest and follows the bed of the canyon. A couple of sharp bends mark the end of the canyon. The trail emerges into Rattlesnake Canyon; turn left on the Rattlesnake Trail at 6.9 miles and continue 0.3 mile to the old ranch site at Powers Garden. The beautiful meadow, set in a picturesque canyon, is graced with towering ponderosa pines. There is seasonal water in Powers Garden Spring, just south of the old ranch site.

The Powers brothers established a homestead here before World War I, and were soon involved in cattle ranching as well as mining. News of the war was slow to reach this isolated country (Arizona had just become a state

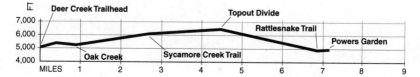

in 1912), and either the Powers brothers didn't know about the draft, or pretended that they didn't. Eventually the authorities came to arrest them for draft evasion. They fled south up the canyon, and according to legend were involved in a shootout with the lawmen at one of their mines.

There are many options for exploring the trail system in the Galiuro Mountains, but be prepared for faint, brushy trails. Many of the trails receive little use or maintenance.

—Bruce Grubbs

90 Ash Creek Falls

Description:	A hike through the alpine forest high on the Pinaleno Mountains, ending at a spectacular waterfall.
Location:	About 35 miles southwest of Safford.
Type of hike:	Out-and-back day hike.
Difficulty:	Easy.
Total distance:	4.8 miles.
Elevation change:	1,380 feet.
Water:	Ash Creek.
Best months:	May–October.
Maps:	Webb Peak USGS; Coronado National Forest, Pinaleno Mountains.
Permit:	None.
For more information:	Coronado National Forest, Safford Ranger District.

The highest of the "Sky Islands," the Pinaleno Mountains have several peaks above 10,000 feet.

Ash Creek Falls • Webb Peak

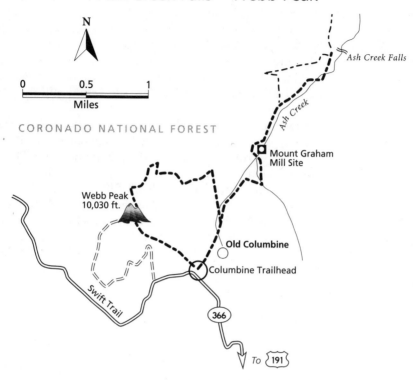

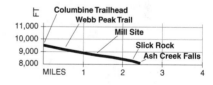

Finding the trailhead: From Safford, drive 7.0 miles south on U.S. 191, then turn right on the Swift Trail (Arizona 366). Go about 28 miles, just past the USFS Columbine Work Center, then turn right into the Columbine Trailhead.

Key points:
- 0.0   Columbine Trailhead.
- 0.5   Webb Peak Trail.
- 1.3   Mount Graham Mill Site.
- 1.7   Horse bypass trail.
- 2.2   Slick Rock.
- 2.4   Ash Creek Falls.

The hike: The trails in the Pinaleno Mountains offer high, cool hikes, a welcome escape from the furnacelike desert below. Snow lingers into May and sometimes returns in October. Access to this hike is provided by the Swift Trail. This amazing road, now paved for most of its length, climbs the north slopes of the range, crosses Ladybug Pass, then traverses high on the south slopes. Numerous trails start from the Swift Trail and its spur roads, and descend the mountain to trailheads in the foothills. These hikes are long, strenuous, and rewarding. The hike to Ash Creek Falls, in contrast, remains in the alpine forest just below the mountain crest, and takes you to a high waterfall.

The Ash Creek Trail starts from the east side of the parking area, and descends gradually into the headwaters of the creek. A delightful mix of quaking aspen and Douglas fir shades the trail. At 0.5 mile, a signed trail forks left to Webb Peak. Our trail continues down Ash Creek, and soon swings around a fine alpine meadow at 1.3 miles, marked MOUNT GRAHAM MILL SITE on the USGS quad. During the settling of Arizona, Sky Island mountains such as the Pinalenos provided timber for the ranches and towns in the valleys below. Often, small mills located near the logging site would mill the logs into lumber.

A short distance below the mill site meadow, a horse bypass trail branches left. The reason for the bypass becomes apparent when you reach Slick Rock, a horse-unfriendly section of trail blasted from the granite bedrock. Below this section, the trail veers left, out of the creekbed. Just where the view to the north opens up, you'll hear and see Ash Creek Falls, a 200-foot waterfall, below the trail to the east. The view includes the Mogollon Mountains in New Mexico, the Mogollon Rim in Arizona, and, far below in the Gila River Valley, the towns of Thatcher and Safford.

—Bruce Grubbs

91 Webb Peak

See Map on Page 249

Description: A hike to a 10,000-foot summit in the Pinaleno Mountains.
Location: About 35 miles southwest of Safford.
Type of hike: Loop day hike.
Difficulty: Easy.
Total distance: 2.7 miles.
Elevation change: 890 feet.
Water: None.
Best months: May–October.
Maps: Webb Peak USGS; Coronado National Forest, Pinaleno Mountains.
Permit: None.
For more information: Coronado National Forest, Safford Ranger District.

Finding the trailhead: From Safford, drive 7.0 miles south on U.S. 191, then turn right on the Swift Trail (Arizona 366). Go about 28 miles, just past the USFS Columbine Work Center, then turn right into the Columbine Trailhead.

Key points:
0.0 Columbine Trailhead.
0.5 Turn left on Webb Peak Trail.
2.1 Webb Peak.
2.7 Columbine Trailhead.

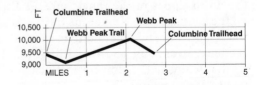

North-facing slopes of the Pinaleno Mountains are covered with an alpine forest of fir and spruce.

The hike: Start on the Ash Creek Trail, then turn left onto the Webb Peak Trail at 0.5 mile. The trail is actually an old road, probably built for logging or fire fighting. Meandering through beautiful alpine forest, the trail eventually reaches an old burn and turns south toward the summit. Follow the trail carefully here, as it is easy to lose in the meadows. There are excellent views into Blair Canyon as the trail climbs steeply to the summit. Turn left on a maintained dirt road and walk the last 100 yards to the old fire lookout on the summit, at 2.1 miles. Next to the U.S. Forest Service cabin, a sign marks the start of the return trail. This trail drops directly down the southeast ridge to the Columbine Trailhead.

The fir forests of the Pinaleno Mountains are home to the endangered red squirrel. Controversy continues over the ongoing development of an astronomical observatory on Mount Graham, the highest peak in the range.

—Bruce Grubbs

92 Safford-Morenci Trail

Description:	An overnight or longer backpack along a historic trail in the Gila Box Riparian National Conservation Area.
Location:	12 miles northeast of Safford.
Type of hike:	Shuttle backpack.
Difficulty:	Difficult.
Total distance:	About 18 miles.
Elevation change:	2,400 feet.
Water:	Bonita Creek; purify before using.
Best months:	March–May, September–November.
Maps:	Bonita Spring, Weber Peak, Copperplate Gulch, Lone Star Mountain USGS.
Permit:	None.
For more information:	Safford Field Office, Bureau of Land Management.

Finding the trailhead: To reach the west trailhead from Safford, drive 8 miles northeast on the San Juan Road, then take the left fork heading for Walnut Springs and the West Ranch and go 4 more miles. The trailhead is signed. To reach the east trailhead, drive west out of Morenci on the Eagle Creek Road about 5 miles to the signed parking area. Both approaches may require four-wheel-drive vehicles, especially in wet weather.

Key points:
- 0.0 West Ranch Trailhead.
- 8.0 Bonita Creek.
- 12.0 Bellmeyer Saddle.
- 18.0 East Trailhead.

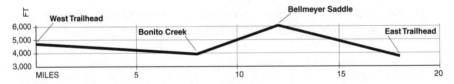

The hike: This well-established but rocky trail winds through rugged and beautiful canyons whose walls are composed of volcanic rocks such as basalt, rhyolite, and andesite. The vegetation varies from mesquite and creosote bush at the West Ranch trailhead to riparian species like Fremont cottonwood, willow, and Arizona sycamore along Bonita Creek to pinyon-juniper-oak woodland in Smith Canyon. Wildlife is abundant. Look for signs of mule deer, mountain lion, javelina, coyote, and gray fox. Bonito Creek, which is located at about the half-way point, makes an excellent camping spot.

Pioneer farmers and ranchers in the Gila River Valley and Bonita Creek area gouged out the Safford-Morenci Trail about 1874. They needed a shorter

Safford-Morenci Trail

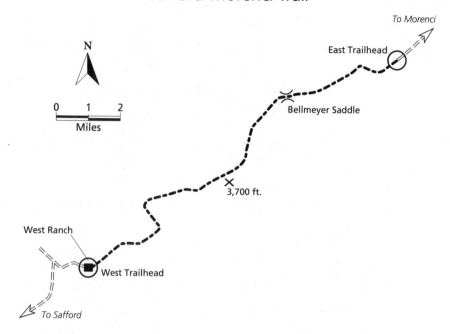

route to Morenci, where booming copper mines offered a market for their produce and meat. The mines also required wood to burn in the smelters, so Mexican wood haulers and their pack trains of mules and burros used the trail.

Horse rancher Albert Bellmeyer and his foreman rode up this trail from the Morenci side on a fine fall day in 1892. They wanted to check on their herd grazing on Turtle Mountain, because there were rumors that renegades from the nearby San Carlos Apache Reservation were in the area. Geronimo had surrendered six years earlier, ending for all practical purposes the threat of hostile Indians. But the ranchers were still concerned.

Exactly what happened next is conjecture, but evidence suggests that the two men were ambushed at Bellmeyer Saddle. Bellmeyer was shot twice and apparently died instantly. The foreman, however, spurred his horse down the trail. Another shot rang out and the foreman fell to the ground. The wound was not fatal, but the attackers crushed his head with a rock. Later, their bodies were discovered and a posse was dispatched to search for the murderers, but no suspects were ever caught.

Other people of note who live near the trail included Toppy Johnson, whose real name was Presley Cantrell. Before coming to Arizona, he had served time in the Santa Fe prison for cattle rustling. The local Fulcher family was also involved in illegal horse-trading. Mother Fulcher committed suicide where the trail crosses Bonita Creek. A couple of cowboys loaded her body onto a large mule and transported her to Morenci.

The eerie howl of the coyote is an integral part of the wilderness. Considered a destructive varmint by many ranchers, the coyote nonetheless helps control rabbits, mice, and other rodents. It is also one of the few mammals that has increased its range over the last two centuries in spite of vigorous predator control programs.

With the advent of the automobile, a road was constructed farther south and the trail was slowly abandoned. Remnants of the old homesteads mark these early days, and prehistoric cliff dwellings tell of even earlier residents.

—Stewart Aitchison

93 Cochise Stronghold East

Description:	A hike through the rugged Dragoon Mountains to the hideout of the famous Apache chief.
Location:	About 37 miles southwest of Willcox.
Type of hike:	Out-and-back day hike.
Difficulty:	Easy.
Total distance:	5.6 miles.
Elevation change:	1,020 feet.
Water:	Seasonal at Cochise Spring.
Best months:	March–May, October–November.
Maps:	Cochise Stronghold USGS, Coronado National Forest (Chiricahua, Peloncillo, and Dragoon Mountain Ranges).
Permit:	None.
For more information:	Coronado National Forest, Douglas Ranger District.

Cochise Stronghold East

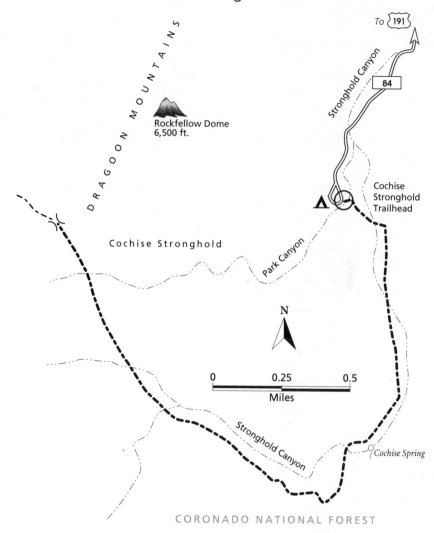

Finding the trailhead: From Willcox, drive 9 miles west on I–10, then about 18 miles south on U.S. 191 to Sunsites, and turn right on the Cochise Stronghold Road (Forest Road 84). Continue on this maintained dirt road to its end and park at Cochise Stronghold Campground.

Key points:

0.0	Cochise Stronghold Trailhead.
0.8	Spur trail.
1.0	Cochise Spring.
2.8	Pass.

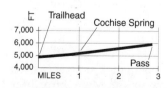

The hike: The trail first climbs south into
upper Stronghold Canyon East. You'll pass a spur trail; stay right here, and

continue past Cochise Spring, at 1.0 mile. Now the canyon turns northwest, and the trail follows it through beautiful rugged country dotted with granite boulders, domes, and cliffs. Finally, the trail swings left onto the south slopes of the canyon and contours to a pass overlooking Stronghold Canyon West, our goal for this hike.

What is now a peaceful hike might have been a different experience when the Chiricahua Apache were using the Dragoon Mountains as a base for raiding settlements in the surrounding valleys. Led by wily Chief Cochise, the warriors led their pursuers into the mountains, where the Apaches' skill at rapid travel through very difficult terrain made them impossible to follow.

—Bruce Grubbs

94 Sugarloaf Mountain

Description:	An easy hike to one of the highest viewpoints in the Chiricahua National Monument.
Location:	35 miles southeast of Willcox.
Type of hike:	Out-and-back day hike.
Difficulty:	Easy.
Total distance:	2 miles.
Elevation change:	470 feet.
Water:	None.
Best months:	All year.
Maps:	Cochise Head USGS.
Permit:	None.
For more information:	Chiricahua National Monument.

Finding the trailhead: From I-10 in Willcox, drive 34 miles east on Arizona 186, then turn left on Arizona 181. Continue 5.1 miles to the Chiricahua National Monument Visitor Center, then take the Bonita Canyon Drive for about 5.5 miles to the Sugarloaf Mountain turnoff. Another mile brings you to a picnic area and the trailhead.

Key points:

0.0 Trailhead.

1.0 Sugarloaf Mountain.

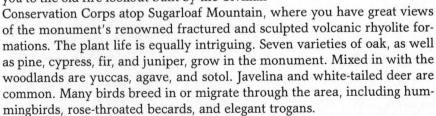

The hike: This well-maintained easy trail takes you to the old fire lookout built by the Civilian Conservation Corps atop Sugarloaf Mountain, where you have great views of the monument's renowned fractured and sculpted volcanic rhyolite formations. The plant life is equally intriguing. Seven varieties of oak, as well as pine, cypress, fir, and juniper, grow in the monument. Mixed in with the woodlands are yuccas, agave, and sotol. Javelina and white-tailed deer are common. Many birds breed in or migrate through the area, including hummingbirds, rose-throated becards, and elegant trogans.

—Stewart Aitchison

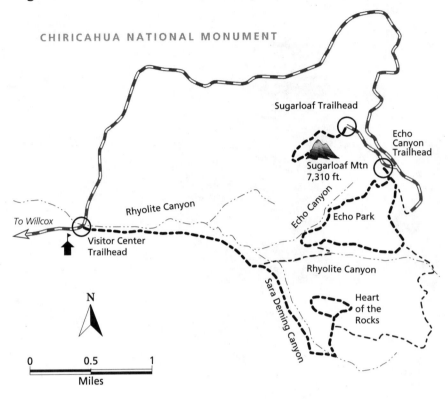

CHIRICAHUA NATIONAL MONUMENT

Sugarloaf Trailhead

Echo Canyon Trailhead

Sugarloaf Mtn 7,310 ft.

Echo Canyon

Echo Park

Rhyolite Canyon

To Willcox

Visitor Center Trailhead

Rhyolite Canyon

Sara Deming Canyon

Heart of the Rocks

N

0   0.5   1
Miles

95 Echo Canyon

	See Map above

Description: A hike through weirdly eroded rock formations in Chiricahua National Monument.

Location: 35 miles southeast of Willcox.

Type of hike: Loop day hike.

Difficulty: Easy.

Total distance: 2.8 miles.

Elevation change: 580 feet.

Water: None.

Best months: All year.

Maps: Cochise Head USGS; Chiricahua National Monument brochure.

Permit: None.

For more information: Chiricahua National Monument.

Finding the trailhead: From I-10 in Willcox, drive 34 miles east on Arizona 186, then turn left on Arizona 181. Continue 5.1 miles to the

A short hike along an easy trail takes you into a wonderland of strange rock formations.

Chiricahua National Monument Visitor Center, then take the Bonita Canyon Drive for about 5.6 miles to the Echo Canyon Trailhead, which is just before the end of the road.

Key points:
- 0.0 Echo Canyon Trailhead.
- 0.2 Rhyolite Canyon Trail.
- 1.2 Rhyolite Canyon Trail.
- 2.1 Inspiration Point Trail.
- 2.6 Turn right on Echo Canyon Trail.
- 2.8 Echo Canyon Trailhead.

The hike: The trail descends gradually from the trailhead, and at 0.2 mile meets the Rhyolite Canyon Trail, which will be the return. Stay right, and follow the Echo Canyon Trail into Echo Park. Here the trail winds between tall rock towers, which remind one of the artificial canyons of a large city.

Next, you'll enter the cool depths of Echo Canyon, which is shaded with Apache and ponderosa pines. The trail swings around a point into Rhyolite Canyon and meets the Rhyolite Canyon Trail at 1.2 miles. Turn left, and follow the trail east along the north side of the canyon. Notice how this slope is brushy, warmer, and drier than the more sheltered bottom of Echo Canyon. You'll have great views of the rock pinnacles and formations on both sides of the canyon. At 2.1 miles, stay left at the Inspiration Point Trail.

The trail swings north and works its way up a side canyon. A side trail to the right leads to Massai Point; stay left. At 2.6 miles, you'll rejoin the Echo Canyon Trail; turn right and walk 0.2 mile back to the Echo Canyon Trailhead.

—Bruce Grubbs

96 Heart of the Rocks

See Map on Page 257

Description: This trail takes you to a strange area of balanced rocks and abundant wildlife in Chiricahua National Monument.

Location: 35 miles southeast of Willcox.

Type of hike: Out-and-back day hike with a short loop section.

Difficulty: Moderate.

Total distance: 6.7 miles.

Elevation change: 1,500 feet.

Water: None.

Best months: All year.

Maps: Cochise Head USGS; Chiricahua National Monument brochure.

Permit: None.

For more information: Chiricahua National Monument.

Finding the trailhead: From I–10 in Willcox, drive 34 miles east on Arizona 186, then turn left on Arizona 181. Continue 5.1 miles into Chiricahua National Monument (entrance fee), to the trailhead at the visitor center.

Key points:
- 0.0   Visitor Center Trailhead.
- 1.5   Turn right on Sara Deming Trail.
- 2.9   Turn left on Heart of the Rocks Trail.
- 3.8   Stay left at Sara Deming Trail.
- 5.2   Turn left on Rhyolite Canyon Trail.
- 6.7   Visitor Center Trailhead.

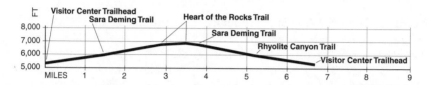

The hike: The trail starts at the national monument visitor center parking lot, and heads east along the south side of Rhyolite Canyon, climbing gradually. At 1.5 miles, turn right onto the Sara Deming Trail, which ascends a little faster as it turns southeast up Sara Deming Canyon. Near the head of the canyon, the trail turns abruptly north and climbs out of the canyon into a land of strangely shaped rock formations. You'll meet the Heart of the Rocks Trail at 2.9 miles; turn left to hike this scenic loop. The trail returns to the same junction at 3.8 miles; stay left and return to the visitor center via the Sara Deming and Rhyolite Canyon Trails.

The Heart of the Rocks Loop features the most massive balanced rock in the monument, as well as rock caricatures of people and animals. There are sweeping views of Sulphur Springs Valley, Cochise Head, and the Chiricahua Mountains.

The story behind this fantastic collection of rocks is not completely understood, but geologists believe that about 27 million years ago, violent volcanic eruptions spewed red-hot pumice and ash over a 1,200-square-mile area. The hot particles became "welded" together to form an 800-foot-thick layer of tuff with a composition of rhyolite. As cooling took place, the tuff contracted and vertical cracks (joints) formed. The extent and thickness of this deposit indicates eruptions substantially greater than the Mount St. Helens eruption in 1980.

From 25 million to 5 million years ago, the earth's crust stretched and broke into large fault-bounded blocks. One uplifted block created the Chiricahua Mountains; the masters of erosion—water, wind, and ice—began to sculpt the rock into odd formations. The horizontal bedding planes and joints provided weak places for erosion to act upon. Fanciful names such as Organ Pipe, Sea Captain, China Boy, Punch and Judy, and Duck on a Rock describe some of the strange rock shapes. Although many pinnacles and rocks appear to be precariously balanced, they were sufficiently stable to withstand the magnitude 7.2 earthquake that shook southeastern Arizona in 1887.

—Chiricahua National Monument, Bruce Grubbs and Stewart Aitchison

"Hoodoos," volcanic rock formations along Rhyolite Canyon, Chiricahua National Monument.

97 Buena Vista Peak

Description:	A hike to a rocky summit with panoramic views of the northern Chiricahua Mountains.
Location:	About 52 miles southeast of Willcox.
Type of hike:	Out-and-back day hike.
Difficulty:	Easy.
Total distance:	2.4 miles.
Elevation change:	300 feet.
Water:	None.
Best months:	May–October.
Maps:	Rustler Park USGS; Coronado National Forest (Chiricahua, Peloncillo, and Dragoon Mountain Ranges).
Permit:	None.
For more information:	Coronado National Forest, Douglas Ranger District.

Finding the trailhead: From I–10 in Willcox, drive 34 miles east on Arizona 186, then turn left on Arizona 181. Continue 3 miles, and then turn left on Pinery Canyon Road (Forest Road 42), a maintained dirt road. Go 12.0 miles to Onion Saddle, and then turn right on the Rustler Park Road (Forest Road 42D). Drive 3 miles; park at Rustler Park Campground.

Buena Vista Peak

Key points:

0.0 Rustler Park Trailhead.
0.5 First saddle and unsigned trail junction.
1.1 Second saddle.
1.2 Buena Vista Peak.

The hike: The trailhead is on the north side of the upper loop of Rustler Park Campground. Turn right at a junction just 100 yards from the start. Now the trail heads north, climbing gradually through the forest on the east slopes of a ridge. It reaches the crest after 0.5 mile; stay right at an unsigned junction.

The trail stays close to the ridge top for a short distance, and then contours the east slope to a second saddle at 1.1 miles. A final short climb brings you to Barfoot Lookout, a USFS fire lookout station built on the rocky summit of Buena Vista Peak.

Buena Vista is Spanish for "good view," and that's certainly true of this 8,700-foot peak at the north end of the Chiricahua Mountains. To the south, you can see the high peaks in the Chiricahua Wilderness, and to the southeast, the exceptionally scenic Portal area along Cave Creek.

—Bruce Grubbs

98 Chiricahua Peak

Description: A hike to the highest point in the Chiricahua Wilderness in the Chiricahua Mountains.
Location: About 50 miles southeast of Willcox.
Type of hike: Loop backpack.
Difficulty: Difficult.
Total distance: 15.5 miles.
Elevation change: 3,670 feet.
Water: Seasonal at Booger and Anita Springs.
Best months: May–November.
Maps: Rustler Park, Chiricahua Peak USGS, Coronado National Forest (Chiricahua, Peloncillo, and Dragoon Mountain Ranges).
Permit: None.
For more information: Coronado National Forest, Douglas Ranger District.

Finding the trailhead: From I-10 in Willcox, take U.S. 191 south 27 miles. Turn left on Arizona 181 and drive east 12 miles. Arizona 181 turns left; continue straight onto maintained dirt Turkey Creek Road (Forest Road 41). Go 9 miles, and then turn left on a short spur road to the Salisbury Trailhead.

Key points:

0.0 Salisbury Trailhead.
2.3 Salisbury Saddle.

Chiricahua Peak

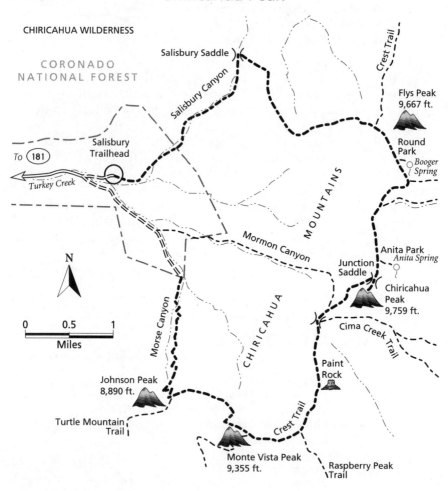

CHIRICAHUA WILDERNESS

CORONADO
NATIONAL FOREST

Salisbury Saddle

Salisbury Canyon

Crest Trail

Flys Peak
9,667 ft.

Salisbury
Trailhead

To 181

Round
Park

Booger
Spring

Turkey Creek

Mormon Canyon

MOUNTAINS

N

Anita Park
Anita Spring

Junction
Saddle

Chiricahua
Peak
9,759 ft.

0   0.5   1
Miles

Morse Canyon

CHIRICAHUA

Cima Creek Trail

Paint
Rock

Johnson Peak
8,890 ft.

Crest Trail

Turtle Mountain
Trail

Monte Vista Peak
9,355 ft.

Raspberry Peak
Trail

4.7   Turn right on Crest Trail.
5.0   Round Park.
5.8   Cima Park.
6.6   Anita Park and Junction Saddle.
6.9   Chiricahua Peak.
7.2   Anita Park and Junction Saddle.
8.1   Chiricahua Saddle.
10.0   Turn right on Morse Canyon Trail.
11.3   Turtle Mountain Trail.
13.5   Morse Canyon Trailhead.
15.2   Salisbury spur road.
15.5   Salisbury Trailhead.

The hike: The trail heads northeast and ambles up through a lovely forest of oak, Apache and Chiricahua pine, and Arizona cypress. The route
steepens, but you are treated to magnificent views across the Chiricahua

264

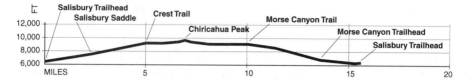

Wilderness and Sulphur Springs Valley. At 2.3 miles, the trail passes through Salisbury Saddle and turns southeast. Generally following a ridge, it climbs over Little Baldy Mountain. As you continue to climb, the vegetation changes to Douglas fir, Engelmann spruce, and eventually some quaking aspen.

At 4.7 miles, turn right on the Crest Trail. You'll pass Round Park and a spur trail that leads to Booger Spring. Back on the Crest Trail, continue south past Cima Park to Anita Park, at 6.6 miles. Another spur trail leads to Anita Spring; like Booger Spring, it may be dry in drought years. A few yards south of Anita Park is a multiple trail junction at Junction Saddle. Continue straight ahead here on the Chiricahua Peak Trail to reach the round, forested summit of the Chiricahua Mountains at 6.9 miles. Unfortunately, the dense forest blocks the view. Return to Junction Saddle, and then turn left on the Crest Trail to resume the loop.

The trail contours along the west slopes of Chiricahua Peak, then passes through Chiricahua Saddle at 8.1 miles. Now the trail stays pretty much on the crest of the range, passing Paint Rock, and then turning west at the junction with Raspberry Peak Trail. At 10.0 miles, the Monte Vista Peak Trail branches left; turn right onto the Morse Canyon Trail. This trail drops down the northwest slopes of the peak, then follows a ridge to a saddle east

The remarkable rhyolite pillars in the Chiricahua National Monument Wilderness Area are the result of fused volcanic magma being eroded into columns. At least eight eruptions are responsible for the accumulation of nearly two thousand feet of volcanic debris.

of Johnson Peak at 11.3 miles, where it meets the trail to Turtle Mountain. Stay right here, and follow the trail as it switchbacks steeply down into Morse Canyon. The grade moderates as the trail drops into the bottom of the canyon, and you'll reach the Morse Canyon Trailhead at 13.5 miles. Walk down the road 1.7 miles, then turn right on the Salisbury spur road and go 0.3 mile to the Salisbury Trailhead.

Many birds are found in the Chiricahua Mountains, not only typical Arizona and Mexican species but also some Eastern birds such as warblers, which pass through on their migrations to and from Mexico. Black bear and mountain lions are also found in these mountains.

—Bruce Grubbs

99 Silver Peak

Description: A hike to a summit offering excellent views of the cliff-bound Portal area and the eastern portion of the Chiricahua Wilderness in the Chiricahua Mountains.
Location: About 65 miles northeast of Douglas.
Type of hike: Out-and-back day hike.
Difficulty: Moderate.
Total distance: 7.8 miles.
Elevation change: 3,050 feet.
Water: None.
Best months: April–November.
Maps: Portal USGS; Coronado National Forest (Chiricahua, Peloncillo, and Dragoon Mountain Ranges).
Permit: None.
For more information: Coronado National Forest, Douglas Ranger District.

Finding the trailhead: From Douglas, drive about 54 miles northeast on Arizona 80, then turn left on the Portal Road. Go 9.1 miles to the Silver Peak Trailhead, which is just past the ranger station.

Key points:
0.0   Silver Peak Trailhead.
3.9   Silver Peak.

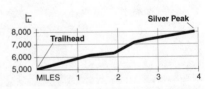

The hike: You'll be climbing Silver Peak, the massive mountain west of the trailhead. The actual summit is hidden from the trailhead. A few yards up the trail, an unsigned trail goes to the ranger station; turn left here and start up the slope toward the west. This slope appears to be gentle, but it's deceiving. The trail actually climbs 700 feet to reach the base of the mountain. This is a good goal for those desiring an easy hike, as it offers good views of the Portal area.

The trail swings around the north slopes of the mountain and enters stands of shady pine forest. Final steep switchbacks lead to the rock summit and

Silver Peak

N

0   0.5   1
Miles

CHIRICAHUA MOUNTAINS

Silver Peak
8,008 ft.

Portal
Ranger
Station

Portal Road

To ⑧⓪

Cave Creek

Silver Peak Trailhead

CORONADO NATIONAL FOREST

Cathedral Rock
6,839 ft.

the precariously perched, abandoned fire lookout building. To the west, the high, forested crest of the Chiricahua Mountains dominates the skyline, and the mountains of New Mexico are visible to the northeast. Closer at hand, to the east and south, lie Portal and Cave Creek.

—Bruce Grubbs

Cave Creek drains a rugged area of deep canyons on the east side of the Chiricahua Mountains.

100 Monte Vista Peak

Description:	This hike takes you to the summit of a 9,000-foot peak in the southern Chiricahua Wilderness in the Chiricahua Mountains.
Location:	About 65 miles north of Douglas.
Type of hike:	Out-and-back day hike.
Difficulty:	Moderate.
Total distance:	7.8 miles.
Elevation change:	2,760 feet.
Water:	Seasonal at Bear Spring.
Best months:	April–November.
Maps:	Chiricahua Peak USGS; Coronado National Forest (Chiricahua, Peloncillo, and Dragoon Mountain Ranges).
Permit:	None.
For more information:	Coronado National Forest, Douglas Ranger District.

Finding the trailhead: From Douglas, drive 34 miles north on U.S. 191, then turn right on Rucker Canyon Road. Go 16 miles and turn left to remain on Rucker Canyon Road. Continue 9 miles, then turn left on Forest Road 74E. Drive 4.6 miles, then turn left on Forest Road 628 and drive 1.8 miles to its end. You'll need a high-clearance vehicle on Forest Road 628.

Key points:

0.0 Trailhead at Forest Road 628.	3.8 Turn left on Crest Trail.
	3.9 Monte Vista Peak.
2.6 Buckskin Saddle.	

Distant ridges, Chiricahua Mountains.

Monte Vista Peak • Rucker Canyon

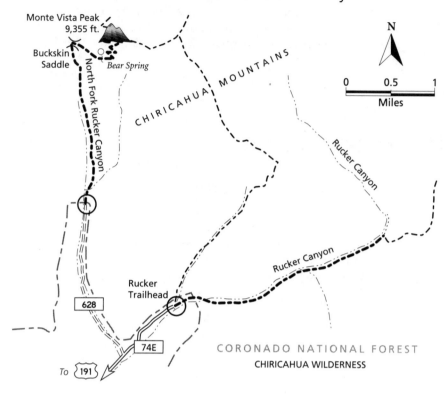

Monte Vista Peak
9,355 ft.

Buckskin
Saddle

Bear Spring

North Fork Rucker Canyon

CHIRICAHUA MOUNTAINS

Rucker Canyon

Rucker Canyon

N

0   0.5   1
Miles

Rucker
Trailhead

628

74E

To 191

CORONADO NATIONAL FOREST
CHIRICAHUA WILDERNESS

The hike: The trail climbs north along the North Fork of Rucker Canyon, in pine-oak woodland. After a couple of switchbacks lead out of the canyon, the trail climbs along the east slopes of the

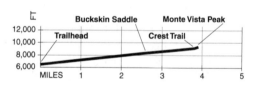

canyon, and the grade becomes steeper. You're hiking through a fine example of a mature ponderosa pine forest. Large trees known as yellow pines predominate, and the forest is open and spacious. You'll also see Apache pine, which is found only in southeast Arizona, southwest New Mexico, and northern Mexico. Its longer, lighter-colored needles distinguish Apache pine from ponderosa pine.

The trail passes through Buckskin Saddle at the head of the canyon at 2.6 miles, and then swings out onto the south slopes for the final ascent of Monte Vista Peak. On this steep slope, the effects of a recent forest fire are plain. Most of the trees were killed. Those that survived lost their lower branches; these are called "flag" trees. Young pines are growing in dense "dog hair" stands. Only a few trees will win the competition for sunlight and grow to maturity.

A spur trail goes to Bear Spring, and shortly afterward the trail ends at the Crest Trail junction, at 3.8 miles. Turn left and walk 0.1 mile to the top. Unlike most Chiricahua summits, Monte Vista Peak is bald and offers terrific views. A fire tower stands on the summit and is used by U.S. Forest Service personnel during the fire season. Ask permission from the observer before climbing the stairs.

—Bruce Grubbs

101 Rucker Canyon

See Map on Page 269

Description: A trail and cross-country walk along lower Rucker Canyon in the Chiricahua Wilderness in the Chiricahua Mountains.
Location: About 65 miles north of Douglas.
Type of hike: Out-and-back day hike.
Difficulty: Easy.
Total distance: 5.6 miles.
Elevation change: 500 feet.
Water: Seasonal in Rucker Canyon.
Best months: April–November.
Maps: Chiricahua Peak USGS; Coronado National Forest (Chiricahua, Peloncillo, and Dragoon Mountain Ranges).
Permit: None.
For more information: Coronado National Forest, Douglas Ranger District.

Finding the trailhead: From Douglas, drive 34 miles north on U.S. 191, then turn right on Rucker Canyon Road. Go 16 miles and turn left to remain on Rucker Canyon Road. Continue 9 miles, then turn left on Forest Road 74E. Drive 5.5 miles to the end of the road at Rucker Campground and trailhead.

Key points:
0.0   Rucker Trailhead.
2.5   Start of cross-country.
2.8   Rucker Canyon.

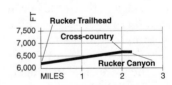

The hike: The Rucker Canyon Trail starts from the east end of the campground, following Rucker Creek upstream to the east through the shady pine forest. At 2.5 miles, the trail abruptly climbs out of the canyon via a series of switchbacks. Leave the trail here and continue up the canyon, following the stream. After 0.3 mile, the canyon turns north and becomes much rougher. This secluded spot is our destination.

Here, beside the musical stream, it's easy to imagine that modern civilization does not exist, and that an Apache warrior may glide into view at

any moment. The wilderness seems complete, and there are ta
views of the crags and forested peaks of upper Rucker Canyon.

Rucker Canyon is named for Lieutenant Rucker, who led ar
tachment based at Fort Bowie at the northern end of the Chiricahua ᴍ
tains in the late 1800s. His mission took him to the Mule Mountains in search
of a band of Apaches who had fled their reservation. Although he found no
trace of the fugitives, he did discover traces of copper near their camp in
what is now downtown Bisbee. The resulting copper strike turned out to be
one of the richest copper mines in the world. Unfortunately, Lieutenant Rucker
was cheated by his partners and didn't share in the bonanza.

—Bruce Grubbs

102 Mount Wrightson

Description:	A well-graded trail to the summit of Mount Wrightson, the highest peak in the Mount Wrightson Wilderness in the Santa Rita Mountains.
Location:	About 35 miles south of Tucson.
Type of hike:	Loop with an out-and-back section; day hike or backpack.
Difficulty:	Difficult.
Total distance:	13.7 miles.
Elevation change:	4,040 feet.
Water:	Seasonally in Madera Canyon, and at Sprung, Baldy, and Bellows Springs.
Best months:	May–November.
Maps:	Mount Wrightson USGS; Coronado National Forest (Nogales and Sierra Vista Ranger Districts).
Permit:	None.
For more information:	Coronado National Forest, Nogales Ranger District.

Finding the trailhead: From Tucson, drive about 24 miles south on I–19; exit at Continental. Drive east through Continental, continue on paved Madera Canyon Road to its end at the Roundup Picnic Area, then park in the signed trailhead parking area.

Key points:
0.0	Roundup Trailhead.
3.5	Josephine Saddle.
3.7	Old Baldy Trail.
5.2	Riley Saddle.
6.8	Baldy Saddle; turn left on Old Baldy Trail.
7.6	Mount Wrightson.
8.4	Baldy Saddle; turn left on Old Baldy Trail.
10.0	Turn right on Super Trail.
10.2	Josephine Saddle.
13.7	Roundup Trailhead.

Mount Wrightson • Santa Rita Crest Trail

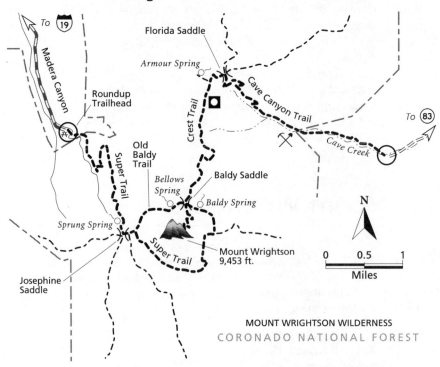

The hike: This hike uses the newer, well-graded Super Trail to take you most of the way to the summit of Mount Wrightson, the highest point in the Santa Rita Mountains. The steeper but shorter Old Baldy Trail is used for the final ascent of the peak, and for part of the return hike.

Leaving the Roundup Trailhead, the Super Trail almost immediately crosses Madera Creek, then switchbacks up the east side of the canyon through chaparral brush and oak. This trail is well named because the ascent, although steady, is always moderate. After climbing along to the east of the creek for a bit, the trail gradually returns to the creek side. Beautiful Arizona sycamores grace the creek, which is nearly always flowing. Madera Canyon is a favorite destination for birders, who come here to see more than 200 species of birds. Many of these birds are found primarily in Mexico, and in a few southern Arizona ranges such as the Santa Ritas. Among these are solitary vireo, acorn woodpeckers, Mexican jays, black-headed grosbeaks, red-shafted flickers, western tanagers, sulphur-bellied flycatchers, yellow-eyed juncos, and the rare elegant trogon.

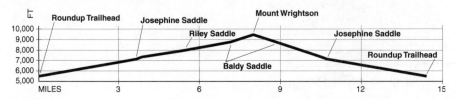

Madera Creek, in the Santa Rita Mountains, is a haven for birds.

Hiking the well-named, gently-graded Super Trail in the Santa Rita Mountains.

More switchbacks take the trail out on the east side of the canyon once again. The trail works its way south toward the head of the canyon, through silverleaf oaks, Arizona white oaks, Emory oaks, Arizona madrone, and alligator junipers. You'll get occasional views of Mount Wrightson high to the east, but usually the summit is hidden behind closer ridges. After the trail passes Sprung Spring, it climbs into Josephine Saddle, at 3.5 miles. A sign memorializes three Boy Scouts who died while camping here during a severe late fall snowstorm.

Several trails depart Josephine Saddle, but our route remains on the Super Trail, which switchbacks northeast out of the saddle. At 3.7 miles, you'll pass the Old Baldy Trail in a minor saddle, which will be our return. The Super Trail now heads southeast across the slopes of Mount Wrightson, passing through Riley Saddle at 5.2 miles. Continuing to circle the mountain, the trail climbs northeast, and then northwest, passing Baldy Spring. The Super Trail ends at Baldy Saddle at 6.8 miles; turn left on the Old Baldy Trail.

At first, the Old Baldy Trail heads across the northeast slopes of Mount Wrightson, but soon begins to switchback steeply, climbing around to the southeast face. The open, rocky terrain gives you great views. Early in the season, snow and ice can be a hazard on this section. A final climb takes you to the rocky summit dome, 7.6 miles from the start.

As you would expect, the view is stupendous from the top of this "sky island." You can see the Tucson area and the Tucson, Santa Catalina, and Rincon Mountains to the north. Eastward, the view includes the Huachuca Mountains and the sweeping oak and grassland country around Sonoita. Southward you can see far into Mexico; closer at hand, the Patagonia Mountains lie just north of the border.

Return to Baldy Saddle, and then stay left to remain on the Old Baldy Trail. This trail switchbacks steeply down the rugged terrain below the saddle, then swings south past Bellows Spring and descends through stands of Mexican white pine and Douglas fir to meet the Super Trail just above Josephine Saddle. Turn right, and follow the Super Trail through Josephine Saddle and back to the Roundup Trailhead.

—Bruce Grubbs and Stewart Aitchison

103 Santa Rita Crest Trail

See Map on Page 272

Description: An alternate, less-traveled route to the Santa Rita crest and the summit of Mount Wrightson.
Location: About 15 miles north of Sonoita.
Type of hike: Out-and-back; day hike or backpack.
Difficulty: Difficult.
Total distance: 13.2 miles.
Elevation change: 3,700 feet.
Water: Seasonally in Cave Creek, and at Armour and Baldy Springs (both springs are side hikes).
Best months: May–November.
Maps: Mount Wrightson USGS; Coronado National Forest (Nogales and Sierra Vista Ranger Districts).
Permit: None.
For more information: Coronado National Forest, Nogales Ranger District.

Finding the trailhead: From Sonoita, take Arizona 83 north 4 miles to Gardner Canyon Road (Forest Road 92). Turn left (west) and drive about 9 miles to its end. The last 2 miles will require a high-clearance vehicle.

Key points:

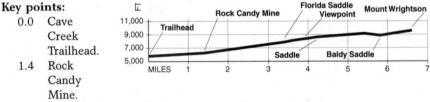

0.0 Cave Creek Trailhead.
1.4 Rock Candy Mine.
3.4 Florida Saddle; turn left on the Crest Trail.
3.6 Armour Spring Trail.
4.0 Viewpoint.
4.2 Saddle.
5.8 Baldy Saddle; go straight ahead onto the Old Baldy Trail.
6.6 Mount Wrightson.

The hike: The trail starts as an old road, following Cave Creek to the west as it climbs steadily. At 1.4 miles you'll pass the old Rock Candy Mine. Shortly after the mine, the trail climbs away from Cave Creek up the north side of the canyon. Steep switchbacks lead to Florida Saddle at 3.4 miles. Turn left onto the Crest Trail, which climbs steeply southward through fine Douglas fir forest past the Armour Spring Trail junction. Now the climb moderates as the Crest Trail continues south along the east slopes of the range. Watch for a clearing below the trail at about 4 miles, where rock outcrops provide a fine view to the east. This point makes a good goal for a shorter day hike.

At 4.2 miles the trail passes through a saddle on the crest of the range, then heads out across the east slopes again. A short, steep climb leads back to the crest, where the trail works its way south to end at Baldy Saddle. At

Florida Saddle and McCleary Peak from the south, Mount Wrightson Wilderness.

this junction, the Super Trail goes left and the Old Baldy Trail goes right; to continue to the summit of Mount Wrightson via the Old Baldy Trail, go straight ahead. The trail swings around the northeast side of the mountain, then switchbacks steeply to the summit, 6.6 miles from the start. From the summit, the Santa Rita Mountains are spread out below you, as well as distant ranges in all directions.

—Bruce Grubbs

104 Carr Peak

Description:	A hike to a 9,000-foot summit in the Miller Peak Wilderness in the Huachuca Mountains.
Location:	About 14 miles south of Sierra Vista.
Type of hike:	Out-and-back day hike.
Difficulty:	Moderate.
Total distance:	6.2 miles.
Elevation change:	1,700 feet.
Water:	None.
Best months:	May–November.
Maps:	Miller Peak USGS; Coronado National Forest (Nogales and Sierra Vista Ranger Districts).
Permit:	None.
For more information:	Coronado National Forest, Sierra Vista Ranger District.

Carr Peak from the Ramsey Canyon Trail, Huachuca Mountains.

Carr Peak • Ramsey Canyon

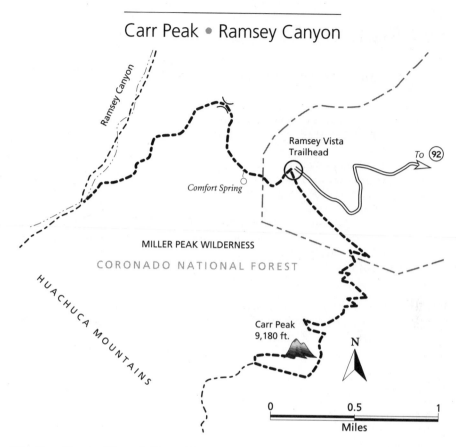

Finding the trailhead: From Sierra Vista, drive about 8 miles south on Arizona 92, then turn right on Carr Canyon Road. Continue to the end of this maintained dirt road at Ramsey Vista Campground, and park in the signed trailhead parking at the west side of the loop road.

Key points:

0.0   Ramsey Vista Trailhead.
2.8   Turn right on Carr Peak Trail.
3.1   Carr Peak.

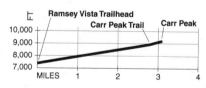

The hike: The Carr Peak Trail heads southeast up a gentle ridge through the 1977 Carr Peak burn. After you pass through a stand of surviving tall timber, the trail steepens as it switchbacks up the north ridge of Carr Peak. The fine, unlimited views are a bit of compensation for the burned forest. On the north side of the peak, the trail passes through thick stands of quaking aspen, and then swings around to the south slopes. Here the forest survived the fire. At 2.8 miles, turn right on the Carr Peak Trail and climb 0.3 mile to the rounded summit.

—Bruce Grubbs

105 Ramsey Canyon

See Map on Page 279

Description: This trail takes you to upper Ramsey Canyon in the Miller Peak Wilderness in the Huachuca Mountains.
Location: About 14 miles south of Sierra Vista.
Type of hike: Out-and-back day hike.
Difficulty: Easy.
Total distance: 4.0 miles.
Elevation change: 600 feet.
Water: Seasonally at Comfort Spring.
Best months: May–November.
Maps: Miller Peak USGS; Coronado National Forest (Nogales and Sierra Vista Ranger Districts).
Permit: None.
For more information: Coronado National Forest, Sierra Vista Ranger District.

Finding the trailhead: From Sierra Vista, drive about 8 miles south on Arizona 92, then turn right on Carr Canyon Road. Continue to the end of this maintained dirt road at Ramsey Vista Campground, and park in the signed trailhead parking at the west side of the loop road.

Key points:
0.0 Ramsey Vista Trailhead.
0.4 Comfort Spring.
0.9 Saddle.
2.0 Ramsey Canyon.

The hike: The trail descends southwest below the campground, and then contours west to Comfort Spring. A very gradual climb through isolated stands of pines leads to a saddle overlooking Ramsey Canyon at 0.9 mile. After the starkness of the Carr Peak burn, it's a relief to

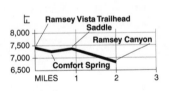

start the descent southwest into Ramsey Canyon, across the cool, forested mountainside. At 2.0 miles, the trail ends at the bottom of Ramsey Canyon. You can explore up or down Ramsey Canyon. This is a popular area for birding; many rare species are found here.

—Bruce Grubbs

106 Miller Peak

Description:	A hike along a section of the Arizona Trail, on the crest of the Huachuca Mountains in the Miller Peak Wilderness, to the highest summit in the range.
Location:	About 23 miles south of Sierra Vista.
Type of hike:	Out-and-back day hike.
Difficulty:	Difficult.
Total distance:	9.2 miles.
Elevation change:	2,900 feet.
Water:	None.
Best months:	May–November.
Maps:	Miller Peak, Montezuma Peak USGS; Coronado National Forest (Nogales and Sierra Vista Ranger Districts).
Permit:	None.
For more information:	Coronado National Forest, Sierra Vista Ranger District.

Finding the trailhead: From Sierra Vista, drive about 15 miles south on Arizona 92, then turn right on the Coronado National Memorial road, which is paved at first but becomes maintained dirt. Continue 8.2 miles to Montezuma Pass, and park.

Key points:
- 0.0 Montezuma Pass Trailhead.
- 2.1 Ridge crest.
- 4.2 Huachuca Crest Trail.
- 4.6 Miller Peak.

The hike: The Miller Peak Trail starts up the grassy slopes south of the parking lot and climbs across the slope to a saddle, then begins switchbacking up a south-facing slope. This section offers

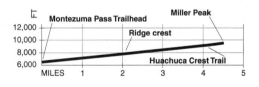

fines views of Montezuma Canyon to the southeast. At 2.1 miles, the trail reaches the ridge crest and follows it north toward Miller Peak.

Notice the contrast between the grassy slopes you have just left and the densely vegetated slopes of Ash Canyon below you. Although the elevations are the same, the north-facing slopes of Ash Canyon are cooler and moister than the south-facing slopes. An alpine mix of vegetation, including ponderosa pine and Douglas fir, begins to dominate as you leave the dry, brushy ridge for the final ascent.

Miller Peak

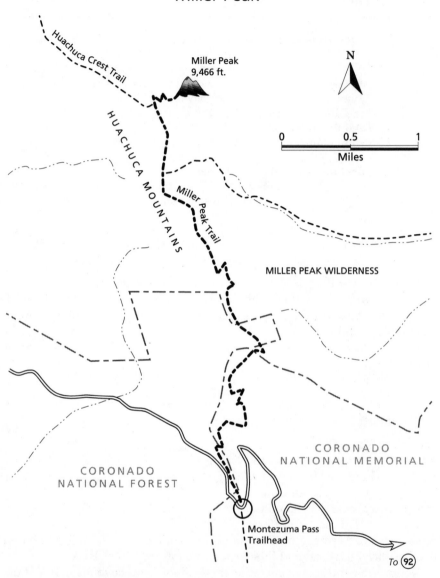

The trail winds through scenic granite terrain before meeting the Huachuca Crest Trail at 4.2 miles. The Miller Peak Trail now swings right and switchbacks to the summit of Miller Peak. The old fire lookout building commands a view far into Mexico as well as near ranges such as the Chiricahua and Pinaleno Mountains.

—Bruce Grubbs

107 San Pedro River Trail

Description:	This is a long-distance hike along the San Pedro River.
Location:	Between Benson and Naco.
Type of hike:	Day hikes to backpacks.
Difficulty:	Easy to moderate.
Total distance:	About 40 miles.
Elevation change:	About 575 feet.
Water:	Although the San Pedro River has some water, it is best to carry your own.
Best months:	October–April.
Maps:	Hereford SW, Stark, Nicksville, Hereford, Lewis Springs, Fairbank, Land USGS.
Permit:	There are entrance and camping fees.
For more information:	San Pedro Riparian National Conservation Area Office.

Finding the trailhead: The northernmost trailhead is at St. David Cienega, about 5 miles southwest of St. David on the Apache Powder Road. The southernmost trailhead is at Palominas, which is located where Arizona 92 crosses the San Pedro River, about 20 miles southeast of Sierra Vista. Palominas is just 4 miles from the Mexican border, but currently this section is open to vehicles.

Key points:

0.0	Northern Trailhead.
10.5	Arizona 82.
18.5	Charleston Road.
24.5	Arizona 90.
33.0	Hereford Road.
36.0	Waters Road.
40.0	Southern Trailhead at Palominas.

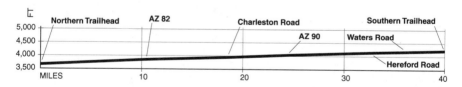

The hike: The San Pedro Trail parallels the river through most of the San Pedro National Conservation Area (NCA). For much of its length, the trial is a fairly level, sandy path. It is open to hiking, mountain biking, and horseback riding. Along the way, you pass old mills, town sites, ranch ruins, and other historic and prehistoric sites. Several highways cross it, as well as

San Pedro River Trail

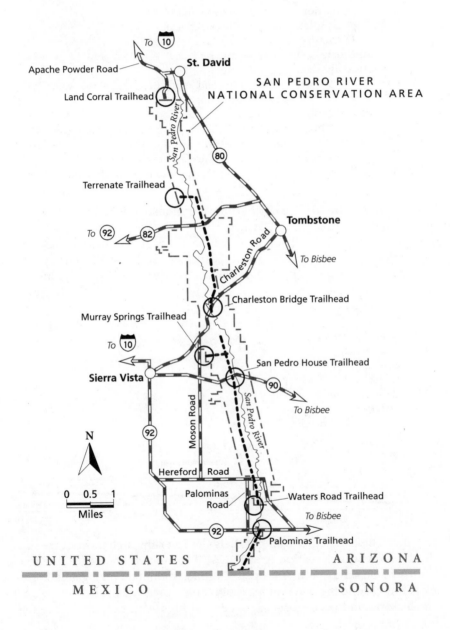

To (10)

Apache Powder Road

St. David

Land Corral Trailhead

SAN PEDRO RIVER NATIONAL CONSERVATION AREA

San Pedro River

(80)

Terrenate Trailhead

To (92)   (82)

Tombstone

Charleston Road

To Bisbee

Charleston Bridge Trailhead

Murray Springs Trailhead

To (10)

San Pedro House Trailhead

Sierra Vista

(90)

To Bisbee

San Pedro River

Moson Road

(92)

N

Hereford   Road

0   0.5   1
Miles

Palominas Road

Waters Road Trailhead

To Bisbee

(92)

Palominas Trailhead

UNITED STATES   ARIZONA

MEXICO   SONORA

The handsome collared lizard is frequently seen basking on boulders in Arizona's wildlands. Male lizards found in the Colorado Plateau area of northern Arizona are usually a striking blue-green color, while those found in the low deserts of southern and western Arizona are often brown. Males, such this one, are usually brighter than females. When alarmed, the collared lizard may flee by running on only its hind legs.

several connector trails, which allow users to do shorter sections. There are seven entrance points scattered the length of the area. A few short sections are still under construction. Most of the hiking is along old roads or the river bank. Wading is sometimes required. The San Pedro Riparian National Conservation Area Office has current trail information.

This area offers opportunities for world-class bird-watching, wildlife viewing and photography, hiking, mountain biking, camping, seasonal hunting, horseback riding, nature study, and environmental education. The San Pedro River has been called one of America's last great places. It's one of the few rivers of any size in the desert Southwest that isn't bone-dry most of the year. Preservation of this riparian habitat was recognized as being so important that in 1988 Congress created the 58,000-acre San Pedro Riparian National Conservation Area, the first such preserve in the nation.

The NCA stretches from the international border nearly 40 miles north to St. David. The San Pedro River enters Arizona from Sonora, Mexico, flows north between the Huachuca and Mule mountain ranges, and joins the Gila River 140 miles downstream near the town of Winkelman. Sometimes the river's flow is only a trickle, but perennial springs keep the ecosystem alive.

Fremont cottonwood and Goodding willow dominate the river corridor. Lesser amounts of Arizona ash, Arizona black walnut, netleaf hackberry, and soapberry occur as well. Chihuahuan desert scrub, typified by thorny species such as tarbush, creosote, and acacia, characterize the uplands bordering both sides of the river, while mesquite and sacaton grass dominate the bottomland adjacent to the riparian corridor.

Wildlife abounds in the NCA because of abundant food, water, and cover. The area supports more than 350 species of birds, eighty species of mammals, two native and several introduced species of fish, and more than forty species of amphibians and reptiles.

Prehistoric and historic sites are also plentiful. The Clovis Culture, named for a unique type of stone projectile point, were the first human occupants in the upper San Pedro River Valley, dating back approximately 11,000 years. Stone tools and weapons used by these people to butcher large mammals, such as mammoths and bison, were found with the bones of their prey at the Lehner Mammoth Kill Site and the Murray Springs Clovis Site. Directions to these sites can be obtained from the San Pedro NCA Office. Remains of other cultures include the Archaic people (6000 B.C.–A.D. 1) and the Mogollon and Hohokam (A.D. 1–1500).

The historic cultures can be divided into three major periods. First came the Spanish. Francisco Vasquez de Coronado led his 1540 expedition through the San Pedro Valley. Around 1775, Spanish troops led by an Irish mercenary began to built the Presidio (fortified settlement) Santa Cruz de Terrenate. It was never completed and was abandoned by 1780 due to continuous Apache raids. Directions to the ruins of the Presidio can be obtained from the San Pedro NCA Office.

Next came the Mexicans. Upon declaring independence from Spain in 1821, Mexicans moved into the San Pedro Valley to homestead and ranch. But they, too, fell victim to the Apaches.

After the Gadsden Purchase of 1853, the area became United States territory. The latter nineteenth century witnessed more cattle ranching, farming, and the discovery of silver in nearby Tombstone and other locations. Most Apache raiding ended in 1886 with the surrender of Geronimo and his followers.

In terms of natural and cultural history, exploring the San Pedro River NCA is one of the most interesting walks in southern Arizona.

—Stewart Aitchison

Tohono O'odham Country

At one time, the Tohono O'odham people ranged over much of southern Arizona and northern Mexico. We have included the best hike on their reservation and other trips in their traditional area.

108 Summit Trail

Description: A day hike to the base of one of the most distinctive peaks in Arizona.
Location: 55 miles southwest of Tucson.
Type of hike: Out-and-back day hike.
Difficulty: Moderate.
Total distance: 8.0 miles.
Elevation change: 2,840 feet.
Water: None.
Best months: October–April.
Maps: Chiuli Shaik, Baboquivari Peak USGS.
Permit: Permit required from Tohono O'odham tribe. Payment for the permit can be made to the manager at Baboquivari Park every day except Wednesday and Thursday. On those days, obtain permits from the Baboquivari District Office in Topawa.
For more information: Tohono O'odham Nation.

Finding the trailhead: The old "standard route" up the west slope on the Tohono O'odham reservation may be reached by taking Indian Highway 19 south of Sells 12.2 miles to Topawa. At Topawa, a sign directs you to the east on a graded road, Indian Highway 10. It's another 12 miles to Baboquivari Park, where there are a picnic area and a primitive campground.

Key points:
  0.0 Trailhead.
  2.5 Saddle.
  4.0 Base of Baboquivari Peak.

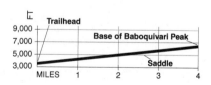

The hike: This trail was constructed by the Civilian Conservation Corps in 1934 and climbs steadily to the base of Baboquivari Peak where the "standard" climbing route begins. The trail is easy to follow. Hikers will need to turn around here.

Distinctive 7,734-foot Baboquivari Peak is a sacred place to the Tohono O'odham. The peak marks the center of the universe and the home of Elder Brother I'itoi, who taught the Tohono O'odham how to live in the desert. Although experienced climbers "free climb" the three pitches, most climbers

Summit Trail

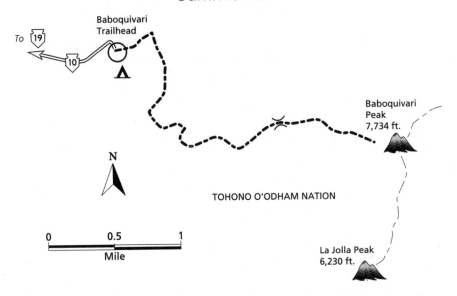

will want the security of a belay. The Tohono O'odham Nation controls access to the west side of the wilderness.

The late Supreme Court Justice William O. Douglas climbed Baboquivari in 1951 and wrote, "It was a mountain wholly detached from the earth—a magic pillar of granite riding high above dark and angry clouds. Lightning briefly played around its base; and then it vanished as quickly as it had appeared—engulfed by black clouds that welled upward in some wind."

Baboquivari Peak from the southeast.

The first recorded climb was by Dr. R. H. Forbes and Jesus Montoya in 1898 after four previously unsuccessful attempts. On the successful climb, the good doctor had brought along a grappling hook fitted with an extension so that, ". . . he was able to extend his arm. . . " Forbes made his sixth and final ascent of Baboquivari in 1949—on his 82nd birthday! He could have gone on to bag the peak a seventh time, but his new bride nixed the plan.

The complexity of terrains and relative abundance of water support a wide variety of plants and animals. Many birds are attracted to the area, including the rare and unusual thick-billed kingbird, five-striped sparrow, northern beardless-tyrannulet, and zone-tailed hawk. Vegetation varies from saguaro, palo verde, and chaparral communities to oak, walnut, and pinyon at the higher elevations.

—Stewart Aitchison

109 Sycamore Creek

Description:	A lovely day hike along a little desert stream in the Pajarita Wilderness.
Location:	20 miles west of Nogales.
Type of hike:	Out-and-back day hike.
Difficulty:	Moderate.
Total distance:	12 miles.
Elevation change:	520 feet.
Water:	Sycamore Creek; purify before drinking.
Best months:	March–May, September–November.
Maps:	Ruby USGS; Coronado National Forest, Nogales District.
Permit:	None.
For more information:	Coronado National Forest, Nogales Ranger District.

Finding the trailhead: From Nogales, drive 3 miles north on I–19; take Arizona 289 west about 9 miles. Then follow Forest Road 39 for 8.8 miles and turn left at the Sycamore Canyon sign. The parking area and trailhead are 0.5 mile down this road at Hank and Yank Spring.

Key points:
- 0.0 Trailhead.
- 2.0 Penasco Canyon.
- 6.0 U.S.–Mexico border.

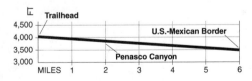

The hike: The route begins at Hank and Yank Spring Picnic Area, the site of an old post–Civil War ranch that was founded by Hank Hewitt and Yank Bartlett. There is no official trail; you just follow the stream. The first mile or so is easy, but then canyon narrows and deeper pools are encountered. To avoid wading, especially when the creek is running high,

289

Sycamore Creek • Atascosa Lookout

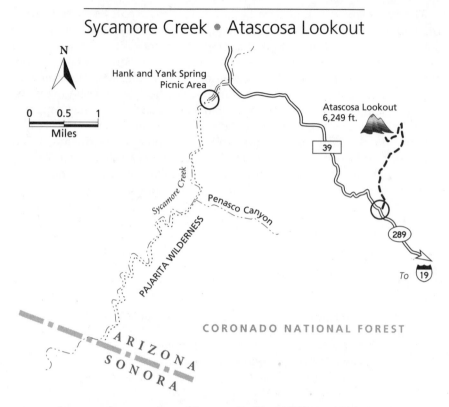

you may have to do some fancy footwork along cliffs and ledges. Two miles downstream, Penasco Canyon enters from the east. Don't do this hike if there is any chance of flooding.

Sycamore Creek, Pajarita Wilderness.

There are probably dozens of Sycamore Canyons in Arizona, but none is as important as this particular one to migrating wildlife, especially birds. Black phoebe, vermilion flycatcher, common black hawk, elegant trogan, green kingfishers, several kinds of herons, and woodpeckers are but a few of the more than 130 species that frequent the canyon. This canyon is also home to the rare Tarahumara frog. Today, people illegally crossing from Mexico into the United States also use the canyon. Be sure to contact the ranger district office to learn the latest on this potentially dangerous activity!

Part of the canyon has been designated as the Goodding Research Natural Area after biologist Leslie Goodding made extensive plant collections in the area between 1935 and the 1950s. He found 624 species of plants including a rare fern, *Asplenium exiguum*, thought to be found only in the Himalayas and in parts of Mexico.

The trail ends at the U.S.–Mexico border, which is marked by a simple barbed wire fence.

—Stewart Aitchison

---

110 Atascosa Lookout

See Map on Page 290

Description: A moderate but rewarding day hike to a lookout.
Location: 18 miles west of Nogales.
Type of hike: Out-and-back day hike.
Difficulty: Moderate.
Total distance: 4.4 miles.
Elevation change: 1,529 feet.
Water: None.
Best months: Year-round.
Maps: Ruby USGS; Coronado National Forest, Nogales District.
Permit: None.
For more information: Coronado National Forest, Nogales Ranger District.

Finding the trailhead: From Nogales, drive about 3 miles north on I–19; take Arizona 289 west 9 miles. Then follow the gravel Forest Road 39 for about 4.8 miles. Look for the trailhead on your right and a small parking area on your left.

Key points:
  0.0   Trailhead.
  2.2   Atascosa Lookout.

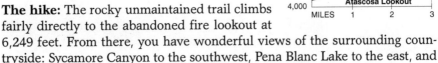

The hike: The rocky unmaintained trail climbs fairly directly to the abandoned fire lookout at 6,249 feet. From there, you have wonderful views of the surrounding countryside: Sycamore Canyon to the southwest, Pena Blanc Lake to the east, and

Atascosa Mountains under a typical Arizona sky.

Nogales to the southeast. Way off to the west are the distinctive hump of Baboquivari Peak and the telescopes crowning Kitt Peak. For an even higher perspective, you can make your way north 0.75 mile to the summit of Atascosa Peak, which is about 200 feet higher than the lookout.

—Stewart Aitchison

Western Desert

This is another part of Arizona best explored from fall through spring. Many of the relatively small desert mountain ranges have been designated wilderness areas since the first edition of this guide. Only a few of the wilderness areas have maintained trails, but experienced desert hikers enjoy making their own cross-country routes.

111 Cherum Peak Trail

Description:	An easy day hike up a desert peak.
Location:	20 miles north of Kingman.
Type of hike:	Out-and-back day hike.
Difficulty:	Easy.
Total distance:	4.0 miles.
Elevation change:	983 feet.
Water:	None.
Best months:	March–May, September–November.
Maps:	Chloride USGS.
Permit:	None.
For more information:	Kingman Field Office, Bureau of Land Management.

Finding the trailhead: From I–40 in Kingman, take U.S. 93 north 20 miles. About 3 miles north of Grasshopper Junction, turn right and drive about 12.5 miles to the end of the road (sometimes called the Big Wash Road) at the Lucky Boy Mine. There are two BLM campgrounds along the road: Packsaddle and Windy Point.

Key points:
0.0   Trailhead.
2.0   Cherum Peak.

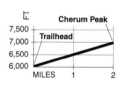

The hike: The trail begins at the end of the road and follows the ridge running southeast to Cherum Peak. This trip is a good introduction to the type of hiking that can be done in the desert ranges of northwestern Arizona. Be sure to carry plenty of water.

Along the lower part of the road to the trailhead, you pass through a mixture of Great Basin and Mojave Desert plants. Joshua trees and creosote are two common species characteristic of the Mojave. Many of the smaller shrubs, such as saltbush, sagebrush, and snakeweed, are typical of the Great Basin Desert. The trail passes through pinyon pine woodland and chaparral. Look for manzanita, silk-tassel bush, and scrub oak.

Cherum Peak Trail

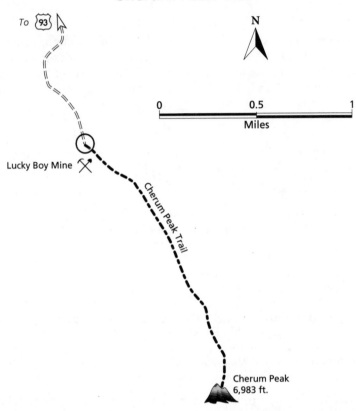

To 93

N

0   0.5   1
Miles

Lucky Boy Mine

Cherum Peak Trail

Cherum Peak
6,983 ft.

From the summit are grand vistas. To the northeast are the Hualapai Valley, the Red Lake Playa, and the Music Mountains. Detrital Valley and the Black Mountains are to the northwest. On a clear day, Mount Charleston near Las Vegas, Nevada, can be seen.

—Stewart Aitchison

112 Wabayuma Peak

Description:	A hike to the top of 7,601-foot Wabayuma Peak in the Wabayuma Peak Wilderness Area.
Location:	About 29 miles south of Kingman.
Type of hike:	Out-and-back day hike.
Difficulty:	Moderate.
Total distance:	6.0 miles.
Elevation change:	1,500 feet.
Water:	None.
Best months:	April–November.
Maps:	Wabayuma Peak USGS.
Permit:	None.
For more information:	Kingman Field Office, Bureau of Land Management.

Finding the trailhead: From Kingman, go south on the paved Hualapai Mountain Road, which climbs through Hualapai Mountain Park. Turn left onto the dirt road marked FLAG MINE ROAD. Continue on this road, through Wild Cow Campground, to reach the signed Wabayuma Peak Trailhead, about 29 miles south of Kingman.

Another, rougher access road leads to the same trailhead from the south. Leave I–40 at Yucca, exit 25, about 22 miles west of Kingman. Drive southwest on paved Boriana Mine Road. About 3.3 miles from I–40, turn left to remain on Boriana Mine Road, which becomes maintained dirt. After about 10 miles, the road meets the wilderness boundary at its southeast corner. To continue, you'll need a four-wheel-drive vehicle. Snowdrifts may close

Granite cliffs near Wabayuma Peak, Hualapai Mountains.

Wabayuma Peak

Wabayuma Peak
7,601 ft.

HUALAPAI MOUNTAINS

Wabayuma Peak Trail

To
Hualapai
Mountain
Park

WABAYUMA PEAK WILDERNESS

N

0   0.5   1
Miles

Wabayuma Peak
Trailhead

To (40)

the upper parts of the road during the winter and early spring. The road crosses a saddle 20.9 miles from I–40; this is the Wabayuma Peak Trailhead.

Key points:
- 0.0 Trailhead.
- 1.0 First saddle.
- 2.0 Leave jeep trail.
- 2.6 Start cross-country.
- 3.0 Wabayuma Peak.

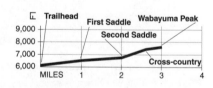

The hike: The trail starts from the Wabayuma Peak Trailhead and climbs along the ridge crest to the northwest through low chaparral brush. This brush plant community is indicative of a warmer climate, which is common on south-facing slopes at this elevation. The views are spectacular right from the trailhead. After a gradual climb, the trail swings through a saddle with a few scattered ponderosa pines, which grow on cooler, north-facing slopes in the Hualapais.

The trail turns sharply west out of this saddle, and climbs over a small hill along the ridge. It now turns north along the ridge and climbs into a saddle at the base of the prominent granite escarpment. Here the summit trail forks left (leaving the jeep trail, which contours north) and starts to climb rapidly in a series of switchbacks. The trail fades out on the ridge crest, which is a pleasant parklike mix of granite outcrops and pine trees.

To reach Wabayuma Peak, work your way north, cross-country, to the foot of the peak. The steep summit block will require some route finding and rock scrambling to reach. Watch for hedgehog cactus growing in the cracks. Alternatively, walk up the easier peak, which is only about 0.1 mile south-west of the end of the trail. This summit is only a few feet lower and provides the same incredible views. The desert ranges of California's Mohave Desert stretch for miles to the west. To the northwest, the 13,000-foot Spring Mountains are visible in Nevada. And on a clear day, you can see the 12,000-foot San Francisco Mountains 135 miles to the east.

—Bruce Grubbs and Rudi Lambrechtse

113 Harquahala Mountain Trail

Description:	A challenging hike in the seldom visited Harquahala Mountain Wilderness.
Location:	15 miles southwest of Aguila.
Type of hike:	Out-and-back day hike.
Difficulty:	Difficult.
Total distance:	12 miles.
Elevation change:	3,290 feet.
Water:	None.
Best months:	October–April.
Maps:	Socorro Peak, Harquahala Mountain USGS.
Permit:	None.
For more information:	Phoenix Field Office, Bureau of Land Management.

Finding the trailhead: From Aguila, drive 13.6 miles southwest on U.S. 60, then turn left (south) onto a four-wheel-drive road. Go 2.2 miles to the trailhead.

Key points:
 0.0   Trailhead.
 6.0   Harquahala Summit.

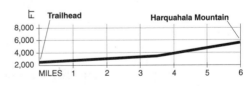

The hike: Although it is possible to drive to the summit from the south on a poor, 10.5-mile-long four-wheel-drive road, the hike is well worth the effort, good for the heart, and easier on your vehicle. The foot trail doesn't waste any time while climbing. The last 0.75 mile ascends more than 1,400 feet! Take your time and enjoy the views.

In 1920 the Smithsonian Institution built an astrophysical observatory here to study the effects of sun activity on the earth's climate. Scientists believed that measuring the amount of energy reaching the earth (dubbed the solar constant) would aid in forecasting weather. After five years, the studies

Harquahala Mountain Trail

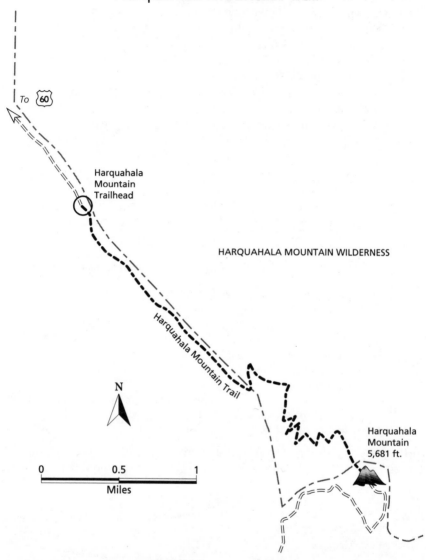

were inconclusive and the facility was abandoned; only ruins remain today. Since 1979, the observatory has shared the summit with a microwave communication facility that controls the water flows in the Central Arizona Project canals that bring Colorado River water to Phoenix. From the summit, long, adventurous cross-country backpacks can be done deep into the Harquahala Mountain Wilderness.

—Stewart Aitchison

114 Vulture Peak

Description:	A great hike through gorgeous Sonoran Desert.
Location:	7 miles south of Wickenburg.
Type of hike:	Out-and-back day hike.
Difficulty:	Easy.
Total distance:	4.0 miles.
Elevation change:	1,180 feet.
Water:	None.
Best months:	September–May.
Maps:	Vulture Peak USGS.
Permit:	None.
For more information:	Phoenix Field Office, Bureau of Land Management.

Finding the trailhead: From U.S. 60 in Wickenburg, drive south 7 miles on the Vulture Mine Road. About 0.7 mile past milepost 30, turn left on the signed Vulture Peak Trail Road. It's another 0.4 mile to the trailhead parking area. If you have a four-wheel-drive vehicle, it is possible to go another 1.6 miles to a different trailhead, but you will miss some of the best part of the hike.

Key points:

0.0   Trailhead.
2.0   Vulture Peak.

The hike: The trail winds through wonderful Sonoran Desert. Saguaro, ocotillo, palo verde, jojoba, creosote bush, teddybear cholla, and staghorn cholla hug the trail. The first 1.6 miles or so offers a fairly gradual climb, then you meet the end of the

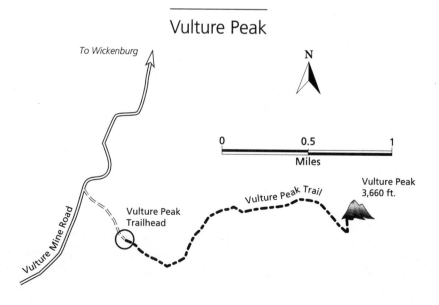

Vulture Peak

four-wheel-drive road, and the trail begins to ascend more steeply. Take your time, enjoy the views, and before long you will reach Vulture Saddle. There are grand vistas from here, but if you have a little more energy, it's only another 240-vertical-foot scramble to the summit of Vulture Peak.

Look for black-throated sparrows, North America's only desert bird that does not have to drink water (it gets moisture from metabolizing the carbohydrates, fats, and proteins in the seeds that it eats); delicate silky flycatchers known as phainopeplas that feed on mistletoe berries in the palo verde trees; and Say's phoebes "hawking" insects out of the air.

—Stewart Aitchison

115 Ben Avery Trail

Description:	A hike in the Eagletail Mountains Wilderness through the Sonoran Desert.
Location:	30 miles west of Tonopah.
Type of hike:	Out-and-back day hike.
Difficulty:	Easy.
Total distance:	7.0 miles.
Elevation change:	150 feet.
Water:	None.
Best months:	October–April.
Maps:	Eagletail Mountains West, Eagletail Mountains East USGS.
Permit:	None.
For more information:	Yuma Field Office, Bureau of Land Management.

Finding the trailhead: From Tonopah, drive about 13 miles on I–10 to exit 81. Turn off for the Harquahala Valley and drive south 5 miles to the Courthouse Rock Road. Follow this road west about 5 miles to a major fork. Take the right fork, a gas pipeline maintenance road, about 6 miles to a marked road going south. Follow this track about 1.5 miles to the Ben Avery Trailhead at the wilderness boundary near the looming hulk of Courthouse Rock. Some lands around and within the wilderness are not federally administered. Please respect the property rights of the owners and do not cross or use these lands without their permission.

Key points:

0.0 Trailhead.

3.5 Indian Spring.

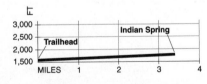

The hike: This trail is named after a well-known Phoenix outdoor writer and covers about 12 miles in all. A nice day hike is to walk in as far as Indian Spring. This is a good area to see wildlife and perhaps evidence of prehistoric cultures. This old jeep trail, now within the Eagletail Mountains Wilderness area and closed to vehicles, meanders gently through impressive Sonoran

Ben Avery Trail

N

0   0.5   1
Miles

EAGLETAIL MOUNTAINS WILDERNESS

To Courthouse
Rock Road

Ben Avery Trailhead

Ben Avery Trail

Courthouse Butte
2,874 ft.

EAGLETAIL MOUNTAINS

Indian Spring

Hikers admire Courthouse Rock in the Eagletail Mountains Wilderness. Rock climbers challenge the monolith's steep sides.

Desert set against rugged, rocky mountains. After a mile, the trail drops into a wash and heads west. The wash narrows, and the trail climbs steeply out of it. The trail crosses a ridge and drops back into another wash.

The topo maps are handy, especially since the trail can be vague where it crosses or follows sandy washes. Camping is prohibited within 0.5 mile of Indian Spring.

—Stewart Aitchison

116 Palm Canyon

Description:	A hike to a desert oasis.
Location:	About 22 miles southeast of Quartzite.
Type of hike:	Out-and-back day hike.
Difficulty:	Easy.
Total distance:	1.5 miles.
Elevation change:	400 feet.
Water:	None.
Best months:	October–April.
Maps:	Palm Canyon USGS.
Permit:	None.
For more information:	Kofa National Wildlife Refuge.

Finding the trailhead: From Quartzite, drive 18 miles south on Arizona 95; from Yuma, drive 63 miles north on Arizona 95. Turn off onto the signed Palm Canyon dirt road that heads east 9 miles toward the Kofa Range.

Key points:

0.0   Trailhead.
0.75 Viewpoint.

The hike: The trail follows the desert wash at the end of the road that eventually takes you into a deep, narrow canyon. Follow the most prominent trail to a small sign on a slightly elevated viewpoint near the middle of the canyon. By looking upward in the

Palm Canyon

KOFA NATIONAL WILDLIFE REFUGE

California fan palms, high in Palm Canyon, Kofa Mountains.

narrow, north-trending side canyon, you will see a grove of Washington palms (also called California fan palms), the only native palms in Arizona. These remarkable trees also grow in other canyons cutting into the Kofa Mountains and at scattered locations in California and Baja. Although the fruits were gathered and eaten by local Indians, this particular population wasn't discovered by botanists until 1923. The palm's name commemorates

President George Washington, who probably never saw a palm, especially this species! Today, this species is commonly planted as an ornamental.

Many people think that Kofa is an Indian word, but it actually is derived from the acronym for the King of Arizona Mine. In the 1890s, prospector Charles Eichelberger discovered gold in these rugged mountains. To mark his property, he had a branding iron forged that read "K of A." Later, when a post office name was being discussed, someone remembered the brand and the name Kofa resulted.

A trail brochure can be picked up from the Kofa National Wildlife Refuge office in Yuma.

—Stewart Aitchison

117 Squaw Lake Nature Trail

Description:	A short nature trail to Squaw Lake.
Location:	About 23 miles north of Yuma.
Type of hike:	Out-and-back day hike.
Difficulty:	Easy.
Total distance:	2.0 miles.
Elevation change:	140 feet.
Water:	Near first set of rest rooms.
Best months:	October–April.
Maps:	Imperial Reservoir USGS.
Permit:	None.
For more information:	Yuma District Office, Bureau of Land Management.

Squaw Lake Nature Trail

Senator Wash Reservoir

Squaw Lake Trailhead

Squaw Lake

N

0   0.25   0.5
Mile

To Yuma

Finding the trailhead: From Yuma, drive north over the Fourth Avenue Bridge into California, then take Highway S-24 in Winterhaven north for 20 miles. Look for the informational signs on the right side of the road to locate the trailhead.

Key points:
- 0.0   Trailhead.
- 1.0   Squaw Lake.

The hike: Like Betty's Kitchen Trail (Hike 118), this is a favorite area with birders, especially in the winter and the spring. More than 200 species have been recorded in the area. Some of the summer residents include summer tanagers, southwestern willow flycatchers, vermilion flycatchers, and yellow-billed cuckoos. Frequent migrants include Townsend's and black-throated gray warblers, western tanagers, and Lazuli buntings. The lake attracts mallards, northern pintails, and common mergansers. The endangered Yuma clapper rail may nest here too.

A trail guide for this very easy, short hike is available from the BLM office in Yuma.

—Stewart Aitchison

118 Bettys Kitchen Interpretive Trail

Description:	An easy, very short but informative nature trail.
Location:	About 15 miles northeast of Yuma.
Type of hike:	Loop day hike.
Difficulty:	Easy.
Total distance:	0.5 mile.
Elevation change:	Negligible.
Water:	None.
Best months:	October–April.
Maps:	Laguna Dam USGS.
Permit:	None.
For more information:	Yuma District Office, Bureau of Land Management.

Finding the trailhead: From Yuma, take U.S. 95 7 miles east to Avenue 7E (Laguna Dam Road) and head north for 9 miles. Just past Laguna Dam, turn left. Proceed another 0.5 mile and look for the Betty's Kitchen Interpretive Trail sign.

Key points:
- 0.0   Trailhead.
- 0.5   Trailhead.

The hike: The Bettys Kitchen area is named after a small cafe that once stood here. This short loop walk following an old access road through a wood-

Bettys Kitchen Interpretive Trail

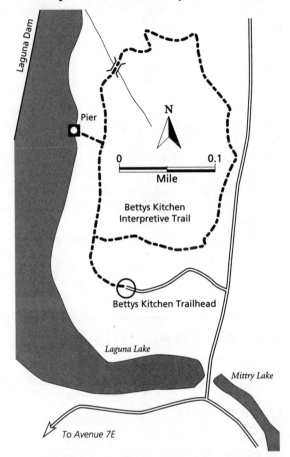

land of tamarisk, Fremont cottonwood, willow, screwbean and honey mesquite, and palo verde offers outstanding bird-watching. Common shorebirds include killdeer and spotted sandpiper. In the winter, look for mallards and cinnamon teal. Anglers try their luck for bluegill, largemouth bass, carp, flathead and channel catfish, and tilapia.

Guided nature tours are offered by the Betty's Kitchen Protective Association (928–627–2773) and the BLM (928–726–6300). At the trailhead, there is box containing a trail guide.

—Stewart Aitchison

306

119 Muggins Peak

Description:	A hike into the Muggins Mountain Wilderness Area through lovely Sonoran desert.
Location:	25 miles east of Yuma.
Type of hike:	Out-and-back day hike.
Difficulty:	Moderate.
Total distance:	4.0 miles.
Elevation change:	1,184 feet.
Water:	None.
Best months:	October–April.
Maps:	Ligurta, Dome, Wellton, Red Bluff Mountain West USGS.
Permit:	None.
For more information:	Yuma Field Office Bureau of Land Management.

Finding the trailhead: To reach the southwest boundary of the wilderness area, take the Dome Valley exit off I–8. Travel 1.25 miles on the frontage road, then turn northwest on County Avenue 20E and continue to County 7th Street. Turn right (east) and drive to foot of the mountains. The Muggins Wash Road continues northeast and drops into Muggins Wash and the wilderness boundary. This route crosses some private land; please stay on the road until reaching the wilderness area.

Key points:
- 0.0   Trailhead.
- 2.0   Muggins Peak.

The Muggins Mountain Wilderness is small, but rugged.

Muggins Peak

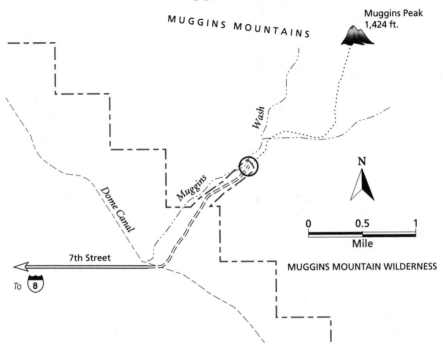

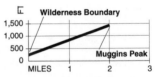

The hike: At the moment there is no official trail, but the BLM is planning to mark one soon. This relatively small but rugged 7,674-acre wilderness is dominated by Klothos Temple, Muggins Peak, and Long Mountain. Washes snake their way up into and around these peaks, making excellent hiking routes. One such hike would be to continue up Muggins Wash about 1.75 miles to the west side of Muggins Peak. An uphill, cross-country scramble takes you to the summit.

Some signs of old placer mine workings from the late 1800s in the western half of the wilderness lend some historic interest to the hike.

Typical Sonoran Desert vegetation covers the area. Along washes may be found blue palo verde, ironwood, mesquite, smoke tree, and bitter condalia. Other species of notable interest are holly-leaved bursage, hoffmanseggia, Wiggins' cholla, and a red-spined barrel cactus. Wildlife includes chuckwalla, Gila monster, cactus wren, desert bighorn sheep, possibly desert tortoise, and elf owl.

—Stewart Aitchison

120 Bull Pasture

Description:	A hike in the Organ Pipe Cactus National Monument Wilderness Area.
Location:	38 miles south of Ajo, east of the Organ Pipe Cactus National Monument Visitor Center.
Type of hike:	Out-and-back day hike.
Difficulty:	Moderate to difficult.
Total distance:	About 7 miles.
Elevation change:	2,500 feet.
Water:	None.
Best months:	October–April.
Maps:	Mount Ajo USGS.
Permit:	None for day hike.
For more information:	Organ Pipe Cactus National Monument.

Finding the trailhead: From Ajo, drive 38 miles south on Arizona 86 to the Organ Pipe Cactus National Monument headquarters. Then take the Ajo Mountain Loop Drive 8 miles to the signed Bull Pasture trailhead at the Estes Canyon Picnic Area.

Key points:

0.0 Trailhead.

1.75 Overlook.

3.5 Mount Ajo.

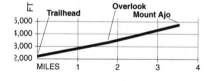

The hike: The maintained trail leaves the picnic area and climbs about 1.75 miles and a thousand feet to a ridge overlooking Bull Pasture, a scenic basin high on the flanks of the Ajo Range. As the name suggests, Bull Basin was a favorite cattle pasture prior to achieving national monument status. (For a variation, on your return trip, take the trail that leads down into Estes Canyon. It ends at the same picnic area where you began.)

From the trail's end at the overlook, a rough but rewarding cross-country hike leads to the summit of Mount Ajo, at 4,808 feet the highest point in the monument. Take time to sign in at the register box; back in 1971, a hiker wandered into Bull Pasture and was never seen again. The route goes around the head of Bull Pasture basin, trending generally eastward toward the steep slopes on the far side. The route then goes northeast to gain the main north-south ridge. You will have to pick your way around some cliff bands. Once on the ridge, the route is a straightforward walk about a mile north to the summit.

Mount Ajo towers above scenic Bull Pasture, Organ Pipe Cactus National Monument.

Bull Pasture

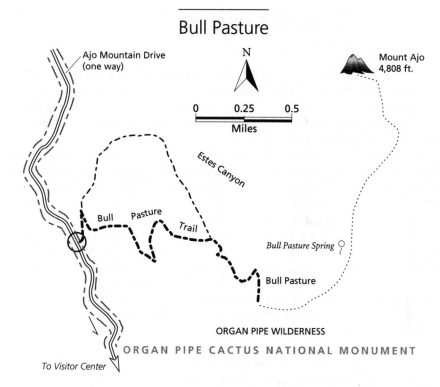

From the top of Mount Ajo, you can see far into Mexico to the south, west across the monument, and north and east across the vast Tohono O'odham Reservation toward the Baboquivari Mountains.

—Bruce Grubbs and Stewart Aitchison

The Arizona Trail

The Arizona Trail, the dream of Flagstaff teacher and hiking enthusiast Dale Shewalter, will eventually be a 800-mile nonmotorized trail that traverses the state from Mexico to Utah. The Arizona Trail is intended to be a primitive long-distance trail that highlights the state's topographic, biologic, historic, and cultural diversity.

The primary users are hikers, equestrians, and mountain bicyclists (outside of wilderness or other specially managed areas). Government agencies, volunteers, and private groups and businesses are working together to make the Arizona Trail a reality.

As of late 2001, most of the 800 miles of trail are open to the public, and 575 miles of the Arizona Trail have been "officially" designated and signed. In most cases, the Arizona Trail utilizes existing trails that are also known by their original names and numbers. Primitive roads are temporarily being used in areas where links are needed, but new trails must be constructed in these areas, especially to maintain the vision of a nonmotorized trail. When completed, the Arizona Trail will become one of the premier long-distance trails in the country.

In late 1993, an Intergovernmental Agreement was established between Arizona State Parks, the U.S. Forest Service, the National Park Service, and the Bureau of Land Management (known as the Arizona Trail Partners) that allows these agencies to cooperatively plan for the development and completion of the Arizona Trail. In 1995, Pima County, Walnut Canyon National Monument, and the Arizona Trail Association joined the Arizona Trail Partners.

The Arizona Trail Association was founded in 1994 to promote the Arizona Trail as a unique and outstanding recreational and educational resource, and to provide opportunities for citizens to become involved in the development, maintenance, use and enjoyment of the Arizona Trail. Volunteers are always welcome; contact the ATA at the address in the Appendix.

Appendix A: For More Information

Apache-Sitgreaves National Forest
Alpine Ranger District, P.O. Box 469, Alpine, AZ 85920; (928) 339–4384
Black Mesa Ranger District, P.O. Box 968, Overgaard, AZ 85933; (928) 535–4481
Clifton Ranger District, HC 1, Box 733, Duncan, AZ 85594; (928) 687–1301
Lakeside Ranger District, RR 3, Box B-50, Lakeside, AZ 85929; (928) 368–5111
Springerville Ranger District, P.O. Box 760, Springerville, AZ 85938; (928) 333–4372
Supervisor's Office, P.O. Box 640, Springerville, AZ 85938; (928) 333–4301

Aravaipa Canyon Preserve, Bureau of Land Management, (520) 828–3443

Arizona Game and Fish Department, 2221 West Greenway Road, Phoenix, AZ 85023-4399; (602) 942–3000

Arizona State Land Department, 1616 West Adams Street., Phoenix AZ 85007; (602) 542–4625

Arizona State Parks, 1300 West Washington, Phoenix, AZ 85007; (602) 542–4174

Picacho State Park, (520) 466–3183

Red Rock State Park, HC - Box 886, Sedona, AZ 86336; (928) 282–6907

Arizona State Trails Program, 1300 West Washington, Phoenix, AZ 85007; (602) 542–4662

Arizona Trail Steward, Arizona State Parks, 1300 West Washington, Phoenix, AZ 85007; (602) 542–7120, www.pr.state.az.us, e-mail clovely@pr.state.az.us

Canyon de Chelly National Monument, P.O. Box 588, Chinle, AZ 86503-0588; (928) 674–5500

Chiricahua National Monument, Dos Cabezas Route, Box 6500, Willcox, AZ 85643; (520) 824–3560

Coconino National Forest
Beaver Creek Ranger District, HC 64, Box 240, Rimrock, AZ 86335; (928) 567–4121
Blue Ridge Ranger District, HC 31, Box 300, Happy Jack, AZ 86024; (928) 477–2255
Mormon Lake Ranger District, 4373 South Lake Mary Road, Flagstaff, AZ 86001; (928) 774–1147
Peaks Ranger District, 5075 North Highway 89, Flagstaff, AZ 86004; (928) 526–0866
Sedona Ranger District, P.O. Box 300, Sedona, AZ 86336-0300; (928) 282–4119
Supervisor's Office, 2323 East Greenlaw Lane, Flagstaff, AZ 86001; (928) 527–3600

Coronado National Forest
Douglas Ranger District, 3081 North Leslie Canyon Road, Douglas, AZ 85607; (520) 364–3468

Nogales Ranger District, 303 Old Tucson Road, Nogales, AZ 85621; (520) 281-2296

Safford Ranger District, P.O. Box 709, Safford, AZ 85548-0709; (928) 428-4150

Santa Catalina Range District, 5700 North Sabino Canyon Road, Tucson, AZ 85750; (520) 749-8700

Sierra Vista Ranger District, 5990 South Highway 92, Hereford, AZ 85615; (520) 366-5515

Supervisor's Office, Federal Building, 300 West Congress, Tucson, AZ 85701; (520) 670-4552

County Agencies

Cave Creek Recreation Area, 37019 North Lava Lane, Phoenix, AZ 85331; (623) 465-0431

Estrella Mountain Regional Park, 14805 West Vineyard Avenue, Goodyear, AZ 85338; (623) 932-3811

Maricopa County Parks and Recreation Department, 411 North Central Avenue, Suite 470, Phoenix, AZ 85004; (602) 506-2930

Usery Mountain Recreation Area, 3939 North Usery Pass Road, #190, Mesa, AZ 85207; (480) 357-1542

Flagstaff Parks and Recreation, 211 West Aspen, Flagstaff, AZ 86001; (928) 779-7690

Grand Canyon National Park, P.O. Box 129, Grand Canyon, AZ 86023; (928) 638-7888

Kaibab National Forest

Chalender Ranger District, 501 West Bill Williams Avenue, Williams, AZ 86046; (928) 635-2676

North Kaibab Ranger District, P.O. Box 248, Fredonia, AZ 86022; (928) 643-7395

Supervisor's Office, 800 South Sixth Street, Williams, AZ 86046; (928) 635-8200

Tusayan Ranger District, P.O. Box 3088, Tusayan, AZ 86023; (928) 638-2443

Williams Ranger District, Route 1, Box 142, Williams, AZ 86046; (928) 635-2633

Kingman Field Office, Bureau of Land Management, 2475 Beverly Avenue, Kingman, AZ 86401, (928) 692-4400

Kofa National Wildlife Refuge, P.O. Box 6290, Yuma, AZ 85366; (928) 783-7861

Navajo Nation Parks and Recreation Department, P.O. Box 9000, Window Rock, AZ 86515; (928) 871-6647

Organ Pipe Cactus National Monument, Route 1, Box 100, Ajo, AZ 85321; (520) 387-6849

Phoenix Field Office, Bureau of Land Management, 2015 West Deer Valley Road, Phoenix, AZ 85027; (623) 580-5500

Phoenix Parks and Recreation, Lookout Mountain, (602) 262-7901

Prescott National Forest
Bradshaw Ranger District, 2230 East Highway 69, Prescott, AZ 86301; (928) 445-7253
Chino Valley Ranger District, P.O. Box 485, 735 North Highway 89, Chino Valley, AZ 86323; (928) 636-2302
Supervisor's Office, 344 South Cortez Street, Prescott, AZ 86303; (928) 771-4700
Verde Ranger District, P.O. Box 670, Camp Verde, AZ 86322-0670; (928) 567-4121

Safford Field Office, Bureau of Land Management, 711-14th Avenue, Safford, AZ 85546; (928) 348-4400

Saguaro National Park, 3693 South Old Spanish Trail, Tucson, AZ 85730; (520) 733-5158

San Pedro Riparian National Conservation Area Office, Bureau of Land Management, 1763 Paseo San Luis, Sierra Vista, AZ 85635; (520) 458-3559

Sedona Parks and Recreation, 525 Posse Grounds Road, Sedona, AZ 86336, (928) 282-7098

Sunset Crater National Monument, 6400 North Highway 89, Flagstaff, AZ 86004; (928) 526-0502

Tohono O'odham Nation, P.O. Box 837, Sells, AZ 85634; (520) 383-2221
Baboquivari District Office, (520) 383-2366

Tonto National Forest
Cave Creek Ranger District, 40202 North Cave Creek Road, Scottsdale, AZ 85262; (928) 595-3300
Globe Ranger District, Route 1, Box 33, Globe, AZ 88501; (928) 402-6200
Mesa Ranger District, P.O. Box 5800, Mesa, AZ 85211-5800; (480) 610-3300
Payson Ranger District, 1009 East Highway 260, Payson, AZ 85541; (928) 474-7900
Supervisor's Office, 2324 East McDowell Road, Phoenix, AZ 85006; (602) 225-5200, www.fs.fed.us/r3/tonto
Tonto Basin Ranger District, Highway 88, HCO 2 Box 4800, Roosevelt, AZ 85545; (928) 467-3200

Yuma Field Office, Bureau of Land Management, 2555 Gila Ridge Road, Yuma, AZ 85365; (928) 317-3200

Walnut Canyon National Monument, 6400 North Highway 89, Flagstaff, AZ 86004; (928) 526-3367

Williams Parks and Recreation, 2200 North Country Club Road, Williams, AZ 86046, (928) 635-1496

Wupatki National Monument, 6400 North Highway 89, Flagstaff, AZ 86004; (928) 679-2365

Appendix B: Local Hiking Clubs and Conservation Groups

Arizona Mountaineering Club, P.O. Box 1695, Phoenix, AZ 85001-1695; (623) 878-2485, azmtnclub@abilnet.com

Arizona Trail Association, P.O. Box 36736, Phoenix, AZ 85067; (602) 252-4794, http://aztrail.org, ata@aztrail.org.

Grand Canyon Trust, 2601 North Fort Valley Road, Flagstaff, AZ 86001; (928) 774-7488

Maricopa Audubon Society, 4619 East Arcadia Lane, Phoenix, AZ 85018; no phone

The Nature Conservancy, 333 East Virginia Avenue, Suite 216, Phoenix, AZ 85004; (602) 712-0048

Sierra Club, Grand Canyon Chapter, 516 East Portland Street, Phoenix, AZ 85004; (602) 267-1649

Appendix C: Map Sources

Beartooth Maps, P.O. Box 160728, Big Sky, MT 59716; (406) 995–3280

Delorme *(3-D TopoQuads Arizona CD-ROM maps)*, Two DeLorme Drive, P.O. Box 298, Yarmouth, ME 04096; (800) 452–5931, www.delorme.com, email info@delorme.com

Maptech (Terrain Navigator CD-ROM maps), 655 Portsmouth Avenue, Greenland, NH 03840; (800) 627–7236, www.maptech.com

Trails Illustrated, P.O. Box 3610, Evergreen, CO 80439-3425; (800) 962–1643, www.trailsillustrated.com

U.S. Geological Survey, Information Services, Box 25286, Denver, CO 80225; (800) HELP–MAP, mapping.usgs.gov

Wildflower Productions *(Topo! CD-ROM maps)*, 375 Alabama Street, Suite 400, San Francisco, CA 94110; (415) 558–8700, www.topo.com, e-mail info@topo.com

Appendix D: Further Reading

Fletcher, Colin. *The Complete Walker III*. New York; Alfred A. Knopf, 1989.

Grubbs, Bruce. *Desert Hiking Tips*. Helena, Montana; Falcon Publishing, 1999.

Harmon, Will. *Leave No Trace*. Helena, Montana; Falcon Publishing, 1997.

Harmon, Will. *Wild Country Companion*. Helena, Montana; Falcon Publishing, 1994.

Harper, Kimball, Larry St. Clair, Kaye Thorne, and Wilford Hess, eds. *Natural History of the Colorado Plateau and Great Basin*. Niwot, Colorado; University Press of Colorado, 1994.

Kricher, John C., and Gordon Morrison. *Ecology of Western Forests*. New York; Houghton Mifflin, 1993.

Larson, Peggy. *Sierra Club Naturalist's Guide to the Deserts of the Southwest*. San Francisco; Sierra Club Books, 1977.

Perry, John, and Jane Greverus. *Guide to the Natural Areas of New Mexico, Arizona, and Nevada*. San Francisco; Sierra Club Books, 1985.

Phillips, Steven and Patricia Wentworth Comus, eds. *A Natural History of the Sonoran Desert*. Tucson; Arizona-Sonora Desert Museum Press, 2000.

Wilkerson, James A. *Medicine for Mountaineering*. Seattle; The Mountaineers, 1992.

Appendix E: Hiker's Checklist

This checklist may be useful for ensuring that nothing essential is forgotten. Of course, it contains far more items than are needed on any individual hiking trip.

Clothing
- [ ] Shirt
- [ ] Pants
- [ ] Extra underwear
- [ ] Swimsuit
- [ ] Walking shorts
- [ ] Belt or suspenders
- [ ] Windbreaker
- [ ] Jacket or parka
- [ ] Rain gear
- [ ] Gloves or mittens
- [ ] Sun hat
- [ ] Watch cap or balaclava
- [ ] Sweater
- [ ] Bandanna

Footwear
- [ ] Boots
- [ ] Extra socks
- [ ] Boot wax
- [ ] Camp shoes

Sleeping
- [ ] Tarp or tent with fly
- [ ] Groundsheet
- [ ] Sleeping pad
- [ ] Sleeping bag

Packing
- [ ] Backpack
- [ ] Daypack
- [ ] Fanny pack

Cooking
- [ ] Matches or lighter
- [ ] Waterproof match case
- [ ] Fire starter
- [ ] Stove

- [ ] Fuel
- [ ] Stove maintenance kit
- [ ] Cooking pot(s)
- [ ] Cup
- [ ] Bowl or plate
- [ ] Utensils
- [ ] Pot scrubber
- [ ] Plastic water bottles with water
- [ ] Collapsible water containers

Food
- [ ] Cereal
- [ ] Bread
- [ ] Crackers
- [ ] Cheese
- [ ] Margarine
- [ ] Dry soup
- [ ] Packaged dinners
- [ ] Snacks
- [ ] Hot chocolate
- [ ] Tea
- [ ] Powdered milk
- [ ] Powdered drink mixes

Navigation
- [ ] Maps
- [ ] Compass
- [ ] GPS receiver

Emergency/Repair
- [ ] Pocketknife
- [ ] First-aid kit
- [ ] Snakebite kit
- [ ] Nylon cord
- [ ] Plastic bags
- [ ] Wallet or ID card
- [ ] Coins for phone calls
- [ ] Space blanket

- [ ] Emergency fishing gear (hooks and a few feet of line)
- [ ] Signal mirror
- [ ] Pack parts
- [ ] Stove parts
- [ ] Tent parts
- [ ] Flashlight bulbs, batteries
- [ ] Scissors
- [ ] Safety pins

Miscellaneous
- [ ] Fishing gear
- [ ] Photographic gear
- [ ] Sunglasses
- [ ] Flashlight
- [ ] Candle lantern
- [ ] Sunscreen
- [ ] Insect repellent
- [ ] Toilet paper
- [ ] Trowel
- [ ] Binoculars
- [ ] Trash bags
- [ ] Notebook and pencils
- [ ] Field guides
- [ ] Book or game
- [ ] Dental and personal items
- [ ] Towel
- [ ] Water purification tablets or water filter
- [ ] Car key
- [ ] Watch
- [ ] Calendar

In the Car
- [ ] Extra water
- [ ] Extra food
- [ ] Extra clothes

About the Authors

Bruce Grubbs is an avid hiker, mountain biker, and cross-country skier who has been exploring the American West for more than thirty years. An outdoor writer and photographer, he's written eleven other Falcon guides, including *Hiking Northern Arizona, Camping Arizona, Mountain Biking Flagstaff and Sedona, Desert Hiking Tips,* and *Using GPS: Finding Your Way with the Global Positioning System.* He lives in Flagstaff, Arizona.

Stewart Aitchison leads natural history trips for Lindblad Expeditions, the Grand Canyon Field Institute, the Museum of Northern Arizona, Elderhostel, and other educational organizations. He has written numerous scientific and popular articles and books, including *Longstreet Highroad Guide to the Arizona Mountains and Grand Canyon, Red Rock–Sacred Mountain: The Canyons and Peaks from Sedona to Flagstaff, Grand Canyon: Window of Time, A Naturalist's San Juan River Guide, Utah Wildlands, A Wilderness Called Grand Canyon,* and *A Traveler's Guide to Monument Valley.* When not out exploring, he lives in Flagstaff with his wife, Ann, and daughter, Kate.